To Daddy With Love on
Christmas 1980

Ron & Gail

VIKINGS!

Magnus Magnusson

VIKINGS!

E. P. DUTTON   NEW YORK

FRONTISPIECE The huge stone ship-
setting at Anundshög in Sweden:
harbinger of the Viking surge that
would reach to the farthest ends of the
known world.

First American edition published 1980 by Elsevier-Dutton Publishing Co., Inc., New York.
Printed and bound by Dai-Nippon Printing Co., Ltd.,
Tokyo, Japan.

For information contact: Elsevier-Dutton Publishing Co., Inc.,
2 Park Avenue, New York, N.Y. 10016

Library of Congress Cataloging in Publication Data: 80-67619

ISBN: 0-525-22892-6

10 9 8 7 6 5 4 3 2 1

Contents

1

The Hammer and the Raven

The so-called 'Viking Age' began around AD 800 and lasted for nearly three centuries. In the pages of history it is presented as a clearly defined period of high drama, with a theatrical opening, a long middle act of mounting power and ferocity, and a spectacular finale on a battlefield in England. The dates are clear-cut, too: 793 to 1066. And throughout that time, war correspondents in the shape of literate monks and clerics kept their goose-quill pens sharpened with alarm, their glossy ink dyed bright with indignation. The Vikings were cast in the role of Antichrist, merciless barbarians who plundered and burned their way across the known world, heedless of their own lives or the lives of others, intent only on destruction and pillage; their emblems were Thór's Hammer and Óðin's Raven, symbolising the violence and black-hearted evil of their pagan gods.

It was never quite as one-sided as that – history seldom is. But it made a good story at the time, and it makes a good story still. It is basically the story that I shall be chronicling in this book; but it was never the whole story. Today there is emerging a much fuller and rounder version, mainly through modern archaeology but with the help of other scientific and literary disciplines as well, which presents the Vikings in a less lurid and more objective light. It is as much a matter of emphasis as anything else: less emphasis on the raiding, more on the trading; less on the pillage, more on the poetry and the artistry; less on the terror, more on the technology of these determined and dynamic people from the northlands of Denmark, Norway and Sweden and the positive impact they had on the countries they affected.

Their influence was much more constructive, more pervasive and extensive than they are generally given credit for. They dominated much of northern Europe for long periods. They brought to the British Isles vigorous new art forms, and vigorous new settlers; they founded and developed great market towns, they injected new forms of administration and justice that have left their mark to this day. (As an Icelandic-born descendant of the Vikings myself, I can never resist reminding my sceptical friends that it was these allegedly pitiless savages who introduced the

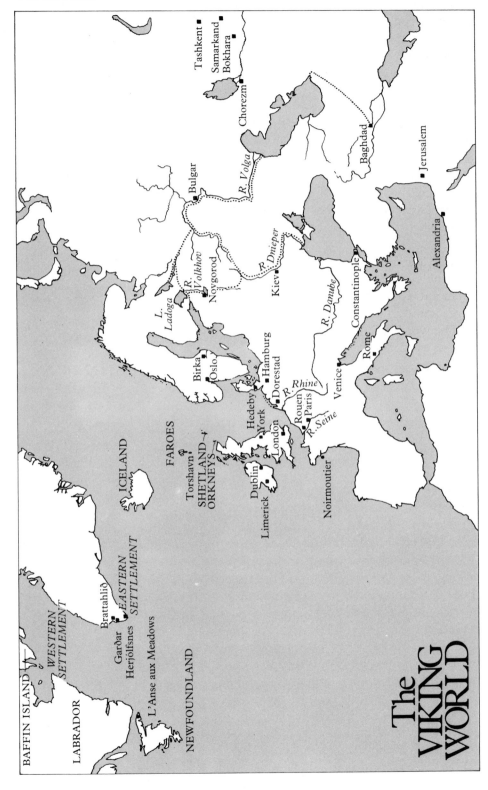

The Viking World

BAFFIN ISLAND

LABRADOR

WESTERN SETTLEMENT

Brattahlið

Garðar EASTERN SETTLEMENT

Herjólfsnes

L'Anse aux Meadows

NEWFOUNDLAND

ICELAND

FAROES

Torshavn

SHETLAND

ORKNEYS

Dublin

Limerick

Noirmoutier

Birka

Oslo

Hedeby

York

London

Rouen

Paris

R. Seine

R. Rhine

Dorestad

Hamburg

Venice

Rome

R. Danube

Constantinople

Alexandria

Jerusalem

L. Ladoga

R. Volkhov

Novgorod

R. Dnieper

Kiev

Bulgar

R. Volga

Chorezm

Baghdad

Tashkent

Samarkand

Bokhara

very word *law* into the English language!) They crisscrossed half the world in their open boats and vastly extended its known boundaries; they voyaged further north and west than any Europeans had ever been before, founding new and lasting colonies in the Faroe Islands and Iceland, discovering and exploring and making settlements in Greenland and even in North America. They penetrated the depths of Russia, founding city-states like Novgorod and Kiev, pioneering new trade routes along formidable rivers like the Volga and the Dnieper, opening up the route to Asia to exploit the exotic markets of Persia and China. They served as hand-picked warriors in the celebrated Varangian Guard, the household troops of the Byzantine Emperor in Constantinople. They went everywhere there was to go, they dared everything there was to dare – and they did it with a robust panache and audacity that has won the grudging admiration even of those who deplore their depredations.

But the Vikings did not happen suddenly; nor did they simply happen. Behind the Viking break-out lay centuries of Scandinavian history that archaeology has been bringing to light – a story of technological development and commercial expansion that helps to explain why the Viking Age came about in the first place.

The word 'Viking' is itself a bit of a puzzle. It may be related to the Old Norse word *vík*, meaning 'bay' or 'creek'; so a 'Viking' meant someone who kept his ship in a bay, either for trading or raiding. Others look for a derivation in the Old English word *wic*, borrowed from the Latin *vicus*, meaning a camp or a trading-place; so a 'Viking' might mean a warrior or a trader – or both.

To the people of the times, 'Viking' meant different things, too. For the Christian communities of western Europe, a Viking was synonymous with barbarian paganism. But to the people of Scandinavia, and especially to the Saga-writers of Iceland in the thirteenth century, the Vikings represented an ideal of heroism and valour; young men went on Viking expeditions to prove their mettle. The Viking life was a sort of open-air university of the manly arts, something for every youngster to aspire to:

> My mother once told me
> She'd buy me a longship,
> A handsome-oared vessel
> To go sailing with Vikings:
> To stand at the stern-post
> And steer a fine warship,
> Then head back for harbour
> And hew down some foemen.

(Egil's Saga, Ch. 40)

Egil's Saga is one of the major medieval Icelandic Sagas, historical narratives written in prose but often studded with verse stanzas. It is the story of a great Viking warrior-poet called Egil Skallagrímsson (*cf* Ch. 6),

Hardangerfjord in south-western Norway – the heartland of the first Vikings.

and that boyish verse was composed in his childhood in Iceland early in the tenth century. His Saga, it is thought, was written by Snorri Sturluson, who lived on the manor farm of Reykholt in southern Iceland.

The Icelandic Sagas, written long after the events they report, were for centuries the major documentary source for the prehistory and history of the Viking lands and the Viking Age. They rank amongst the finest achievements of medieval European literature, but as historical sources they cannot be taken too literally. Snorri Sturluson, one of the few Saga-writers whose name we know, was the outstanding scholar of his age. As a distinguished statesman deeply embroiled in Icelandic politics of the thirteenth century, he was fascinated by the politics and people of the Viking period; as an erudite Christian intellectual he was also fascinated by the pagan mythology of the Vikings, which he helped to preserve by recording and explaining some of the most ancient Germanic myths and legends. Building his work on earlier written sources, on oral traditions and on the remembered skaldic poetry of Scandinavian court poets, he tried to create a coherent framework for the past, a context within which to understand and illuminate the Viking experience.

At Reykholt, Snorri Sturluson wrote some of the towering masterpieces of the thirteenth century. His systematic account of Norse mythology is contained in a work called the *Prose Edda*, or *Snorri's Edda*, which is in effect a handbook for poets, designed to teach the traditional techniques of the ancients and to explain the pagan literary allusions to be found in their poetry. He also wrote a monumental *History of the Kings of Norway*, popularly known as *Heimskringla* ('Orb of the World') from its opening words: '*Kringla heimsins, sú er mannfólkit byggvir . . .*' – 'The orb of the world, which mankind inhabits . . .'

What a majestic opening! I always like to reflect that at the time when, out in the far east, Genghis Khan was trying to subjugate the world by the sword, up in the far north a learned Christian antiquarian was trying to subject it to the power of the pen:

> The orb of the world, which mankind inhabits, is riven by many fjords, so that great seas run into the land from the Outer Ocean. Thus, it is known that a great sea goes in through Nörvasund [Straits of Gibraltar] all the way to the land of Jerusalem. From that same sea a long bight stretches towards the north-east, called the Black Sea, which divides the three continents of the earth: to the east lies Asia, to the west lies Europe (which some call *Aeneas-land*), but to the north of the Black Sea lies Greater Sweden or Sweden the Cold [Russia] . . .
>
> Through Greater Sweden [Russia], from the range of mountains that lie to the north beyond the edge of human habitation, there runs a river properly called the Tanais [Don], which flows into the Black Sea. In Asia to the east of the Tanais [Don] there was a land called Ásaland or Ásaheim [Land of the Æsir]; its chief city was called Ásgarð [Home of the Æsir]. That city was ruled by a chieftain called Óðin, and it was a great centre for sacrifices . . .
>
> (*Heimskringla: Ynglinga saga*, Ch. 1)

That was how Snorri Sturluson tried to rationalise the origin of the Norse gods, the Æsir, who lived in a heaven called Ásgarð. According to Snorri, they had been an Asiatic tribe who had migrated to Scandinavia in ancient times under the chieftain Óðin, who in Norse mythology became the chief god of the Viking pantheon, Óðin the All-Father.

The cult of Óðin was a dark and sacrificial business. Whole armies and individual enemies would be sacrificed to him. He was the god of the occult, and the god of war. From his throne in Ásgarð he could see out over all the universe. On his shoulders perched his two constant companions, two ravens called Hugin and Munin (Mind and Memory) which kept him informed of what was happening; they were birds of carrion, the scavengers of the battlefield. In Ásgarð he had a palace called Valhöll (wrongly transliterated in English in its genetival plural form, Valhalla), where fallen warriors spent the afterlife in an orgy of feasting and fighting, preparing for the Last Battle which would spell the Doom of the Gods (*Ragnarök*).

Óðin was essentially the Lord of the Slain, the god of kings and chieftains; but he was also the god of poetry and wisdom. He sacrificed one of his eyes in his constant search for knowledge, and is usually portrayed as a one-eyed figure in disguise. He is also credited with the discovery of runes, the semi-magical system of writing incised on bone, wood or stone by the Norsemen before the introduction of the Roman alphabet. The runic alphabet consisted originally of sixteen twig-like letters known as the *futhark* from the values of its first six symbols; the full alphabet is to be

Tiny tenth-century bronze figurine of a seated Thór, found in the north of Iceland. It shows Thór holding his beard, which is metamorphosed into his Hammer resting on his knees. Actual height, 7.6 cm.

found on an incised rib-bone now in the Culture History Museum in Lund, Sweden. Runes were mostly used for memorial inscriptions, but they were also used for secret charms or curses. Their magical association goes all the way back to an enigmatic myth about their discovery by Óðin after he had ritually hanged and stabbed himself:

> I know that I hung
> On the windswept tree
> For nine whole nights,
> Pierced by the spear
> And given to Óðin –
> Myself given to myself
> On that tree
> Whose roots
> No one knows.
>
> They gave me not bread
> Nor drink from the horn;
> Into the depths I peered,
> I grasped the runes,
> Screaming I grasped them,
> And then fell back.

(*Hávamál*)

The Norse pantheon was dominated by a trinity of gods. Óðin was nominally the chief god, All-Father. But another very important god was Thór, the Thunderer, who was probably the most widely venerated of all the Viking gods. Where Óðin was the aristocratic god, Thór was the patron god of seamen and farmers. He was a huge bluff figure, red-haired, red-bearded, red-eyed. He was god of the sky, the ruler of storms and tempests, wielder of thunderbolts. He rode the heavens in a chariot drawn by two sacred goats, and at his passage thunder crashed, the earth quaked and lightning cracked. He was the Lord Protector of the Universe, guarding the world with his mighty hammer Mjöllnir against the menace of the Giants who lurked just beyond the limits of civilisation. Thór's Hammer, however, was more than just a symbol of supernatural strength and violence; it was also a fertility emblem, which was used to hallow weddings and marital homes as horse-shoes were to do later. Numerous Thór's Hammers have been found in the form of amulets and good-luck charms, as well as some moulds for casting them.

The third god of the Norse trinity was the fertility god, Frey, closely associated with his twin sister, Freyja. Frey was the paramount god of the Swedes, and the divine ancestor of their royal dynasty at Uppsala (cf Ch. 4). He is usually portrayed with a giant penis erect, symbolising his powers of fertility and prosperous increase. Snorri Sturluson wrote of him: 'Frey is the noblest of the gods. He controls the rain and the sunshine and therefore the natural increase of the earth, and it is good to call upon him for fruitful seasons and for peace. He also controls the good fortunes of men.' Freyja was his female mirror-image, loveliest and most lascivious of the goddesses, wanton and fecund.

There are now innumerable artefacts in museums throughout northern Europe that are thought to portray or allude to these gods: a beautiful little cast bronze figurine of a seated Thór grasping his beard and his hammer, dating from the tenth century and found in northern Iceland; an eleventh-century bronze statuette of a squatting Frey from Rällinge in Sweden; various representations of a one-eyed man accompanied by bird motifs to suggest Óðin. But it is only in the poetry of the *Edda* (usually called the *Poetic Edda* or the *Elder Edda* to differentiate it from *Snorri's Edda*) that the old gods and heroes come to life.

The *Edda* is a collection of thirty-nine poems, compiled in Iceland in the thirteenth century. The poems or lays themselves are very much older, however, and have their roots deep in the pre-Viking world of Germanic legend. Ten are mythological, for the most part stories about the gods and their adventures. The others are heroic lays about the great figures of Germanic folklore – Sigurð the Dragon-Slayer, Attila the Hun, Ermaneric the Goth.

One of the longest of the poems is a mythological lay called *Hávamál* ('The Words of the High One'). It is a ninth-century compilation made from five or six earlier poems and consisting of gnomic advice and prag-

VIKINGS!

matic sayings attributed to Óðin. Apart from the strange passages about Óðin hanging himself from a tree in search of the magic of the runes, it has nothing to do with mysticism or religion; it is a series of down-to-earth, sometimes cynical maxims for the ordinary Viking to live by – a sort of do-it-yourself Viking handbook for survival:

> Look carefully round doorways before you walk in; you never know when an enemy might be there.

> There is no better load a man can carry than much common sense; no worse a load than too much drink.

> Never part with your weapons when out in the fields; you never know when you will need your spear.

ABOVE Small eleventh-century statuette of a squatting Frey with penis erect, found at Rällinge in Sweden.

RIGHT Carved panel from Hylestad Church in Norway, depicting scenes from the legend of Sigurð the Dragon-Slayer. Here Sigurð sucks his finger after burning it on the dragon's roasted heart – thereby learning the language of the birds, who warn him of impending treachery.

Upper section of the Hunninge Stone in Gotland: the Viking in his ship skimming over the sea, and later (*top*) being welcomed to Valhöll by a Valkyrie (*top right*) while warriors engage in endless battle (*uppermost*).

Be a friend to your friend, match gift with gift; meet smiles with smiles, and lies with dissimulation.

No need to give too much to a man, a little can buy much thanks; with half a loaf and a tilted jug I often won me a friend.

Confide in one, never in two; confide in three, and the whole world knows.

Praise no day until evening, no wife until buried, no sword until tested, no maid until bedded, no ice until crossed, no ale until drunk.

The halt can ride, the handless can herd, the deaf can fight with spirit; a blind man is better than a corpse on a pyre – a corpse is no good to anyone.

Wealth dies, kinsmen die, a man himself must likewise die; but word-fame never dies, for him who achieves it well.

One particular area has provided a priceless source of graphic material to supplement the literary sources, a whole portfolio of pictures on stones

from the Baltic island of Gotland, off the east coast of Sweden (*cf* Ch. 4).
Nearly four hundred of these carved and painted picture-stones have been
found on Gotland, dating from the Migration Period in the fifth century to
the eleventh. They have given posterity a marvellously vivid archive of the
pre-Viking and Viking view of life and death in this world and the next.

One particular specimen, the Hunninge Stone from Klinte in Gotland,
dating from the eighth century, tells the whole story of the Ages of Viking
Man. It is a sculpted Saga in itself. It is a very large stone – just on three
metres high – and now forms part of the magnificent collection of picture-
stones in Gotland's Historical Museum (*Fornsalen*) in Visby, the capital
town of Gotland. At the bottom we see the Viking as farmer, carefully
husbanding his land and livestock. In the middle section we see him on a
Viking longship, skimming over the curling waves of the 'whale's-path' to
augment his income with a bit of private enterprise – the less acceptable
face of Viking capitalism to medieval eyes. And at the top we see him
arriving in the afterworld which welcomed all true Vikings who died in
battle: free transport on Óðin's eight-legged magic steed, Sleipnir, to
Valhöll, the Hall of the Slain; a welcome by a Valkyrie serving endless
horns of ale; and an eternity of friendly battle in which the dead and the
wounded are miraculously restored every evening.

The Valkyries were the Choosers of the Slain. In later myths they were
represented somewhat romantically as the warrior handmaidens of Óðin,
and they appear as such in Wagnerian opera. But originally they were
demons of carnage and death who devoured corpses on the battlefield like
wolves and ravens; in this they resembled the Greek Furies with their
manic thirst for retribution and blood-revenge. After the Viking defeat at
the Battle of Clontarf in Ireland in 1014 (*cf* Ch. 6), a Norse poet portrayed
them in their primitive form, exulting in blood and weaving the web of
war; the poem, known as the *Darraðarljóð*, is preserved in *Njál's Saga* (*cf*
Ch. 7):

> Blood rains
> From the cloudy web
> On the broad loom of slaughter.
> The web of man,
> Grey as armour,
> Is now being woven;
> The Valkyries
> Will cross it
> With a crimson weft.
>
> The warp is made
> Of human entrails;
> Human heads
> Are used as weights;
> The heddle-rods

Are blood-wet spears;
The shafts are iron-bound,
And arrows are the shuttles.
With swords we will weave
This web of battle.

It is terrible now
To look around,
As a blood-red cloud
Darkens the sky.
The heavens are stained
With the blood of men,
As the Valkyries
Sing their song . . .

(*Njál's Saga*, Ch. 157)

Such was the background of belief and conduct in the Viking Age and the centuries that preceded it. Such was the life of the mind that informed and reflected the reality of everyday activity in the Viking Age. And that reality, it is now recognised, involved the same kind of preoccupations that affect the realities of the twentieth century: technological development, commercial competition, economic expansion – in a word, survival.

For centuries before the start of the Viking Age, the northlands had been engaged in trade with the south, the east and the west. The earliest Scandinavian trading-post we know of was Helgö, a settlement on an island in Lake Mälar in the Uppland province of Sweden; it was founded in the fifth century, or perhaps even earlier. Excavation there in the past few years has revealed terraces of houses and craftsmen's workshops, and a variety of imported goods from western and eastern Europe and even further afield, perhaps from as far away as India, in the shape of a bronze figure of a Buddha dating from the sixth or seventh century. Helgö was a predecessor of the larger trade centre of Birka, a few kilometres to the west on Lake Mälar, which sprang up right at the start of the Viking Age in the early ninth century (*cf* Ch. 4).

In a paper delivered at a symposium on 'The Vikings' to celebrate the 500th Anniversary of the University of Uppsala in Sweden in June 1977, Professor Peter Sawyer of Leeds University emphasised the growing scholarly awareness of the importance of trading activity in Dark Age Scandinavia.[1] Furs from the far north and the countries east of the Baltic were highly prized in the royal courts and noble households of Continental Europe, especially marten pelts, beaver and winter squirrel. Ivory from walrus tusks was also in great demand, for ornaments or as a costly substitute for wood in making caskets. Amber from the Baltic coasts was another luxury raw product, to be made into jewellery or amulets. Falcons

[1] 'Wics, Kings and Vikings' in *The Vikings* (Acta Universitatis Upsaliensis, Uppsala, 1978).

VIKINGS!

from the far north were noted for their speed and rapacity when hunting. And there was always a ready market for that most perishable but in-exhaustible of commodities – human slaves.

Germanic society was essentially reciprocal, and friendships were cemented by the constant exchange of costly gifts. Loyalty to one's lord was reinforced by the distribution of largesse in the form of treasure, and poets sang the praises of open-handed 'ring-givers' and 'bestowers of gold'. Precious objects and beautiful things were valued as status symbols in those days no less than they are today; conspicuous wealth and ostentatious generosity were considered virtues.

The growth of trade was clearly an important factor in the development of kingship. Trade was an obvious source of steady revenue for anyone who could control and exploit it; traders required protection that only kings could provide. Tolls and taxes on mercantile traffic through a king's territory provided the wealth to finance armed forces that could supply that protection.

The growth of trade also required better forms of transport. In the early days, much of the trade was conducted overland; and here the Swedish trading towns like Helgö and Birka, with access to the Baltic through Lake Mälar, had an immense natural advantage. During the winter, which was the optimum time for fur-trading, these island ports became in effect inland towns, because the waterways for hundreds of kilometres in all directions were frozen solid, becoming easily-negotiated highways for sledges. The Scandinavians were pioneers in the use of skis and skates. Bone skates fashioned from the metapodials of horses, cattle and deer have

The Vikings used bone skates for trading journeys during winter. In Norway the author tried out a pair from the University Museum of Antiquities in Oslo – and found they worked!

been found in vast numbers at many archaeological sites in Scandinavia, and also in the Viking city of York in England (*cf* Ch. 5); the Old Norse word for skate, *ísleggr*, means literally 'ice leg-bone'. They were simply smoothed down on one side, and cut to fit a foot. The skate would be attached by thongs at heel and sometimes toe, and the skater would propel himself with a spiked stick, not lifting his feet from the ice. It sounds clumsy; but I tried them out myself on a frozen lake in Norway, and found it easy to work up to very respectable speeds after a minimum of practice.

However, the major form of transport would become the ship, which helped to make the Viking Age possible and has remained its most evocative symbol in the public's mind. Oddly enough, the evolution of the Viking ship was a very slow and gradual business; and the key factor was the development of a keel capable of supporting a mast. For many centuries, apparently, the Scandinavians were content to travel about their fjords and inshore waters in rowing-boats. The importance of the sail was that it enabled them to expand their horizons so dramatically.

But why did it take so long, and why did it come to fruition at the particular time we call the Viking Age? After all, there was nothing new or revolutionary about the use of sails as such; the Vikings did not invent them. It seems to have come about as a function of the expansionism encouraged, in part at least, by new trade potential. The horizons *needed* extending, and so the Scandinavian shipwrights set about making it possible.

In ancient times, the Scandinavians seem to have used primitive dug-outs or hollowed logs. But it is more than likely that they also used skin boats – boats with wooden frames over which ox-hides would be stretched and fastened. This possibility was brilliantly demonstrated in the early 1970s by Professor Sverre Marstrander, Director of the University Museum of National Antiquities in Oslo. He had made a close study of the elaborate rock carvings of boats, dating from the Bronze Age 3000 years ago, that are found all over southern Norway. Earlier scholars had suggested that they represented rafts, or dug-outs with outriggers, or even planked boats; but Professor Marstrander became convinced that these carvings, although doubtless ritualistic in intent, were realistic depictions of skin boats. He set out to prove his theory in the only practical way possible – by actually building one. Sponsored by the BBC TV archaeological programme *Chronicle* and with the enthusiastic encouragement of its founder and executive producer, the late Paul Johnstone, Professor Marstrander commissioned boat-builder Odd Johnsen of Frederikstad to create to his specifications a Bronze Age skin boat based on the rock carvings he had come to know so intimately. The result was a memorable television programme about experimental archaeology – and a Bronze Age boat that worked.

Professor Marstrander argued that the skin boats of the Bronze Age with their sturdy ribs would have developed naturally into the earliest

Bronze Age rock carvings at Kalnes in Norway. The framework of the craft is visible through its sides.

plank-built vessels of the Iron Age that we know from archaeology. The oldest Nordic boat yet found, the Als Boat (also known as the Hjörtspring Boat), which was found in a bog in southern Denmark in 1921, dates to around 300 BC. It is thought by scholars to be a direct imitation of a skin boat, using wood instead of cow-hides; it was round-bottomed, and made from five overlapping planks fastened together with stitching.

Next in the archaeological record comes the Björke Boat, found on an island west of Stockholm, which has been dated to around AD 100. It was basically a dug-out canoe to which a plank had been riveted, clinker-style, to give additional freeboard.

The next major development is seen in the Nydam oak boat, now on display in the Schleswig-Holstein Museum of Early and Pre-History at Schloss Gottorp. It was found in a bog in southern Jutland in 1864 and is dated to around AD 400 – the period of the great Continental migrations (AD 300–600). It is surely no coincidence that ship-building innovations should be found from a time when there was an urgent demand for transport. The Nydam Boat was a very large one, long and narrow, clinker-built of broad oaken planks, with rowlocks for thirty oars on each side. It is the earliest boat yet found that was specifically designed to be rowed, not paddled. It did not have a proper keel, merely an extra-heavy plank at the bottom to take the strain of beaching. It had the high stem and stern that would become such a familiar feature of Viking Age boats, and a large steering-paddle on the starboard side. It was in warships of this kind that the first Angles and Saxons reached England in the fifth century; and although there is still much learned argument about the exact way the Nydam Boat looked and performed, it can surely be seen as a direct forerunner of the Viking longship. It is also a clear precursor of the magnificent Anglo-Saxon galley excavated from a burial mound at Sutton Hoo in England in 1939, dated to around AD 600.

Chronologically, the last 'pre-Viking' boat in the sequence is the Kvalsund Boat from western Norway, which is dated to around AD 700. Despite its fragmentary condition when found, it had the familiar full-bodied hull we associate with Viking boats; but more importantly, it had a rudimentary keel. It seems to have been designed as a rowing-boat, and there is no evidence that it ever carried a mast; but we can view the Kvalsund Boat with its sweeping prow as standing at the very threshold of the Viking Age – an intermediate boat in which we can recognise the immense sailing potential that would soon be realised to the full by the shipwrights of the Viking Age proper.

The Kvalsund Boat brings us hard up against the two most celebrated boat finds in Scandinavia – the Gokstad Ship and the Oseberg Ship (*cf* Ch. 2). The combination of sail and oars gave them a speed and manoeuvrability that took Europe totally by surprise; their shallowness of draught allowed them to penetrate rivers that gave them access to rich inland cities like London and Paris. They needed no harbours, for they were designed

to be beached on any shelving sandy shore. They could land warriors and horses anywhere and everywhere, and in retreat they could reach islets in the shallow waters of estuaries that other boats could not navigate. They gave the Vikings a huge advantage over their opponents: for coastal attacks their boats were ocean-going landing-craft, while for attacks on inland cities their capacity to navigate shallow rivers gave them the element of surprise of airborne paratroops dropped behind the enemy defence lines.

Ships and the sea played an overwhelming part in the life and imagination of the Norsemen. They were a constant factor in their everyday activities. After death, the ship was apparently supposed to carry the dead man to the afterworld, either as a funeral pyre as described by the Arab traveller Ibn Fadlan amongst the Vikings in Russia in 922 (*cf* Ch. 4), or in boats that were buried and securely anchored in heaped burial mounds (*cf* Ch. 2), or in graves whose outlines were boldly marked by stone-settings in the form of ships (*cf* Ch. 3). In Norse mythology, the god Frey counted among his greatest treasures a magic ship called *Skíðblaðnir* which had been built by those consummate craftsmen of legend, the dwarves; according to Snorri Sturluson it always had a following wind, and it was so ingeniously constructed that it was large enough to carry the entire pantheon of the gods of Ásgarð, yet could be folded up and tucked into a pouch when not in use.

21

The Oseberg Ship in Norway with its richly carved prow.

Viking poets waxed lyrical about their ships. In their esoteric skaldic court poetry, the ship constantly appears in elaborate figures of speech known as 'kennings': the ship was an 'oar-steed', a 'horse of the breakers', an 'ocean-striding bison', a 'surf-dragon', a 'fjord-elk', a 'horse of the lobster's heath'; a flotilla of ships was a 'fleet of the otter's world'.

To the Viking, his ship was not just his means of transport; it was his home, his way of life, his pilgrim's way, something to love but also to fear. The storm and stress of the seafarer's life, the love-hate relationship with his ship, is magnificently expressed in the elegiac Anglo-Saxon poem called *The Seafarer*:

> I can sing   my own true story,
> Tell of my travels,   how I have oft suffered
> Times of hardship   in days of toil;
> Bitter cares   have I often harboured,
> And often learned   how troubled a home
> Is a ship in a storm,   when I took my turn
> At the arduous night-watch   at the vessel's prow
> As it beat past cliffs.   Oft were my feet
> Fettered by frost   in frozen bonds,
> Tortured by cold,   while searing anguish

OPPOSITE Professor Marstrander's replica Bronze Age boat afloat.

23

Exact scale replica of the smallest dinghy (*færing*) found with the Gokstad Ship in Norway, with the author rowing stroke.

Clutched at my heart,
My sea-weary mind . . .   and longing rent

My heart's blood stirs me   . . . Yet now once more
        The towering seas,   to try again
        My heart's desires   the salt waves' play;
    To go on the journey,   always urge me
        Of foreign peoples   to visit the lands
                                    far over sea . . .
                            (*The Seafarer: Exeter Book*)

The bulk of Viking shipping will have consisted of small ferry boats or larger cargo boats like the *knörr* (*cf* Ch. 7). But in the Sagas, the limelight is always on the longships, the thoroughbred racing warships. The longships were for heroes, for warriors. Naval warfare was simply an extension of hand-to-hand combat on land; the ships were roped close together in line abreast, and this floating line would then attack the enemy line head-on. The brunt of the battle was borne by the selected champions who stood at the prow and absorbed the first fury of the impact; if the prow-man (*stafnbúi*) fell, another would step forward to take his place, while the men

24

aft in the ship rained missiles and arrows on the opposing ranks. Victory would come when resistance on a ship had been so worn down that it was possible to board it and clear the decks of survivors. There were few niceties of tactics; it was a grim process of attrition, hammering away at each other until exhaustion or weight of numbers swung the balance. A Viking sea-battle was no place for the faint-hearted.

The ultimate in sea-heroism is enshrined in a late and semi-legendary Icelandic Saga called *Jómsvíkinga saga*. It concerns the activities of a warrior community of Baltic Vikings who lived in a fortress called Jómsborg; one of their alleged leaders, Thorkel the Tall, would play a prominent part in the Danish invasions of England in the early eleventh century led by King Svein Fork-Beard (*cf* Ch. 9). The fortress of Jómsborg, if it ever existed at all, could perhaps be identified with the town of Wollin at the mouth of the Oder; archaeological excavations there in the 1930s revealed that Wollin in the late tenth century was a large and well-garrisoned trade centre with a mixed Norse and Slav population.

In the Saga, the Jómsvíkings were in their heyday during this period, when King Harald 'Blue-Tooth' Gormsson was on the throne of Denmark (*cf* Ch. 3). They were said to be a close-knit band of mercenaries greatly prized and feared for their fighting prowess; their fortress was a monastic community which no woman was ever allowed to enter, they were all between the ages of eighteen and fifty, and they were pledged by unbreakable oaths to keep the peace amongst themselves and to avenge one another's deaths.

The climax and logical culmination of their *raison d'être* came around the year 980. One Yuletide they all got mortally drunk, and were goaded by the crafty Harald Gormsson of Denmark into making rash vows to crush his arch-enemy, Earl Hákon of Norway, or die in the attempt. Next morning, nursing vile hangovers, they trudged down to their ships and sailed away, sore-headed and frozen-bearded, to a famous battle, the Battle of Hjörungavágr, where they were soundly trounced. Only seventy of them survived the slaughter; they were taken alive and roped together to await execution.

Jómsvíkinga saga gives a marvellous description of how the executions began, as one man after another was freed from the rope and beheaded. The victorious Norwegians wanted to see if these Danish Jómsvíkings were as brave in the face of death as they were reputed to be, and the Jómsvíkings obliged with a show of nonchalant bravado. One asked his colleagues to watch carefully to see if any spark of life remained after his head flew off; he would try to lift the dagger in his hand if he could – but the axe fell, and so did the dagger. Another asked to be struck by the axe full in the face, so that all could see that he did not pale: 'He did not pale, but his eyes closed as death overtook him.'

The eleventh man to be led to his execution was an eighteen-year-old boy with long silky golden hair. He asked that someone of warrior rank

John Anstee at work on the complex process of making a pattern-welded sword in Viking style. The lower picture shows four of the stages when the iron is being worked into its patterns – 'Immensely difficult and immensely rewarding,' he says. 'Viking smiths were second to none.'

Karl Heinz Gloy in Denmark, carving patterns on the verge-boards of his Viking longhouse.

should hold his hair away from his head to prevent it becoming blood-stained. One of the earl's henchmen stepped forward, took hold of the hair and twisted it round his hands. But as the axe fell, the young man jerked his head back sharply so that the blow fell on the man who was holding his hair, cutting off both his arms at the elbows. This brilliant ploy so delighted the Norwegians that the young Jómsvíking was offered his life; but he only accepted on condition that the rest of his companions were spared, too. And so they were.

Such preposterous heroics were meat and drink to the post-Viking Age readers of the Icelandic Sagas. And they have continued to exert a strange fascination on people ever since. At Kendal in the north of England, museum-curator and archaeologist John Anstee has spent many years trying to learn and emulate the subtle blacksmith's art that produced the superb pattern-welded swords of the Vikings. In the United States, Mr Bob Asp of Hawley, Minnesota, has spent eight years building a full-scale replica of the Gokstad Ship in an old potato warehouse – a private dream that he hopes to realise eventually with an actual sea-voyage in it to Norway. In Denmark, a cabinet-maker called Karl Heinz Gloy has built himself, single-handed, a perfect replica of a Viking longhouse in his back garden, complete with beautifully carved verge-boards to keep the wind from lifting the turf roof. In Iceland, a farmer called Sveinbjörn Beinteinsson has started a revival of interest in the ancient Viking religion, the *Ásatrú* (Belief in the Æsir), which now attracts several score of unfanatical adherents. And throughout England the four hundred members of the Norse Film and Pageant Society, now the largest active Medieval Society in Britain, feel impelled to spend their weekends enacting full-dress displays of dramatic episodes in Viking history – especially the more spectacularly bloody battles.

The power of the smith, the poetry of the sword and the ship, the heroism in the face of the hereafter: all these are the living ingredients still of the Viking experience. 'Men do not limp while their legs are the same length,' said one young Icelander, badly injured, as he walked straight and steadfastly into the presence of a king of Norway.

And yet this heroism was hammered from a credo that was essentially fatalistic and without hope. The afterworld held no promise of redemption, no easy bribe of eternal bliss. The world of the Norse gods was doomed from the start, and the gods themselves knew it; Óðin the All-Father knew all the time that their destiny was destruction, remorseless and fore-ordained, when their world would be overwhelmed by the forces of chaos:

Brothers will battle	to bloody end,
And sister's kin	commit foul acts.
There's woe in the world,	wantonness rampant;
An axe-age, a sword-age,	shields are sundered;
A storm-age, a wolf-age,	before the world crumbles.
No mercy or quarter	will man give to man.
The sun grows dark,	earth sinks in the sea,
The bright stars	fall from the skies;
Flames rage	and fires leap high,
Heaven itself	is seared by heat.

(*Völuspá – The Sibyl's Prophecy*)

The Viking gods were doomed to die in a cataclysmic Last Battle, at Ragnarök (Doom of the Gods). It took the Christian poet who wrote *Völuspá*, the opening poem in the *Poetic Edda*, to add, as consolation, a glimpse of a better world to come:

She sees arise	a second time
Earth from the sea	green with growth.
Falls cascade,	the eagle flies high,
The one from the mountains	who stoops for fish.

> She sees a hall, more fair than the sun,
> Thatched with gold, at Gimlé;
> There shall the gods in innocence dwell,
> Live for ever a life of bliss.
>
> And there once again, rare and wonderful,
> Golden chessmen will be found on the grass,
> Which the gods had owned in olden times.
>
> Then shall the Mighty One come to his kingdom,
> The strong from above, Who rules over all . . .

But even so, the Sibyl in *Völuspá* can see even further, towards another turn in the relentless cyclical ordeal of purification by fire and sword; for the last stanza echoes the dark and brooding images of the future that would befall the Viking gods:

> Now comes the dark dragon flying,
> The glittering serpent from Niðafell;
> It soars over the plain, and on its pinions
> It bears the bodies of slaughtered men.

Destiny was inexorable. The absolute finality of death was inevitable. Even the gods themselves had to face it. And in the end they would face it with the same stoicism, the same heroic fatalism, as the best of heroes. They had only one consolation:

> Wealth dies, kinsmen die,
> A man himself must likewise die;
> But one thing I know that never dies –
> The verdict on each man dead.

(Hávamál)

The 'word-fame' has lasted a thousand years. The 'verdict on each man dead' is changing. It is this word-fame, this changing verdict, that we will be exploring in this book.

2

Bolt from the Blue

England in the year of grace 793: a green and pleasant land, relatively peaceful in an era of general turbulence, islanded and apparently secure from outside attack. It was not yet a united nation, but a number of separate and often warring kingdoms: Northumbria in the north, Mercia in the Midlands, East Anglia to the east, Kent to the south-east, Wessex to the south-west. Northumbria was dominant in the seventh century, Mercia in the eighth, Wessex would come into its own in the ninth.

While kings fought and kings fell, their deeds and misdeeds claiming most of the attention of chroniclers and annalists, the general populace apparently prospered. Farmlands yielded good produce, trade expanded. The Church, founded by St Augustine late in the sixth century, had gradually tamed the 'barbarian' instincts of the hordes of pagan Angles and Saxons from Continental Europe who had overrun England after the Roman legions had been withdrawn from Britain in AD 410. Learning and literature blossomed, craftsmen flourished. Saintly men founded monasteries, where scholars like the Venerable Bede could write great works; it was at the monastery of Wearmouth and Jarrow in the first half of the eighth century that Bede wrote his monumental *Ecclesiastical History of the English People*. And it was in these monasteries that books were embellished with superb illumination, like the magnificent eighth-century *Codex Aureus* (now in the Royal Library in Stockholm). Golden books, golden chalices, silver plate, carved ivories, precious jewellery, decorated weapons, artistic metalwork of every kind; and the finest of all this great outpouring of creative Anglo-Saxon art was the book known as the Lindisfarne Gospels, produced during the 690s on the Holy Island of Lindisfarne, just off the north-eastern shoulder of England.

It is one of the most splendid manuscript books in the world, 258 folio pages of beautiful half-uncial script and magnificent coloured illustrations: a matchless masterpiece from the early English Church in the so-called 'Dark Ages', when Northumbria was one of the foremost centres of culture and scholarship in all Europe.

And then, suddenly, came terror:

Imago aequilae

Manuscript illumination from the Lindisfarne Gospels, produced on the Holy Island of Lindisfarne in the 690s and now in the British Museum.

793. In this year terrible portents appeared over Northumbria which sorely affrighted the inhabitants: there were exceptional flashes of lightning, and fiery dragons were seen flying through the air. A great famine followed hard upon these signs; and a little later in that same year, on the 8th of June, the harrying of the heathen miserably destroyed God's church on Lindisfarne by rapine and slaughter.

(Anglo-Saxon Chronicle, Laud MS)

The Viking raid on Lindisfarne in 793, a smash-and-grab assault by a prowling band of Norwegian marauders, is cited in every textbook as the start of the Viking Age. It makes a hauntingly evocative scene. On the bare and windswept tidal islet of Lindisfarne, long revered as a cradle of Christianity, peaceful monks are going about their devotions as usual. Suddenly all hell breaks loose, we are told. Grim-prowed ships with

The Lindisfarne Stone: grave-marker found on Lindisfarne, formerly thought to commemorate the first recorded Viking raid in 793. The original is now in the British Museum.

square sails and snarling dragon-heads loom menacingly over the sea-horizon to the east; oaken keels scrape noisily up the shelving sandy beaches; fierce-bearded Vikings, ravening for Christian blood and plunder, leap ashore with manic abandon, and in a trice all is confusion and slaughter:

> And they came to the church of Lindisfarne, laid everything waste with grievous plundering, trampled the holy places with polluted feet, dug up the altars and seized all the treasures of the holy church. They killed some of the brothers; some they took away with them in fetters; many they drove out, naked and loaded with insults; and some they drowned in the sea. (Simeon of Durham)

Lindisfarne was only a curtain-raiser. In the next few years there was a flurry of raids on other monasteries and abbeys: Wearmouth and Jarrow, Bede's old monastery, in 794, Iona in 795, and again in 802 and 806, Rathlin Island off Ireland in 795. By 799 the first raiders were reported at various islands off the Aquitaine coast of France. The flood-gates had opened.

But Lindisfarne was exceptional. The attack on Lindisfarne was construed as an attack on civilisation itself, a shocking affront. An early church and monastery had been founded there in the 630s by a missionary monk, St Aidan, from that other 'Holy Island' of Iona, where St Columba had established a mother church of Celtic monasticism off the west coast of Scotland. Fifty years later, in 687, Lindisfarne had become the burial place of the most celebrated of Northumbrian saints, St Cuthbert, whose relics are now enshrined in Durham Cathedral (cf Ch. 6).

To this day, the memory of 793 still seems to haunt the island. There are the sombre ruins of the medieval church and priory, all weathered red sandstone and Romanesque arches, and it is all too easy for the thousands of visitors who go there on pilgrimage every year to associate them with that historic Viking raid. In fact, though, they are the ruins of a Norman priory which was not built until three centuries later, and it owed its dereliction more to the ravages of time and the Tudor Dissolution than anything else.

Then there is the celebrated Lindisfarne Stone, which was dug up more than fifty years ago from under the ruins of the Norman priory. It has always been taken to commemorate the actual Viking raid of 793. On one side it depicts a menacing file of seven warriors brandishing swords and axes, wearing heavy jerkins and tight trousers; on the other side are carved the Cross, the sun and moon, God's hands, and two worshippers. But is it really a commemorative picture-stone, a cartoon, in effect, of that Viking bolt from the blue?

Dr Brian Hope-Taylor, the most recent archaeologist to have studied the area in depth, thinks not. He points out that the stone is a grave-marker from a cemetery, not a commemorative stone, and that although it can be dated stylistically to the ninth century, the Viking battle scene is of a type best known from carved and engraved stones in pagan Scandinavia. So who carved it? And for whom? Was it done by a Christian Anglo-Saxon craftsman on Lindisfarne who had been quick to pick up the Viking artistic idiom? Is it realistic to suppose that the Vikings themselves were so pleased with their handiwork of 793 that they went back to commemorate it?

The Lindisfarne Stone, which is now in the British Museum (there is also a rather raw-looking replica in the small museum on the island), is an evocative little riddle which we are never really likely to solve. But whatever its provenance it has a symbolic significance, as part of the greater symbolic importance of Lindisfarne itself. There may well have been isolated raids on undefended churches elsewhere before 793, because churches and monasteries were the repositories of harvest wealth and craft skills – the local banks of the time, in effect. But because of its position as a major centre of Christian learning, it was Lindisfarne that sent the first shock-waves of real alarm spreading through Europe.

At the time of the raid the great Northumbrian scholar, Alcuin, was working in France as a teacher at the invitation of the Emperor Charlemagne. He was the scion of a noble Northumbrian family and had been

The ruins of the late medieval church and priory on Lindisfarne today.

OPPOSITE The Gokstad Ship, excavated in 1880 and now in the Viking Ship Hall at Bygdøy in Oslo.

educated at the monastic school in York. Not unnaturally he took the news hard. He reacted by writing no fewer than five letters to England about the raid – a positive barrage of correspondence for those days. They contain suitable expressions of horror and dismay, of course; but for the most part their tone is admonitory: Alcuin used the raid as occasion for a sermon, but a sermon against the English rather than the Vikings. The Viking attack, he claimed, was a direct visitation of divine wrath against the sins of the English: sins that included peccadillos like fornications, adulteries and incests; avarice, robbery and violent judgements; luxuriousness, long hair and flashy clothing . . .

But the most intriguing passage comes in his letter to the king of Northumbria, King Æthelred:

> Lo, it is nearly 350 years that we and our forefathers have inhabited this most lovely land, and never before has such terror appeared in Britain as we have now suffered from a pagan race; nor was it thought that such an inroad from the sea could be made [*or* such a sea-disaster could happen].
> (Dorothy Whitelock: *English Historical Documents*)

Evidently what was so shattering about Lindisfarne was the stark fact that it could have happened at all. Churches and monasteries all over Europe had been built in exposed coastal positions in the blithe belief that they were invulnerable from the sea. Yet here was deadly proof of

34

The excavation of the Gokstad Ship from a funeral mound in Norway in 1880.

the rise of a new sea-power that was quite capable of achieving such 'inroads from the sea' or 'sea-disasters' all the way across the North Sea from Norway.

Obviously it was the Viking ship with its advanced technology that made this possible. And when we think of Viking ships, we think inevitably of the Gokstad Ship, which was excavated from a burial mound in south-western Norway in 1880 and is now proudly displayed in the Viking Ship Hall at Bygdøy in Oslo.

It is little short of a miracle that the Gokstad Ship has survived. It was built around AD 850, and some time afterwards – perhaps ten, perhaps fifty years later – it was hauled ashore to provide the setting for a royal funeral. Near the town of Sandefjord on the western side of Oslo Fjord, some three kilometres from the sea, it was lowered into a deep trench cut into the blue clay underlying the ground surface. Just aft of amidships a wooden burial chamber was set into the ship, and a dead king was laid on the bed inside. He was a powerfully-built man in his fifties who had suffered severely from arthritis or gout. Round the body the mourners laid out his weapons and accoutrements and personal possessions, and an odd menagerie of slaughtered animals – twelve horses, six dogs and a peacock. Then they heaped the blue clay over the grave to form a high, elongated barrow which from then on would be known locally as *Kongshaugen*, the King's Mound.

36

As good luck would have it, the blue clay had remarkable preservative properties because it sealed the ship completely from any contact with the air; only where the tall stem and stern posts had protruded above the bed of clay was there any decaying of the timbers. Grave-robbers broke into the mound some time in antiquity to steal the valuables that had been buried with the king; apart from that, the Gokstad Ship lay undisturbed and unmouldering for a thousand years until it was excavated by Nicolay Nicolaysen, president of the Antiquarian Society in Oslo.

To my mind, quite simply, Gokstad is the most beautiful ship ever built – such is its grace of line, the lean power of its hull. Its vital statistics are: 23.33 metres long overall; 5.25 metres broad; 1.95 metres deep from the gunwale amidships to the bottom of the keel. It was built almost entirely of oak; the hull weighs over seven tons, yet even when fully laden with another ten tons of equipment and freight it drew only about one metre of water. It carried a stout pine mast with a large sail made up of double-thickness strips of red and white woven cloth (*vaðmál*), which would have given either a striped or a chequered effect depending on how the sail was made up. The ship was steered by a rudder-paddle ingeniously mounted aft on the starboard ('steer-board') quarter.

Gokstad was essentially a sailing ship, but it could also be rowed: there were oar-holes for sixteen pairs of long, narrow-bladed spruce oars, cut to differing lengths so that they would all strike the water simultaneously in short choppy strokes. There were no fixed rowing benches; the oarsmen must have used their sea-chests to sit on when rowing was called for, either for manoeuvring in close waters or when the wind failed. It suggests a crew of about thirty-two men; but surprisingly enough, Gokstad was found with not thirty-two but sixty-four shields slung inboard from a pierced lath just below the gunwales. Arne Emil Christensen, a curator at the University Museum of National Antiquities in Oslo and a leading authority on Viking ships, interprets this as meaning that the Gokstad Ship carried a double crew, one resting while the other rowed. To have two men to an oar would have been very useful when it came to hand-to-hand fighting, but it must have made conditions on board during long voyages incredibly cramped and uncomfortable. Imagine seventy burly men curled up in sleeping-bags on the deck!

The remains of three smaller boats were found in the Gokstad mound,

Drawing of the Gokstad Ship, prow to the left. The steering-paddle at the stern is on the far (starboard) side.

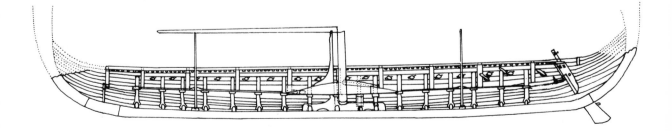

beautifully made and measuring 9.75, 8 and 6.6 metres respectively. An exact replica of the smallest boat, a four-oared sailing dinghy (*færing*), has recently been built and sea-tested by the National Maritime Museum at Greenwich; it is now on display at the Viking excavation site at Coppergate in York (*cf* Ch. 5).

Constructing likenesses of Gokstad has become something of an industry nowadays. Everyone with any interest in the history of ships, both lay and learned alike, is fascinated to know just how good Gokstad would have been in the water: would its performance have matched the perfection of its lines?

The first and most celebrated replica, or near-replica, was built in 1893 to show the flag for Norway at the Chicago World Fair of that year. This project was sparked off by the news that Spain was planning to send replicas of the three caravels with which Christopher Columbus had discovered South America four centuries earlier. The challenge was taken up by Magnus Andersen, the editor of a Norwegian shipping journal, as a means not only of proving that the Vikings had discovered America (*Vínland* – *cf* Ch. 8) long before Columbus, but also of demonstrating the continuing virility of Norwegian shipping in a highly competitive field. The idea met with predictable hostility from the archaeological establishment of his day, especially from the Gokstad excavator, Nicolay Nicolaysen, but Andersen went ahead with it none the less, buoyed up by a wave of nationalist feeling both at home and amongst Norwegian émigrés in the United States.

Alan L. Binns, senior lecturer in the department of English at Hull University, has noted that Andersen was no academic purist when it came to building his replica, the *Viking*, and made several modifications to the original specifications; but the *Viking* is still the most accurate Gokstad replica yet built. The keel was deeper, to give greater stability; the draught was 1.5 metres; there was a big fender made of reindeer hair along the outside of the top strakes of the gunwales to give the ship extra buoyancy if it should be swamped; and it carried extra sails. In addition to the single rectangular sail of the Viking ships, Andersen rigged up a pair of small triangular topsails from the ends of the yard-arm up to the mast-head, and also rigged a pair of stunsails or studding-sails on extra yards on either side of the main sail. Even so, as Arne Emil Christensen points out, with all extra sails set, the sail area of the *Viking* was still less than some of the suggested rigging reconstructions of Gokstad.

The *Viking* left Bergen at noon on Sunday, 30 April 1893, with a crew of twelve, two chronometers, spare fittings galore, and a thousand bottles of beer. Fully laden, the total weight of the ship was over thirty tons – much higher than seems feasible for the historical Gokstad. The voyage was frequently stormy, but the rudder proved equal to all occasions, and the hull turned out to be amazingly supple:

The bottom together with the keel gave with every movement of the ship, and in a strong head-sea the keel could move up and down as much as three-quarters of an inch. But strangely enough the ship stayed completely watertight.

The ship's remarkable elasticity was also apparent in other ways; in heavy seas, for instance, the gunwales would twist out of true by as much as six inches.

(Magnus Andersen: *Vikingfærden*, 1895)

The *Viking* in Chicago in 1893, after the epic voyage by Magnus Andersen from Norway.

The serpentine flexibility of the hull proved a distinct advantage in sailing, and the *Viking* regularly logged speeds of ten knots or more. They saw Bacalao light on Newfoundland at 4 a.m. on 27 May; they were then twenty-eight days out from Bergen – a tremendous achievement, to have crossed from Norway to North America in four weeks in an open sailing boat. The *Viking* caused a stir wherever it docked, and was the hit of the Chicago World Fair; it had achieved its primary purpose of putting old Norse and modern Norwegian ship-building on the map. The *Viking* itself ended up in a park at Chicago Zoo, where it is now said to be rather the worse for wear.

The original Gokstad Ship was designed as an all-purpose vessel that could go anywhere, and fight anywhere. It was the kind of ship that made the Viking Age possible – fast, versatile and predatory: a thoroughbred, descended from centuries of experience of sea-faring, built with consummate skill, craftsmanship and assurance. Gokstad, for me, is a poem carved in wood:

> Men will quake with terror
> Ere the seventy sea-oars
> Gain their well-earned respite
> From the labours of the ocean.
> 'Norwegian arms are driving
> This iron-studded dragon
> Down the storm-tossed river,
> Like an eagle with wings beating.
> (Snorri Sturluson: King Harald's Saga, Ch. 60)

Gokstad was a medium-sized ship. The largest ship recorded in the Icelandic Sagas was the *Long Serpent (Ormurinn langi)*, which was built for King Ólaf Tryggvason of Norway at Trondheim in the year 998. It had thirty-four pairs of oars, compared to Gokstad's sixteen; at King Ólaf's final sea-battle at Svold in the year 1000, the *Long Serpent* was said to have carried more than two hundred warriors on board – a formidable floating garrison for the centre of the line.

In his *Ólaf Tryggvason's Saga* in *Heimskringla*, Snorri Sturluson describes the making of *Long Serpent* (Ch. 88). Quite apart from his other talents, Snorri was a born journalist who liked nothing better than a good yarn; and his story about *Long Serpent* illustrates perfectly the way in which Viking shipwrights worked entirely by eye, by feel, by instinct.

The shipwright who fashioned the stem and stern of the vessel was called Thorberg *skafhögg* ('Trimmer'); but there were many others involved, some to do the planking, some to trim the wood, some to make rivets, some to carry timber; and all the materials used in the construction were very carefully chosen. The ship was both long and broad and high-sided, and stoutly timbered.

While they were planking the sides of the ship, it so happened that Thorberg had to go home on urgent business; by the time he came back, the ship was fully planked. That same evening the king went to see how the vessel looked, along with Thorberg and others, and everybody said that never had such a large and handsome longship been seen before....

Snorri goes on to say that when the king went back to the ship next morning, all the carpenters were standing around with their hands in their pockets, doing nothing. The king asked them what the matter was. They replied that the ship was ruined; during the night some vandal with an axe had hacked deep notches into the gunwale all the way down one side. The king went puce with rage and swore that he would have the culprit's head if he ever found out who did it: 'And anyone who can tell me who did it will be richly rewarded.'

At that, Thorberg stepped forward and said, 'I can tell you who did this job, sire.'

'I might have known I could rely on you to find out the truth and tell me it, Thorberg,' said the king, all smiles.

'Yes,' said Thorberg, 'I can tell you who did it, sire. I did it.'

The king could hardly believe his ears. At last he said, 'Either restore it to the way it was before, or you will die for this!'

Then Thorberg went and trimmed and pared the ship's gunwale until all the notches had disappeared. The king realised that the line of the top strake was now much more elegant, and asked Thorberg to do the same to the other side, thanking him warmly for the improvement.

And the king was now well pleased.

Aesthetic satisfaction was, I am sure, a very real factor in the Viking ship-building tradition. I saw it for myself in action in 1979 in a little Norwegian boatyard, the Rød Båtbyggeri at Frederikstad on the east side of Oslo Fjord. Here a small family of master shipwrights were commissioned to build a two-thirds scale replica of the Gokstad ship to celebrate the millennium of the Isle of Man on 5 July 1979 (*cf* Ch. 6). It was a fascinating experience to watch it take shape from the keel upwards, swelling gracefully in a series of overlapping clinker-built strakes, riveted together and caulked with animal hair dipped in tar, fitting the ribs as snugly and flexibly as skin.

Operation *Odin's Raven*, as the boat was named, was the brainchild of a young Manx insurance company director and entrepreneur, Robin Bigland, who has reason to believe that his family originally came 'west-over-sea' with the Vikings from Byglandsfjord in southern Norway. The skipper of the boat was an equally flamboyant and determined Manxman, Eddie Kaighan (his name in Manx means 'Son of the Horseman'), the harbourmaster at Castletown on the Isle of Man and holder of a master mariner's ticket. The academic consultant was Alan L. Binns of Hull University, a seasoned sailor who could provide the unusual combination of practical expertise and historical knowledge; he had acted as the adviser and shipmaster for the famous Kirk Douglas film *The Vikings*, and must therefore be the only scholar alive ever to have commanded a fleet of five Viking ships, one of which he even converted into a fireship!

Odin's Raven had a crew of sixteen – five Norwegians and eleven Manxmen. I went with them on the sea-trials. It was at that point that the whole exercise changed from being merely a spectacular stunt into a valid experiment for historian and archaeologist alike. All the Viking ships that have been recovered by archaeology have been little more than hulls, which are easy enough to reconstruct; but no evidence of how they were rigged is available – and it is the kind of rigging, the height of the mast, the area and consistency of the sail, that really determine how Viking ships

Odin's Raven, the Manx millennium boat built in 1979 as a scaled-down replica of the Gokstad Ship.

were actually sailed. The sailing of *Odin's Raven* from Trondheim in the north of Norway to Peel in the Isle of Man in 1979 may well provide some of the answers, or at least suggest further questions to be explored even though a scaled-down replica would obviously display different characteristics in the water.

To the Vikings, sailing or rowing a ship came as naturally as driving a car does to us today. But there was one extra dimension that I had not experienced until I went out with *Odin's Raven*: the sheer physical exhilaration of it. It is quite literally thrilling, to feel the timbers vibrating to the oar-strokes, the rigging thrumming to the wind, the whole ship undulating like a serpent over the sea. It was by no means an easy life, being a Viking. You rowed till your muscles cracked, the sea-spray froze on your beard, the ship bucked and corkscrewed. But there must always have been this physical exhilaration, this sense of mastery over the elements through this marvellous instrument whose technology had been evolving, slowly and surely, over the centuries.

Obviously it was the Viking ship that made the Scandinavian break-out possible, and so effective. But why the break-out in the first place? What causes some nations or races at some particular period in their history to come to the boil and start seething over their neighbours?

There is never any one single reason, one dominant factor, to explain it. In the case of Scandinavia, which the sixth-century Ostrogoth historian Jordanes referred to as 'the womb of nations', several causes have been

42

suggested, any or all of which may have combined to produce the interplay of social and economic pressures and opportunities, of needs and means, to make it possible.

One catalyst that has been suggested was a massive expansion of the production of iron in Scandinavia in the seventh and eighth centuries. Another theory concerns the apparent population explosion that was taking place then. Other scholars point to the growth in international trade at this time, with its inevitable and concomitant growth in piracy, for pirates are the parasites of trade-routes. Another school of thought talks in terms of the growth of royal authority, both as a means of driving piracy to other waters and exploiting both trade and piracy more purposefully.

All of them are no doubt at least partly right. Improved iron production created better tools for the easier clearance of forest-land for farmland, and also required the development of new markets to absorb any surplus production. As we all know from history, the development of any new primary product, whether it be bronze or iron or coal or oil, has a profound effect on the society involved in its production. In Norway, the evidence of place-names and archaeology suggests that there was movement in the seventh century to colonise new farmland higher up in the mountain valleys than before; this is an indication both of increasing population pressure and improved agricultural techniques. Better farming would lead to better farm produce, which in turn would lead to better fed and healthier populations. Within a system of primogeniture, whereby only the eldest son inherited land, an abundance of sturdy younger sons is created, all intent on carving out a place in the sun for themselves elsewhere.

It can all be made to sound very neat, if somewhat circular. That is the prerogative of the theorist. Other theorists will emphasise other aspects to produce other, equally pat answers. Trade was on the increase in northern Europe as kingdoms and empires stabilised, they argue. Trade attracted pirates, so better ships had to be developed to escape the attentions of pirates, which led to even better ships being developed by the pirates: escalation of effort to maximise profit, an economist would call it.

In an expansionist situation of that kind there would always be powerful and ambitious men to seize the opportunity of increasing their wealth by getting their hands on this trade by fair means or foul. Kings would seek to channel and exploit the trade through their own territory by creating market-towns where they could exact tolls and dues in return for royal protection: the larger their territories, the larger their revenues and the larger their reservoir of available manpower for defence or aggression.

The early historians interpreted the imperatives of history solely in terms of great personages and great events, not causes and factors. Snorri Sturluson's *Heimskringla* is not a history of Norway as such but a *History of the Kings of Norway*:

VIKINGS!

> In this book I have had written down old stories of the chieftains who held dominion in the northlands and who spoke the Norse tongue, according to what I have heard learned men tell, and also of their descendants, according to what I have been told. Some of this is to be found in old genealogies, wherein kings and others of noble birth have traced their pedigree, while the rest has been composed from old poems or ballads in which people have found entertainment. Although we cannot be sure what truth there is in them, we know for a fact that old men of learning held them to be true.
>
> (Snorri Sturluson: Prologue to *Heimskringla*)

The first Saga in *Heimskringla* is *Ynglinga saga*, the Saga of the Yngling dynasty of Sweden, so named because they claimed to be descended from the ancient fertility god/king, Yngvi-Frey. It was a branch of this dynasty, according to Snorri, that founded the first royal house in Norway, as monarchs of the kingdom of Vestfold in south-eastern Norway. Snorri based his information on the verse compilation known as *Ynglingatal* (*Ynglings' List*), composed by the ninth-century poet Thjóðólf of Hvin, a contemporary and court poet of King Harald Fine-Hair of Norway.

In *Ynglingatal*, two semi-legendary kings of Vestfold are said to have been buried at a place called Borre: King Eystein Fart, who drowned after being knocked overboard by the swinging sail-yard (*beitiáss*) of a passing ship, and his son Hálfdan, nicknamed *inn mildi ok inn matarilli* for his generosity with money but stinginess at table. This Hálfdan, according to Snorri's genealogy, was the great-grandfather of Harald Fine-Hair; and at this point, legend and history and archaeology come within hailing distance of one another.

Borre lies on the western shore of the Oslo Fjord, near the township of Horten. Today it is a protected National Park; but in the nineteenth century it was part of the glebelands of the parsonage of Borre. It had been a royal cemetery in antiquity, a clutch of imposing burial mounds housing the ship-graves of kings or powerful chieftains; these have been associated with the early Yngling sea-kings, buried in their ships within sight and close proximity of their natural element, the sea. It is a beautiful spot now, girt with dignified oaks and beeches and birch trees, but to the archaeologist it presents a mournful sight. The surviving mounds all have a deep depression or cleft in them, like a wound from a great axe-blow, caused either by grave-robbers in olden times, or by internal collapse, or by indiscriminate quarrying for road-making material.

There are five of these burial mounds left now, each one surrounded by a moat with a causeway for access. In 1852 one of them was excavated in the most unfortunate manner imaginable. It was sold to the district roads department for quarrying; soon after work began, the labourers started coming across rivets and nails and other evidence of a ship-burial. A local antiquarian heard about this and did his best to protect the site by offering

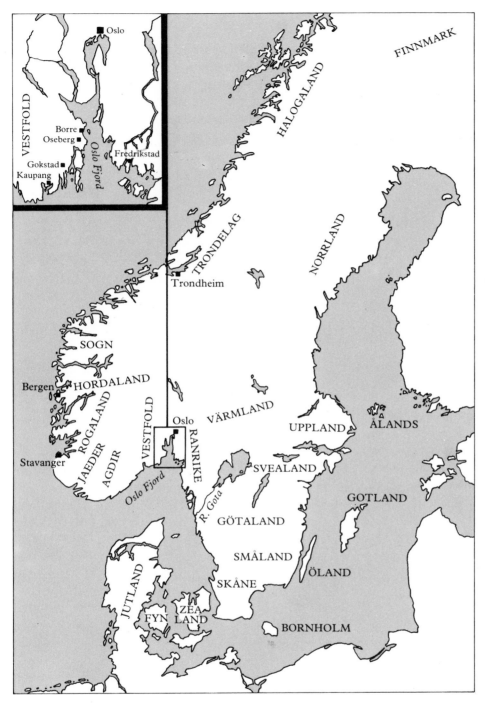

small rewards for any finds the men might make. He also arranged that if
they found anything that looked really important they would suspend
work until he had time to reach the scene.

This well-meaning precaution proved unavailing, however; indeed, it
only served to whet the workmen's appetite. One day when they came
across something that glinted yellow in the sunshine they started hacking

45

One of the ruined burial mounds at Borre, now a National Park, once believed to be the grave-field of the early Yngling kings of Norway.

at the mound in a fever of excitement, thinking they had struck gold. As a result of their frenzied digging, the tunnel that had been bored into the centre of the mound collapsed, and several labourers were very nearly killed. What they had actually seen was a bronze-mounted saddle, which was destroyed in the process of 'excavation' apart from a few broken fragments.

Late in May of that year, a much younger Nicolay Nicolaysen of later Gokstad fame was sent down from Oslo to try to salvage what was left. His investigation threw some light on the character of the mound, but its contents had been irretrievably damaged. He also investigated another mound, right at the northern end of the row, but it turned out to have been robbed in antiquity and yielded nothing but some horse-bones.

It was a sorry tale, and it did not end there. Nicolaysen's sketch-map of the site marks no fewer than nine mounds that were clearly visible at that time; today, due to further vandalism of one kind or another, there are only the five and the stumps of two more. The mounds had obviously contained ship-burials, from all accounts on a par with the Gokstad burial, although there had been no providential blue clay to prevent the timbers from rotting. It is doubtful whether the rudimentary conservation techniques then available would have coped with the problem of recovering the finds intact even if the mound had been undisturbed; but Borre will always be mourned as a great archaeological opportunity ruined.

In the mood of nationalistic fervour that prevailed in Norway in the nineteenth century as the country moved towards full independence from

Sweden, the royal cemetery at Borre was regarded as a shrine, the birthplace of the Norwegian nation, for it was the Yngling dynasty of Vestfold which would eventually bring all the scattered petty kingdoms and chieftainries of Norway under the authority of a single monarch in the person of Harald Fine-Hair.

Working back from the presumed date of Harald Fine-Hair's accession in the second half of the ninth century, and using Snorri Sturluson's Yngling genealogy as a guide, the earliest Borre mounds were dated to the start of the ninth century. The northernmost mound was associated with King Eystein Fart, who had been buried 'at the end of the moraine', according to *Ynglingatal*. But sceptical modern scholars tend to regard Snorri's stories about the Yngling ancestors and their burials at Borre as pure legend – a view which they think Snorri himself shared, judging by his cautious words in his Prologue to *Heimskringla*. They prefer to base their dating on comparative art styles. In 1915 the formidable Norwegian scholar, Professor A. W. Brøgger of Oslo University, made a close study of the ornamentation on the series of cast gilt-bronze harness mounts that had survived the depredations at Borre and lain forgotten on a museum shelf since then. His conclusion was that the so-called 'Borre style' should be dated to around 850. More recently there have been suggestions that even this is too early, and that the Borre style did not develop until the very end of the ninth century. This would make the Borre mounds contemporary with Harald Fine-Hair himself, and put paid to the romantic notion of Borre as the last resting-place of the first Ynglings: but comparative dating on the basis of art styles alone can be just as imprecise and subjective as legend itself.

But one burial mound, a few miles south of Borre, which was successfully excavated in 1904, has provided both archaeology and Saga-history with a find of unbelievable richness and inexhaustible interest: the celebrated ship-burial mound at Oseberg.

The Oseberg mound stands six metres high in splendid isolation in the middle of a grassy plain beside the river Slagenbekken. On the surrounding hills there are numerous satellite mounds, all unimposing in comparison. It is an area of richly fertile farmland, and in Viking times the river would have been navigable all the way up to the present farm of Stora Oseberg.

The Oseberg excavation was attended by circumstances scarcely less fraught than those of Borre, but with infinitely happier results. In August 1903 the owner of the farm came to the University Museum in Oslo with some timber remains he had found in a large mound on his land, known locally as the 'Foxes' Mound'. The director of the Museum at that time was a Swedish scholar, Professor Gabriel Gustafsson. Gustafsson had occasion to remember the visit vividly, because that day happened to be his fiftieth birthday. He investigated the mound at once, and confirmed his preliminary impression that he had a ship-burial on his hands.

The magnificently carved cart from the Oseberg Ship.

The landowner was a greedy man who knew his rights: if the mound contained anything of value, he would be entitled to a 'find reward' (the equivalent of 'treasure trove' in England), and he wanted it at once. Gustafsson managed to fob him off until the following spring, to give himself time to mount a proper excavation, and on 6 May 1904 he started work. That *annus mirabilis*, which lasted until 16 December, has gone down in the annals of archaeology as the 'Oseberg summer'.

Inside the mound, Gustafsson uncovered a most beautiful ninth-century Viking ship, magnificently decorated with wood carvings. All its timbers had been miraculously preserved by the mound of blue clay that had been heaped over it. Gustafsson dismantled the boat with great care and stored all the parts in the castle of Akershus in Oslo. The truculent farmer was still threatening to sell everything to the highest bidder; but in October a private landowner in Vestfold bought the ship and presented it to the nation, thus sparing Norway the humiliation of seeing one of her greatest historical treasures being sold to a foreign museum. It was this crisis, incidentally, that led to the enlightened Norwegian legislation which now protects archaeological sites and ancient monuments.

The Oseberg Ship, which now shares pride of place with the Gokstad Ship in the Viking Ship Hall at Bygdøy in Oslo, was built around 800, some fifty years earlier than Gokstad, and is thought to have been buried around 850.

Oseberg also contained the largest assemblage of Viking Age wooden objects ever found in Scandinavia, a whole inventory of contemporary furniture and equipment and implements: a chair, a four-wheeled cart, four sledges, three beds with their bedding, chests and boxes, tapestries, looms, buckets, casks, kitchen utensils, riding harness, spades, a dung-fork, a hoe. There was also an iron ship's cauldron complete with chain and collapsible tripod, and much else besides. Many of the objects had been broken by the stones that had been thrown into the ship to anchor it firmly in the mound, but they have now been restored and reconstructed, to give an unparalleled picture of the arts and crafts of Viking Norway.

The quality of the carving on the Oseberg Ship and its furniture is breathtakingly spectacular: snarling dragon-heads on posts, menacing Viking faces on the four-wheeled cart, superbly intricate patterns on the sledges. Arne Emil Christensen of the University Museum in Oslo draws an illuminating comparison between the Oseberg carvings and the style of Viking court poetry ('skaldic' poetry) with its elaborate poetic diction: both are esoteric, allusive, close-clenched and complicated. It is essentially art for the connoisseur, winding and convoluted like the syntax of skaldic verse. In the poetry, the line and the metre condition the content, and so it is with the carvings; the artist did not so much carve an animal, as carve a complex pattern with an animal in it. You have to know the pattern to see the animal, just as you have to know the pattern of skaldic poetry to see the tree for the wood.

The ship itself is also invaluable as an example of the evolution of Viking

Some of the kitchen utensils, implements and storage vessels from the Oseberg Ship.

Leather shoes from the Oseberg Ship, specially made for the swollen feet of the older skeleton.

ship technology. Oseberg has been interpreted as a kind of State barge, a royal yacht; it may well have been used for that purpose in its old age, but it was originally built as an all-purpose vessel at the time of the earliest Norwegian raids on Lindisfarne and other holy places. It represents a distinctly earlier stage in ship-building than Gokstad, which was built fifty years later and had clearly learned from Oseberg's mistakes. For instance, the mast-fish on Oseberg showed signs of emergency repairs at sea; in Gokstad, that inherent weakness of design had been noted, and circumvented. The early raiders had come back with a number of technical problems to solve regarding the seaworthiness of their ships; Gokstad was the culmination of what Oseberg began.

But Oseberg and Gokstad have another, more personalised significance for the history of Viking Norway: the identity of the people who were buried in them. Gokstad contained the skeleton of a man in his fifties; Oseberg contained the skeletons of two women, one elderly, the other young. As at Borre, the question arises – who were they? A possible scenario is provided by Snorri Sturluson in *Heimskringla*; it involves the continuation of the Yngling line from those 'Borre kings' of Vestfold, Eystein Fart and Hálfdan *inn mildi ok inn matarilli*.

Hálfdan was succeeded by his son, Guðrøð the Hunting-King. By his first wife, Guðrøð had a son called Ólaf Geirstaða-Álf; but when his wife died, Guðrøð's calculating eye fell upon a beautiful young princess in the neighbouring kingdom of Agdir to the south, a huge territory stretching from Larvik to Kristiansand and deep inland. Her name was Ása, the daughter of King Harald Red-Beard of Agdir. Guðrøð duly sent a proposal of marriage to Agdir, which was refused. But Guðrøð the Hunting-

50

King of Vestfold was not a man to take no for an answer. He launched his warships and descended on Agdir without warning. Despite a valiant defence, Ása's father and brother were killed, and Ása herself was forcibly abducted to Vestfold.

The outcome of this rough wooing was a son called Hálfdan the Black, who was destined to become the father of the celebrated Harald Fine-Hair. A year after her baby was born, Ása took her revenge; she had her husband murdered in his cups, then coolly took her baby son back to Agdir where she assumed power as Queen Mother and regent. In Vestfold, the throne passed to Guðrøð's elder son, Ólaf Geirstaða-Álf. He is described as a great warrior and very able, handsome and powerfully built. He was twenty years old when his father was murdered, probably not much older than his vengeful step-mother, Queen Ása.

Nearly two decades now pass. When Ása's son, Hálfdan the Black, reached his majority at the age of eighteen, he took over the kingship of Agdir from his mother. He then demanded, and received, his paternal inheritance of half the kingdom of Vestfold from his half-brother, Ólaf Geirstaða-Álf. This apparently amicable settlement gave Hálfdan a power-base from which he launched a series of campaigns against neighbouring territories, 'and he became a mighty king'.

One of the snarling animal-heads from the Oseberg Ship.

Whether all this is half-remembered history or pure folklore is impossible to tell. But if the main outline is correct, then the murder of Guðrøð the Hunting-King of Vestfold would have taken place around 840, and Hálfdan the Black would have succeeded to the throne of Agdir and half of Vestfold around 860, when both his mother and his half-brother would have been about forty years old. The trouble is that the historical traditions, which are notoriously unreliable, do not quite match the archaeological evidence – whose interpretation is itself not always entirely reliable.

Ólaf Geirstaða-Álf died, according to *Heimskringla*, of a disease of the leg, and was buried in a mound at Geirstaðir. The superficial similarity of the names 'Geirstaðir' and 'Gokstad' (earlier 'Gjekstad') is tempting. Also, the first anatomical examination of the Gokstad skeleton indicated a well-built man in his fifties who had suffered severely from arthritis in the left knee and ankle: the 'leg disease' of the Saga? At the time that the Gokstad Ship was interred, around 880 it is now thought, Ólaf Geirstaða-Álf would have been about sixty years old. If the date and the medical evidence are correct, there is nothing inconsistent with the theory that Gokstad housed the mortal remains of Ólaf Geirstaða-Álf.

And what of Queen Ása? We are told nothing more about her in the Sagas, but it is not improbable that she went with her son to Vestfold and set up house there in 860. Once again, there is a tempting similarity of names: 'Ása' and 'Oseberg'. Oseberg was clearly a queenly burial, with a richly furnished ship that was eminently fit for a queen. Could it have been Queen Ása? But there were not one but two female skeletons in the Oseberg ship, the one a young girl in her twenties, the other aged around fifty. So which one was the queen?

Both of the Oseberg bodies had been roughly handled by grave-robbers who broke into the mound not long after the funeral. They had been dragged out of the wooden burial chamber amidships. The older woman had lost her right hand and left upper-arm in the process, perhaps for the sake of any precious rings and bracelets she might have been wearing. Among the grave goods were two pairs of costly leather shoes specially made for her swollen, arthritic feet. On the face of it, the older skeleton would appear to be the 'royal' of the two; the younger woman would then have been a handmaid who had elected, or been selected, to accompany her mistress to the afterworld.

But that raises chronological problems. The older Oseberg woman and the Gokstad man had died at about the same age, or with a difference of ten years at most; and Ása and her stepson Ólaf, as we have noted, were near contemporaries. But the Oseberg burial is considered by most scholars, on stylistic grounds, to have been as much as thirty years earlier than Gokstad, which would suggest that if either of the Oseberg skeletons was Ása, it must have been the younger one.

However, not every scholar believes that relative dating on stylistic

52

grounds alone can be so precise; the gap between the two burials, it is argued, could have been as little as ten or fifteen years – which would be compatible with a fifty-year-old Queen Ása in Oseberg and a sixty-year-old King Ólaf in Gokstad. We shall probably never know for certain; but Saga-sentiment makes me want to believe that the Lady of Oseberg was indeed Queen Ása, that resourceful and implacable queen who took such uncompromising vengeance for her ravished maidenhood. She was a fitting queen to be the grandmother of modern Norway through her equally determined and ruthless grandson, Harald Fine-Hair, the first king of all Norway.

According to *Heimskringla*, Harald was ten years old when his father, Hálfdan the Black, died in a drowning accident at the age of forty. His mother, a princess of the kingdom of Ringerike, had already dreamed the kind of prophetic dream that Saga-writers found irresistible. While standing in her herb-garden she had plucked a thorn from her shift, and this thorn had grown into a mighty tree that seemed to cover the whole of Norway. The lower part of the tree-trunk was red as blood, the upper part was green and beautiful, while the topmost branches were white as snow. The dream presaged a serene and fulfilled old age, a procreant and successful middle age, but a blood-spattered and arduous youth. And so it turned out.

The Saga chronologies are difficult to reconcile where Harald is concerned, but it seems as if Hálfdan the Black died around 870–80. From his ambitious father, Harald inherited the realm of Vestfold and an aggressive, acquisitive disposition. Under the regency of his uncle, Harald had first to fend off the wolves who scented possible spoils in a kingdom ruled by a minor. There were scores to be paid off, too, against the memory of his father. But gradually, under his uncle's constantly loyal tutelage, Harald established himself in Vestfold and made himself master of neighbouring kingdoms as well: the blood-red stem had taken root.

At that time Norway was not a political entity; it was a scatter of petty kingdoms often at each other's throats. Even its name was symptomatic of this fragmentation: *Norvegr*, the 'North Way', not so much a nation as a trade-route. Harald Hálfdanarson is remembered chiefly on two accounts: for creating a unified Norwegian realm, and for the romantic origin of his nickname, 'Fine-Hair'.

According to Snorri Sturluson, the young Harald, flushed with success against his immediate enemies, took a fancy to a beautiful young princess of Hordaland called Gyða. When Harald's emissaries went to invite her to become the king's concubine, she replied haughtily that she was not prepared to surrender her maidenhood to some petty kingling who did not have a proper kingdom to his name.

Surprisingly, this dusty answer did not infuriate Harald; it only seems, in the current phrase, to have 'motivated' him. Then and there he swore that he would neither cut nor comb his hair until he had subdued the whole

Harald Fine-Hair rescuing his foster-father, the giant Dofri, by cutting his bonds. Illumination for the capital letter H. A folklore incident from *Harald Fine-Hair's Saga* in Snorri Sturluson's *Heimskringla*, in the great manuscript codex known as *Flateyjarbók*.

of Norway. It took him a long time, but eventually he did it, nominally at least, by dint of arduous campaigning and wily alliances. Even the imperious Gyða was now convinced, and when Harald sent his emissaries again she went willingly to his bed, to join what seems to have been a royal harem of political wives and personal concubines. But Harald himself was not yet satisfied, until he had dealt with the nests of Viking marauders west-over-sea who had fled Norway to escape his heavy hand and were now raiding his coastal shipping from bases in the Northern Isles of Scotland; then, and only then, did he carry out his pledge:

> King Harald now went to the baths, and had his hair dressed; and Earl Rögnvald of Möre clipped his hair, which had been unshorn and uncombed for ten years. Previously he had been known as Harald *lúfa* – Harald Mop-Hair – but Earl Rögnvald now gave him a new nickname and called him Harald *hárfagri*, Harald Fine-Hair, and everyone who saw him agreed that it was most appropriate, for he had a truly magnificent head of hair.

> (*Harald Fine-Hair's Saga*, Ch. 23)

'King Harald was now master of all Norway,' says Snorri Sturluson; but what did being 'master of all Norway' mean in reality? In Harald's case it was probably much less than the phrase implies. Norway was as intractable geographically as it was politically. Far to the north, reaching to

54

North Cape and the White Sea (Norway's present frontiers with Finland and the Soviet Union), lay Hálogaland ('Aurora Borealis Land'), a desolate region of scattered farmers, hunters and trappers. There was wealth to be won there, in the form of furs, hides and walrus-ivory.

The major region of the north was the Trøndelag, the rich farming area around Trondheim, a stubborn redoubt of an aristocratic dynasty of *jarls* (earls) intent on protecting and exploiting the trade-route from the north. The incumbent during Harald's rise to power was the formidable Earl Hákon Grjótgarðsson, with whom Harald prudently came to terms: Earl Hákon recognised Harald's 'overlordship', which probably just meant a mutual recognition of geographical spheres of influence, and gave him a daughter in marriage.

Harald's own power-base was the kingdom of Vestfold. But the crucial area of Norway for Harald's ambitions was the south-west, the serrated stretch of fjord-riven coastline now bounded by Bergen and Stavanger. Every fjord there, it seems, was the private principality of a self-styled sea-king, battening on the agricultural wealth of the hinterland valleys and preying on the lucrative sea-trade that tried to sail past his lair. This area became Harald's prime target: he who controls the coastal shipping lanes controls the land. Year by year, from his new base in the Trøndelag, Harald and his northern allies pushed southward, crushing whatever opposition they might meet.

The crunch came in a major naval battle in Hafrsfjord, just to the west of the modern oil-boom town of Stavanger. It is clearly visible from the road from Sola Airport to Stavanger itself, now superintended by the radio communications tower at Ullandhaug. It was here that Harald Fine-Hair

Hafrsfjord, near Stavanger, scene of Harald Fine-Hair's crucial sea-battle in his bid for the crown of all Norway.

had his final showdown with a confederacy of recalcitrant chieftains from all over south-western Norway:

> Did you hear in Hafrsfjord
> How armies battled,
> How noble King Harald
> Fought Kjötvi the Wealthy?
> Ships sailed southward,
> Thirsting for battle,
> Prow-heads snarling
> On well-carved hulls.
>
> (Thorbjörn Hornklofi: *Haraldskvæði*)

Thorbjörn Hornklofi was one of Harald's favourite court poets, and Snorri Sturluson relied on his verses for a circumstantial account of the battle. 'It was a long, hard fight,' says Snorri, 'but eventually King Harald won the day.' Many of the sea-kings fell. The defeated survivors struggled to safety on an island on which there was a fortified redoubt (*vígi mikit*), and from there they waded ashore, their shields slung across their backs, and fled ignominiously to their homes.

Norwegian scholars now think they can pinpoint the exact site of the Battle of Hafrsfjord. Some years ago, divers found the remains of water-logged timbers on the sea-bed. The timber was in poor condition and disintegrated when it was brought to the surface; but when sufficient conservation effort is available, the area will be properly excavated in order to clarify whether these really are the remains of the ships that were destroyed in that crucial battle. Certainly the topography is right. Not far from the timber finds is a promontory called Ytraberget ('Outer Rock'), which used to be an island in the Viking Age, when the sea-level was some two metres higher than it is now. It is a steep and rocky headland which still has the remains of a Migration Period (AD 300–600) fortification on it. The director of the Stavanger Maritime Museum (Stavanger Sjøfartsmuseum), Dr Arne Bang Andersen, has little doubt that this was the place where the fugitives from the battle scrambled ashore before running for home. The present owner of the land, Bjarne Valvik, has no doubts either, and intends to leave it to the nation. In 1972, on the eleventh centenary of the traditional date of the battle, King Olaf V of Norway visited Ytraberget to commemorate the Hafrsfjord victory that, in effect, created his throne. Part of the Migration Period fortification was restored for the occasion, and one of the larger stones from the wall was erected in a solo position with the dignified inscription: 'Harald 872. Olav 1972'.

That traditional date of 872 is probably wrong. It is drawn from the works of the early Icelandic historians, who saw the settlement of Iceland itself as a direct outcome of Harald's subjugation of the independent chieftains of Norway (*cf* Ch. 7). The latest scholarly thinking indicates that the Battle of Hafrsfjord probably took place around 890.

The stakes at Hafrsfjord were high, and not just in terms of pride and prestige and battle honour, not even just a matter of life or death. What was in the balance was the ultimate control of Norway's trade wealth; and a spectacular post-war archaeological excavation in the heart of Harald's realm of Vestfold has strongly underlined its importance.

The site is known as Kaupang, in the Tjølling district of Vestfold county; it lies just off the major land-route south from Oslo along the ridge of a glacial moraine that strides through Vestfold, the *Raveien* ('Moraine Way'), now the E18 motorway. The name 'Kaupang' simply means 'market-place', as in the English place-name 'Chipping', and there are several Kaupangs or Kaupangers in Norway. But Kaupang in Tjølling was once known as *Skiringssal*, and that gives it a very special significance for Viking Age history.

Skiringssal (*Sciringes heal* in Old English) is mentioned in the Anglo-Saxon translation of the *Universal History* of Orosius, dating to the late ninth century and usually attributed to King Alfred the Great himself (*cf* Ch. 5). It appears in an interpolated section which describes the visit to Alfred's court of a wealthy Norwegian merchant called Óttar (Ohthere in Old English), who came from Hálogaland in the far north. He owned a huge herd of reindeer, but his main source of income, he told King Alfred, was tribute from the Lapps in the form of skins and furs, walrus-ivory and whale-bone, ship's rope made from whale-hide and seal-hide, and eider-down. With a shipload of these luxury goods, he had sailed down the coast of Norway and across to England, there to sell his cargo and present exotic gifts to Alfred. On the way, he had stopped at 'a port in the south of Norway which is called *Sciringes heal*'.

There has been much debate about the location of Óttar's Skiringssal. But it has now been positively identified as Kaupang in Tjølling by Dr Charlotte Blindheim, a senior curator at the University Museum of National Antiquities in Oslo and head of its Viking department, who excavated the Kaupang site for seventeen arduous seasons from 1950 to 1967. Skiringssal proper seems to have been Tjølling itself, a rural parish now dominated by a fine church but in Viking times evidently a seat of royal power in Vestfold. The 'port' at Kaupang/Skiringssal turned out to be a small but densely populated trading settlement with its own snug harbour on the shores of Viksfjord, which cuts into the land off Larviksfjord. It flourished for more than a hundred years right at the start of the Viking Age, throughout the ninth century and into the tenth, until lack of space for expansion led to its decline.

Óttar/Ohthere is the only merchant we know by name to have visited Kaupang/Skiringssal with a costly cargo from northern Norway. But from the quantity and high quality and cosmopolitan nature of the finds from the Blindheim excavations we know that it was an extremely prosperous and busy place, comparable in importance if not in size with the more celebrated marts of Hedeby in Denmark (*cf* Ch. 3) and Birka in Sweden

Kaupang, the site of Norway's first Viking Age town.

(*cf* Ch. 4). It was an orderly and peaceful community of merchants and artisans, very different to the conventional Viking image of constant pillage and rapine; it had no walls or defences of any kind and apparently required none, for Dr Blindheim found not a trace of evidence of destruction by fire or any other marks of violence.

There is nothing to be seen today of the market town that once flourished there – only a belt of dark, greasy soil called the 'Black Earth', sloping gently down towards the western side of the bay. It looks totally unremarkable. But when Dr Blindheim excavated in that area, she found substantial remains of a packed settlement of irregular groups of buildings, with stone jetties all along the original sea-front – now inland because of the fall in the sea-level since Viking times. The backbone of the economy of Kaupang/Skiringssal had clearly been trade and handicrafts: iron processing, bronze casting, textiles, soapstone utensils, and the specialised manufacture of beads from rock crystal, amber and perhaps also glass.

Dr Blindheim had already excavated a hitherto unsuspected grave field of sixty small boat-burials which had been the exclusive preserve of a merchant class who were probably incomers to Kaupang/Skiringssal. From the finds it was clear that Kaupang had been a distribution centre for all manner of goods in all directions. The major overseas market was probably Jutland, via Hedeby, which lay directly south from the mouth of Viksfjord. But the imported goods demonstrated strong commercial and cultural contacts with the British Isles in particular, as well as with Continental Europe and the Baltic.

The degree of wealth generated by Kaupang/Skiringssal in its heyday during Harald Fine-Hair's reign, when merchant princes like Óttar/ Ohthere were using it, must have meant very substantial revenues in tolls and taxes for the royal coffers. But Skiringssal was never Harald Fine-Hair's 'capital' town – he never had one in the modern sense of the term. Instead, he travelled between a number of royal residences with his retinue, staying as long at each as the political situation or the availability of supplies dictated.

Most of these manor estates were in the south-west of Norway, where Harald based himself after the Battle of Hafrsfjord, and Dr Arne Bang Andersen of Stavanger has identified five of them in that area: Seim, to the north of Bergen; Fitjar, on the island of Stord, near Selbjornsfjord to the south of Bergen; Útstein, an island to the north-east of Stavanger which now boasts a handsomely restored thirteenth-century monastery which is open to the public; Ávaldsnes, on the island of Karmøy, strategically situated at a narrow sound off the mainland through which all coastal traffic had to pass; and Álreksstaðir (modern Årstad), which now lies within the conurbation of Bergen itself.

Bergen is arguably the most attractive city in Norway, with its striking waterfront of late medieval mercantile buildings. It has not only a fine Historical Museum, but a splendid 'site' museum known as the Bryggens Museum, which is built over and round a recent archaeological excavation of a section of the medieval quayside (*brygge*) of Bergen.

The Bryggens Museum is a vividly laid out exposition of the history of medieval Bergen. The town does not seem to have started developing into a mart until the late eleventh or early twelfth century, and so falls outside the scope of a book on the Viking Age. But there is one enchanting find that no one can resist including – the celebrated 'Bergen Stick'.

The 'Bergen Stick' is precisely that: a roughly whittled piece of stick, only 25 centimetres long, cut from a branch of a deciduous tree and split lengthwise. Where it was split, the surface was not properly smoothed; the outside, or bark, side was undressed, apart from cutting off a couple of twigs at the knots. On the main surface some anonymous doodler incised a

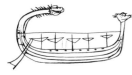

Viking ship incised
on the back of the
thirteenth-century
'Bergen Stick'.

panoramic view of the prows of a mighty fleet of Viking ships, forty-five in all; the vessels in the centre of the line sport ornamental bronze wind-vanes. It would be nice to think it represented Harald Fine-Hair's fleet at Hafrsfjord! But, alas, it was found in a thirteenth-century level at the Bryggens site, and has been dated by the Museum director, Dr Asbjørn Herteig, to the middle of that century at the earliest.

On the back of the stick there is a stylised sketch of a single ship, and a vignette of three longship prows. Underneath there is a brief inscription in runic characters: 'Here comes the sea-bold one.'

'Here comes the sea-bold one.' It would have fitted Harald Fine-Hair admirably. With his accession to a unified throne for the first time, the character of the Viking Age changed for Norway. Centralisation of power meant that the early sporadic raids by freelance marauders would evolve into larger and more purposeful royal expeditions, financed by the growing revenues of organised trade.

It also gave fresh impetus to Viking movement westwards. According to the early Icelandic historians, it was Harald's 'tyranny' that provoked a mass exodus of free-minded Norwegians to found new colonies west-over-sea, where memories of the past would harden into Saga traditions, especially in Iceland (*cf* Ch. 7):

> Iceland was first settled from Norway in the days of Harald Fine-Hair, the son of Hálfdan the Black... and that was 870 years after the birth of Christ...
>
> And then there came such a great movement of people out here from Norway that King Harald laid a ban on emigration, because he feared that Norway was being depopulated....
>
> It is said that Harald was king for seventy years, and lived to be eighty years old.
>
> (Ari the Learned: *Book of Icelanders*)

3

'From the Fury of the Northmen...'

A furore Normannorum, libera nos Domine – 'From the fury of the Northmen, O Lord, deliver us!' That is probably the most hackneyed line in all the vast literature about the Vikings and their evil ways. It is alleged to have been the fervent litany chanted in every medieval church throughout Europe once the Viking ravages started.

In fact it is quite certainly apocryphal, as the Belgian scholar Albert D'Haenens has documented.[1] No scholar has ever been able to find a ninth-century text containing these words, although there are various litanies in which the faithful prayed to Heaven to deliver them from the menace of enemies; but it is difficult to date those prayers or to identify the enemies – they could have been Vikings, or Saracens, or Hungarians. Only one sentence, from an antiphony intended for churches with a particular cult dedicated to St Vaast or St Medard, bears any resemblance to the celebrated slogan: *Summa pia gratia nostra conservando corpora et custodita, de gente fera Normannica nos libera, quae nostra vastat, Deus, regna* – 'Our supreme and holy Grace, protecting us and ours, deliver us, God, from the savage Northman race which lays waste our realms.'

The famous 'fury litany', so freely quoted in practically every book about the Vikings, seems to have been cobbled together in modern times from a selection of such Latin invocations as *Ab incursione alienigenarum, libera nos Domine* ('From the invasion of foreigners, deliver us, O Lord'). But there is no denying its force, or its aptness. It is undoubtedly what Continental clerics would *like* to have said. The 'fury of the Northmen' must have been very real, and very frightening, even in an age almost inured to violence. And when that fury was unleashed on Europe, systematically and purposefully, the full force of it came from the smallest of the Viking countries – Denmark.

The prehistory of Denmark reaches back to the Old Stone Age, with the first traces of occupation occurring around 240,000 BC. The Ice Ages put an end to human settlement in Scandinavia, and Man did not return to Denmark until groups of hunter-gatherers arrived around 15,000 BC.

---

[1] *Les Invasions Normandes en Belgique au IXᵉ Siecle*, Louvain, 1967.

61

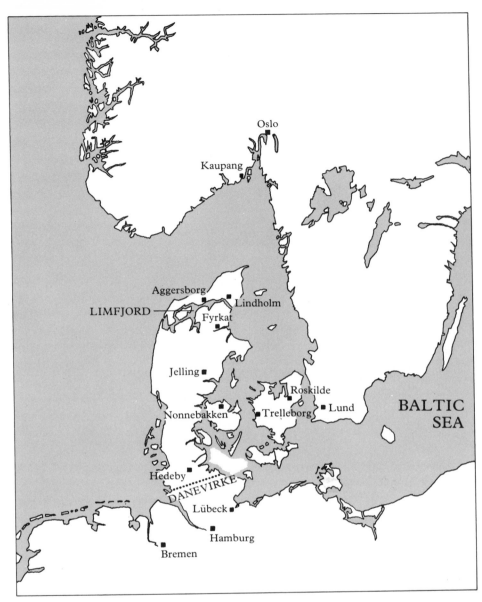

Denmark and her
Continental neighbours
in the Viking Age.

These were superseded around 3500 BC by the first Neolithic farmers,
who introduced new patterns of settlement and land management which
would begin to shape the face of modern Denmark.

There is not space here to trace the sweep of the centuries that took
Denmark through the Stone Ages, the Bronze Age and the Iron Ages to
the threshold of the Viking Age. But they are splendidly displayed at the
'living museum' of Moesgård near Århus, the second city in Denmark.
Under the direction of Dr Ole Klindt-Jensen, himself an authority on
Viking art,[1] Moesgård has become the most adventurous open-air
museum in Scandinavia – which is saying a lot, considering that it was

[1] *Viking Art* by D. M. Wilson and O. Klindt-Jensen, London, 1966.

62

Scandinavia that pioneered the whole concept of open-air museums back in the nineteenth century.

Moesgård Forhistorisk Museum is based in a manor house that was built some two centuries ago, in 1776, set in a hundred hectares of parkland. The galleries are brilliantly laid out in modern 'stable-blocks' flanking the manor house itself; in them, the visitor is led irresistibly past a series of vivid tableaux of the past – reconstructions of actual excavations, replicas of great finds like the Gundestrup cauldron, a silver bowl of Celtic workmanship dating from the second century BC and depicting sacrificial victory rites, and the actual remains of the sacrificed Grauballe Man, found naked in a peat-bog with his throat cut and dating from the Roman Iron Age of the first four centuries AD. The surrounding parkland of Moesgård is being built up as the setting for a 'prehistoric trackway' which leads through fields and woods and beaches, interspersed with rescued ancient monuments and archaeological reconstructions carefully resited in landscaped settings. Taken together, they provide an unforgettable experience of the way in which the flair and brilliance of Viking technology and art evolved from long centuries of developing skills and social customs.

The climax of the Moesgård experience is now the annual *Vikingetræf* (Viking Moot), which takes place during the last weekend in July to commemorate the feast day of St Ólaf, the patron saint of Scandinavia (*cf* Ch. 10). The *Træf* is the brainchild of an English archaeologist, Geoffrey Bibby, who is on the staff at Moesgård and who launched this

The Viking regatta at Moesgård in Denmark at the annual *Vikingetræf*; on shore, the *naust* (boat-shed) which is used as an ale-hall during the *Træf*.

idea of an open-air Viking festival in 1977. It has a wonderfully informal mood, with tented booths stretching along the sea-shore: a Viking Age fair at which visitors can get the feel of what a Viking mart must have been like. There are craftsmen using traditional techniques to weave textiles, plait decorative bands, forge iron implements, strike silver coins, make baskets, and fashion leather fighting-masks styled on a design taken from a rune-stone at Moesgård. Vendors sell Viking sausages ('cauldron-snakes'!) spiced with thyme and garlic, Viking bread, and Viking ale made chiefly from bog-myrtle with apples and cranberries.

Also at Moesgård, visitors can try for themselves the two major forms of Viking transport – the ship and the pony. Down on the sea-shore there is a large *naust* (boat-shed) which was built in 1969 to house a full-size replica of a Viking cargo ship, the *Imme Aros*. During the *Træf* the *naust* is converted into an ale-hall while the *Imme Aros* takes to the water, there to be joined by a number of other ship replicas from all over Scandinavia in a Viking regatta. On land, horse-lovers put on display their Viking ponies (*equus scandinavicus*), which survived as a pure-bred strain only in Iceland (*cf* Ch. 7) but which are now being exported back to the Viking heartlands.

Moesgård and its *Vikingetræf* celebrate not only the constructive aspects of the Viking Age but also a historic sense of national identity through the Vikings. That national identity is hard to establish through archaeology or history or Saga alone; no single site or documentary source can do it. However, there is one great site in northern Jutland, a huge cemetery containing more than seven hundred graves, which dramatically reflects the continuity of Denmark's story in the centuries immediately before and during the Viking Age. It is a site called Lindholm Høje.

Lindholm Høje lies on an eminence near Nørresundby overlooking the Limfjord, some five kilometres from the city of Ålborg. It has always been a site of strategic importance because it commands the Limfjord, which provides a sheltered navigational route through northern Jutland. That is probably why, during the Second World War, German occupation troops in Denmark were set to digging trenches in the area; and as they dug, they came across substantial traces of stone-set graves all over the top of Lindholm Høje.

Late in the Viking Age the whole of Lindholm Høje had been covered with a thick layer of wind-blown sand to a depth of some four metres. A few stone-set graves had been noticed and cursorily excavated late in the nineteenth century, enough to provoke curiosity at least; but it was not until after the accidental wartime discoveries revealed the extent of the site that a full-scale excavation was mounted in the 1950s by Danish archaeologists led by Dr Thorkild Ramskou of the National Museum of Denmark.

Lindholm Høje turned out to be one of the greatest Viking burial grounds yet found in Scandinavia. The majority of the graves contained cremations and dated from AD 500 onwards; many of these had been marked out with patterns of stones. These patterns were either triangular, rectangular, round or oval. But coinciding with the start of the Viking period, around AD 800, there was a significant change in the stone-settings; they became boat-shaped (*skibsætning*). Most of them were about eight metres in length, but there was one really impressive specimen of twenty-three metres.

These ship-settings were not a new feature in Scandinavia: they had been found in Bronze Age burials on the island of Gotland, for instance (*cf* Ch. 4). But the Lindholm Høje ship-settings represent a revival of interest in the role of the ship in Scandinavian society, not simply as a means of transport for trade or fishing or piracy but also as a continuing require-ment for some symbolic voyage to the afterworld. The great ship-burials at Gokstad and Oseberg in Norway (*cf* Ch. 2) and the remarkable de-scription of a Viking ship-funeral in Russia by Ibn Fadlan (*cf* Ch. 4) are vivid illustrations of this intense preoccupation with ships for this life and the next.

Associated with the Lindholm Høje cemetery, and just to the north of it, an extensive township was uncovered by the Danish archaeologists in the 1950s. After the cemetery was first inundated with sand, around AD 950–1000, the township encroached on it. One of the new buildings was a huge four-winged structure that may have been an exceptionally large manor-farm, or a monastic building. In a rubbish-pit between these new buildings was found one of the most celebrated artefacts of the Viking Age – a beautiful silver brooch in the Urnes style, a graceful animal motif with intertwining tendrils dating from about AD 1050 and now in the Ålborg Historical Museum. Silver replicas of this motif are now among the most popular Viking souvenirs in production.

The excavators also came across poignant evidence of the final abandon-ment of the Lindholm Høje settlement right at the end of the Viking Age. It was a farm field, newly ploughed, with high-backed beds making it look like a gigantic washing-board. Sand had obviously covered it very quickly one day; and across the field there were the wheel-tracks of the farmer's last journey over it – a blind, swerving dash for safety, perhaps, once he realised that his farm was going to be engulfed.

The importance of Lindholm Høje was due to its commanding position, for whoever held it was well placed to control any traffic through the Limfjord. So it is disappointing that no reference to it appears in the early historical sources. Snorri Sturluson in *Ynglinga saga* mentions, briefly, a place called 'Vendil at Limafjord' which was razed by an early Swedish king around AD 700, and which wishful thinking might associate with Lindholm Høje; but the picture of pre-Viking Denmark proffered by the historians is merely a mishmash of guesswork and supposition, involving a legendary king called 'Dan' to explain the name Denmark. It is to archaeology, not Saga, that we must turn for a comprehensible account of how Denmark became a Viking nation.

The most considerable surviving antiquity in Denmark is the *Danevirke*

RIGHT Stone ship-settings on graves at the huge necropolis of Lindholm Høje in Denmark.

BELOW An Icelandic pony on a Viking ship replica at Moesgård.

('Danish Work'), a series of fortifications built in several stages across the base of the Jutland peninsula between the North Sea and the Baltic, from the River Treene to the head of the Schleifjord. It is a complicated system of massive earthworks thrown up at different times to defend Jutland from attack. It shielded the land route between the River Eider and the Schlei-fjord, and was frequently rebuilt and strengthened as control of southern Jutland changed hands. Danes, Swedes and Franks all battled for it, and won and lost it in turn.

Urnes-style brooch from Lindholm Høje.

Unlike Hadrian's Wall across the north of England, it is not a clearly defined stone rampart, signed and dated by the Roman engineers who made it. Instead it is a somewhat confusing complex of defensive embankments and fortlets, now much eroded by time and redevelopment, straggling across the waist of Jutland with a number of spurs and offshoots.

It used to be thought that the Danevirke had originally been built by the first Danish king of real eminence to emerge from the mists of legend: King Godfred, contemporary and rival of the illustrious Emperor Charlemagne of the Franks early in the ninth century (c. 800–10). Charlemagne's reign (771–814) is well documented in many sources, and from them we can piece together a picture of Godfred as an able, energetic and aggressive monarch, fully alive to the threat of his powerful neighbour in the south. It was all too easy to assume that Godfred must have built the Danevirke, because no other king of such stature was known to us by name – nor any other enemy of such puissance as Charlemagne.

Recent scientific research, however, has ruined this tidy view of the past. In the 1970s, 178 samples of timber from the substructures of four sections of the Danevirke earthworks were subjected to dendrochronological tests. Dendrochronology (tree-ring dating) can give an absolute date for the year in which the tree was felled and presumably used. The results were uncompromising: the first stages of the ramparts (Danevirke I) were built in the 730s, with the year 737 preponderant. So what does this unexpectedly early date mean?

It can only mean that there were kings of substance in Denmark, long before Godfred, who were capable of organising the resources of their realms for major building projects like the Danevirke – and that there was something correspondingly important and valuable to defend. Jutland had little agricultural wealth to speak of; its significance lay in its strategic position astride the gateway between the North Sea and the Baltic. Trade between the two had to brave the hostile pirate-ridden waters of the Skagerrak, or go through Jutland: either through the Limfjord past Lindholm Høje, or overland – either the long haul from Ribe to Kolding, or the shorter twelve-kilometre portage in the shelter of the Danevirke from the Eider to the great Viking market-town of Hedeby.

Hedeby (German *Haithabu*, 'the place on the moor') lay on the east side of Jutland at the head of the Schleifjord, three kilometres to the south of the modern town of Schleswig in the *Land* of Schleswig-Holstein in West

Germany. It grew up late in the eighth century on the shores of the lagoon of Haddeby Noor, just off the Schlei, which offered easy and sheltered access to the Baltic. Just behind it, on the landward side, lay the major north–south land route, the so-called *Hærvej* ('Army Road').

Hedeby occupied an area of twenty-four hectares, bounded by a semi-circular rampart about a kilometre in length. This rampart was connected by a spur to the main line of the Danevirke three kilometres away, and is known as the *Forbindelsesvold*, the 'Connecting Dyke'. Hedeby's defences had started as a modest wooden stockade – timbers from this earliest phase have been dendrochronologically dated to 810 – but as Hedeby increased in importance the fortifications were scaled up into a massive earthwork, ten metres high in places, which is still the major feature of the site today. It would be surprising if the real growth of Hedeby did not start under the energetic patronage of King Godfred, who may also have strengthened the existing Danevirke during his reign.

The site of Viking Age Hedeby has been intensively excavated in this century. There was a major dig in the 1930s, and another large-scale excavation, from 1962–9, was led by Dr Kurt Schietzel of the Schleswig-Holstein Landesmuseum at Schloss Gottorp. This produced hundreds of thousands of finds which are still being studied by specialist teams all over Europe. A major new excavation, concentrating on the harbour area of the town, began in 1979 (*cf* Ch. 10).

From all these excavations, as well as many contemporary documentary references, it is clear that Hedeby was one of the major trade centres in northern Europe throughout the Viking Age, and the most important emporium in Scandinavia. It was a busy, bustling, prosperous place, its wooden houses tightly packed together alongside workshops, warehouses, storage-sheds, stables and barns. In the 'Craftsmen's Quarter' lived potters and weavers, jewellers and leather-workers, carpenters and smiths, and Hedeby had its own mint, possibly the earliest in Scandinavia. Daily life there must have been rather like a perpetual *Vikingetræf* at Moesgård, but it was not apparently as decorous; an Arab merchant from Cordoba, Al-Tartushi, was less than flattering about it:

> They hold a festival where they assemble to honour their god and eat and drink. Anyone who slaughters an animal by way of sacrifice has a pole outside his house door and hangs the sacrificed animal there, whether it be ox or ram, he-goat or boar, so that people may know that he makes sacrifice in honour of his god. The town is poorly off for goods and wealth. The people's chief food is fish, for there is so much of it. If a child is born there it is thrown into the sea to save bringing it up . . . I have never heard more horrible singing than the Slesvigers' – it is like a growl coming out of their throats, like the barking of dogs, only much more beastly.[1]

[1]From the *Travel Book* of Ibrahim ibn Jakub, *c.* 975.

Compared with Cordoba, Hedeby must have seemed primitive to a fastidious Moorish traveller; but all the archaeological evidence emphasises the immense amount of trade in luxury goods that flowed through the town, from east to west and west to east: slaves from the Baltic, glassware and wine and weapons from western Europe, soapstone utensils from Norway, and from the hunting-grounds of the North the winter furs and skins so highly prized on the Continent.

Domestic life in Hedeby can now be vividly experienced at Moesgård, in the shape of a full-size reconstruction of a town house of the Viking period, based on tangible evidence from the 1962–9 excavations. Because the sub-soil at Hedeby is now waterlogged, a great deal of the wooden structure of this particular house had been preserved. One of the side-walls and a gable-end had collapsed, enabling archaeologists to measure the height of the house exactly. There is some doubt about the roofing material – whether it was turf or reed-thatch – but it is clear from buttress beams that survived that the upper part of the walls was supported from the outside, to prevent the walls bulging outwards under the weight of the roof. One of the doors also survived, as well as a hanging shelf, and the foundations of the hearth and the oven.

From all this evidence the Moesgård staff have been able to construct a faithful copy of the house as it once was. It measured thirteen metres by five, and was divided into three compartments. One room had low earthen benches facing the hearth and a large clay oven; and today in the Hedeby house visitors can bake Viking bread for themselves or make Viking pancakes on Viking griddles over sweet-smelling pine-log fires, or watch Viking textiles being woven on a warp-weighted loom.

Viking Hedeby also saw an early attempt to convert pagan Scandinavia to Christianity. For Viking kings, conversion seems to have been as much a matter of political expediency as piety; baptism was often the price of alliance with a powerful Christian neighbour. After Godfred's death in 810 (he was murdered by one of his retainers), Denmark's history became once again a welter of warring rivals for the crown; and in 826 one such contender, Harald Klak, made a deal with Charlemagne's successor, his son, Louis the Pious. In return for Frankish support for his claim to the Danish throne, Harald Klak and four hundred of his followers were solemnly baptised into the Church at the imperial palace at Ingelheim, near Mainz; and when Harald Klak returned to Denmark with the Emperor's backing, he brought with him a Christian missionary, a twenty-five-year-old monk called Anskar.

Anskar, later canonised for his efforts, has been dubbed the 'Apostle of the North'. But his first effort was short-lived. According to his contemporary biographer, Rimbert, he established a small school in Denmark, probably in Hedeby; but Harald Klak proved unpopular and was soon driven out, and Anskar had to leave with him. He was back in Hedeby in 849, this time as Archbishop of Hamburg and titular papal legate to the

RIGHT The Danevirke
near Hedeby, now
overgrown with trees.

BELOW Danish
schoolchildren bake
Viking pancakes at
Moesgård, in a
reconstruction of a
Viking Age house
excavated at Hedeby.

peoples of the Nōrth. He was given permission to build a church in Hedeby which, despite many vicissitudes, seems to have survived the turbulent years until Denmark was formally converted to Christianity more than a century later by King Harald Blue-Tooth.

It is difficult to assess the significance of this early church. It may well have been little more than a kind of spiritual Seamen's Mission for foreign merchants in Hedeby who were already Christian, sometimes threatened, sometimes tolerated. According to the records, the three earliest churches built in Scandinavia were all in trading centres – Hedeby and Ribe in Denmark, and Birka in Sweden (cf Ch. 4). It was in these marts that the fledgeling churches would expect to find ready-made adherents, either resident or transient. In addition, many of the Viking traders did more than merely rub shoulders with their Christian neighbours; when occasion required it, they cheerfully submitted to a ceremony of provisional baptism (prima signatio) as a condition for being allowed to trade in Christian communities:

> This was a common custom of the time, both among merchants and those mercenaries who joined up with Christians, since those who accepted provisional baptism had full communion with Christians and pagans alike, yet could keep whatever faith was most agreeable to them.
>
> (Egil's Saga)

For the time being at least, these early churches retained only a toe-hold in the pagan North, no doubt keeping a low profile rather than trying to be aggressively evangelistic. But with the tide of Carolingian Christianity lapping at the Danevirke on Denmark's southern borders, it was only a matter of time before the paganism of the North would be overthrown.

When the Viking break-out from Denmark came – when the 'fury of the Northmen' was unleashed on Continental Europe – it was not directed against Christianity or Christian church establishments; it was directed first and foremost against great trade centres like Dorestad on the Rhine, in the Low Countries of Frisia. And it did not start until 834 – somewhat later than the first Norwegian raids at the end of the eighth century.

The attacks by Norwegian sea-rovers on island monasteries, starting with Lindisfarne in 793 (cf Ch. 2), seem to have been a false dawn to the Viking Age proper. However alarming they were to monastic communities at the time, they were sporadic and uncoordinated, by-products of the more generalised Norse settlement and colonisation of the islands of northern Britain at the time (cf Ch. 9). After the initial flurry of Norwegian assaults, lasting some ten years, the Continental sources are silent about Viking raids, apart from a reference to a fleet from 'Nordmannia' that was repulsed from the mouth of the Seine in 820.

One explanation for this lull is surely the political situation in Europe. Charlemagne had welded together a vast empire that embraced modern

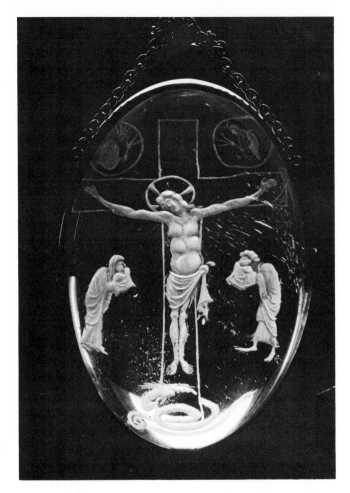

Ninth-century rock-crystal reliquary from the Carolingian empire.

France, West Germany, Holland, Belgium, Switzerland and Italy. This was Frankia, the kingdom of the Franks. He had modelled his ambitions on those of the classical Roman Emperors, but an empire transformed by Christianity. The culmination came on Christmas Day in 800 when Charlemagne was crowned in Rome as the first Holy Roman Emperor of the West. It was his achievement that from his capital at Aachen he inspired an organised revival of administration and literature and the arts throughout Europe, despite being illiterate himself.

However, it was a huge unwieldy empire, and Charlemagne was constantly engaged in military enterprises to defend it or hold it together, not least against King Godfred of Denmark. Charlemagne clearly divined the Viking threat as early as anyone else, and the last years of his reign saw him busying himself with building up the defences of his northern seaboard – the organisation of naval flotillas, the patrolling of the River Scheldt, the setting up of a system of guards and watches along the North Sea.

His empire had depended to a crucial extent on the dominating force of his personality and leadership. When he died in 814 he was succeeded by a son, Louis the Pious, who although more cultivated than his father, lacked his forcefulness. While Louis pursued his policy of spreading the Christian faith wherever he could, civil wars started breaking out within his kingdom, and by the 830s the Frankish empire was beginning to fall apart. The Vikings had an unerring nose for weakness in others, and Continental Europe now smelt vulnerable – although it was not the Vikings who were to destroy the Frankish empire; they were to be the catalysts of its collapse.

In 834 the first Danish raiders struck:

834. A fleet of Danes came to Frisia and laid waste a part of it. From there they came through Utrecht to the trading place called Dorestad and destroyed everything. They slaughtered some people, took others away, and burned the surrounding region.

(*Annals of St Bertin's*)

Dorestad (Dutch *Wijk bij Duurstede*) lay at the junction of the River Lek and an arm of the Rhine, right in the centre of the Netherlands. Archaeological excavations there began as long ago as the 1840s, and for the oddest of reasons: it had long been known that the fields in the area contained large quantities of animal bones, and during the grim winter of 1840–1 the starving villagers dug them up in huge numbers to make glue and bone-meal – it is said that 500,000 kilograms of bones were collected that winter. In the course of these diggings, large numbers of antiquities came to light. As a result, a formal excavation was started by one of the great pioneers of Dutch archaeology, Dr L. J. F. Janssen; despite the rather primitive techniques of field archaeology at that time, Janssen laid the groundwork for all the excavations that have since taken place there.

Dorestad was a huge place – some 240 hectares, ten times larger than Hedeby, perhaps the biggest mart in northern Europe – with its own mint, whose coins were used as exemplars for many other mints throughout Europe. Although it was reasonably well fortified, the Danish raiders broke through, and for the next generation Dorestad was to be a prime target for plunder or tribute until it was finally overwhelmed in 863, when the River Rhine changed its course for a time and flooded the town.

Dorestad was only the forerunner. In 836 Antwerp on the Scheldt was plundered and burned, as was the trade centre of Witla at the mouth of the Meuse. Across the Channel, southern England was also under attack by Danish Vikings, with a raid on the island of Sheppey in the Thames estuary in 835 (*cf* Ch. 5). In the Bay of Biscay, the island trade centre of Noirmoutier at the mouth of the Loire was plundered and its monastic site abandoned.

In 840 Louis the Pious died, and the great empire he had inherited was divided up between his three bickering sons – the eastern part to Louis the German, the west to Charles the Bald, and the centre and Italy to Lothar. And now the disintegration of the Frankish empire set in with a vengeance. Any political unity that Charlemagne had imposed was gone, and Frankish society became splintered and localised, racked with feuds and treacheries.

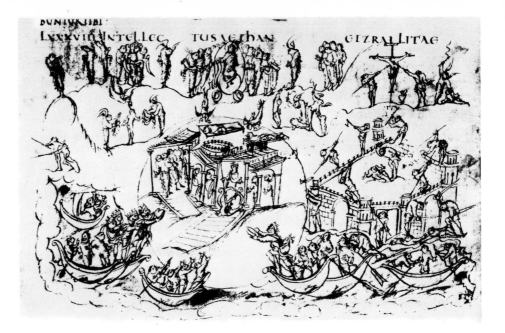

Detail from the Utrecht Psalter: river-borne attack on a European city.

It was a situation tailor-made for the Vikings, and they were not slow to exploit it. In 842 they were back on the Loire – in all probability Norwegians this time, following the trail the Danes had blazed – with a fleet of sixty-seven ships. It was rumoured that they had come at the invitation of a rebel Count, one Lambert, who coveted the city of Nantes for himself. It was Lambert's pilots who guided the Viking fleet past abandoned Noirmoutier and up the intricate channels of the Loire to Nantes.

Their timing was perfect. They struck on St John's Day, 24 June, when the town was crammed with visitors. What followed was indiscriminate slaughter, from which neither church nor churchmen were immune. Through the calculated timing of the raid, ecclesiastical traffic and commercial trade were the joint targets. Nantes in 842 was an appalling paradigm of what was to come: a perfidious local baron had won himself a town from his king, Charles the Bald, with Viking help; the Vikings had filled their ships with plunder and slaves to ransom or sell; and the raiders had learned that piracy could be a full-time occupation because, instead of going home for the winter, they settled on the island of Noirmoutier 'as if they meant to stay for ever'.

The year 840 and the death of Louis the Pious can be seen as a watershed. With the Frankish lords at one another's throats, the old Carolingian empire became a Viking hunting ground. Rouen on the Seine was sacked in 841; next year it was the turn of another great trade centre, Quentovic, near modern Étaples, south of Boulogne. In 845, a huge royal Danish fleet of reputedly six hundred ships led by King Horik sacked Hamburg, seat of Anskar's new arch-diocese – an assault from which Anskar himself barely escaped with his life and a few sacred relics.

In that same year, 845, a Danish Viking known only as Ragnar entered the Seine with a fleet of 120 ships – later embroidery would associate him

74

with the legendary Ragnar *loðbrók*, Ragnar Hairy-Breeks (*cf* Ch. 5). To check him, Charles the Bald deployed his army on both banks of the river – a tactical blunder which played right into Ragnar's hands. Ragnar attacked the smaller contingent, routed it, and then hanged 111 prisoners on an island in full view of the second Frankish force. The Franks, their morale shattered, offered no further resistance, and Ragnar sailed on to his planned destination. On Easter Sunday he pounced on Paris and sacked it; and Charles the Bald paid him 7000 pounds of silver to depart in peace with all his loot. It was the first recorded payment of protection money to the Vikings (in England, it would be called *Danegeld*, *cf* Ch. 5); it bought him six years of freedom from invasion while he tried to deal with his enemies and rivals at home, but it set a precedent that later marauders would follow with pleasure and profit.

For now, nowhere was safe. Viking fleets cruised up the Gironde and Garonne to ravage Aquitaine and Bordeaux. Spain and Portugal, then under Moorish rule, were attacked, but not always successfully – a daring raid on Seville on the River Guadalquivir was eventually repulsed at a cost of a thousand Vikings killed in battle and four hundred taken prisoner and hanged. By the middle of the ninth century, the whole Frankish empire was in a state of calamity:

> The number of ships increases, the endless flood of Vikings never ceases to grow. Everywhere Christ's people are the victims of massacre, burn-

The River Seine, from Château Gaillard; the Viking route to the heart of France.

75

ing and plunder, clear proof of which will remain as long as the world itself endures. The Vikings overrun all that lies before them, and none can withstand them. They seize the cities of Bordeaux, Périgueux, Limoges, Angoulême, Toulouse; Angers, Tours and Orléans are made deserts; the ashes of many a saint are carried away. Thus little by little is coming to pass the prophecy spoken by the Lord through the mouth of his prophet [Jeremiah]: 'Out of the North a scourge shall break forth upon all the inhabitants of the earth.'

Ships past counting voyage up the Seine, and throughout the entire region evil grows strong. Rouen is invaded, sacked and set on fire; Paris, Beauvais and Meaux are taken, the fortress of Melun is laid waste, Chartres occupied, Evreux and Bayeux looted, and every town invested.

(Ermentarius of Noirmoutier)

Ermentarius was one of the monks who abandoned the monastery at Noirmoutier in the face of the first Viking assault in 835 and fled, eventually reaching Tournus in Burgundy. His great contemporary work, *History of the Miracles and Translations of Saint Philibert*, gives a sober and moving account of the general terror the Vikings caused, the panic-stricken flight of inhabitants, the paralysis of the will to resist, the craven payment of huge amounts of tribute to make the invaders go away. Every major river in northern Europe, it seemed, was now swarming with Viking fleets; they used them as freely as we use motorways today – and nothing, it seemed, could stop them.

The effect of all this unrelenting Viking onslaught must have been horrifying and traumatic. Although the modern tendency is to modify the popular image of the Vikings as being mindless savages and to emphasise instead their positive contributions to trade and art and technology and so on, the ravaging of Frankia (however exaggerated some of the monkish chronicles may be) leaves even the most fervent Viking apologist speechless. In a brutal and murderous age, the Vikings' behaviour in Frankia was simply that much more brutal and murderous than most.

The raids were becoming more organised, more confident, more ambitious. And one particular expedition was destined to sail straight into the pages of the Sagas – the epic, four-year cruise of Björn Ironside and his fellow commander Hastein.

It started from Paris, in the year 857:

Paris! There you sit in the middle of the Seine, in the midst of the rich lands of the Franks, calling out: 'I am a city above all others, sparkling like a queen above them all!' All know you by the splendour of your bearing. Whoever lusts after the wealth of France is paying you homage. An island rejoices to support you, a river embraces you, its arms caressing your walls. Bridges stand on the river banks to left and right, towers keep watch on every side, in the city itself and beyond the river.

(Abbo of St Germain de Près)

Nineteenth-century
French impression of
the Danish river assaults
on the cities of France.

Paris was not the formal capital of France then – there was no capital in
those days. It was basically just the bastion of the Île de Paris in the
middle of the Seine, dominated today by the Cathedral of Notre Dame. It
had first been attacked by Ragnar in 845; now, in 857, it was sacked again,
allegedly by Ragnar's son, Björn Ironside, as shadowy a figure in history as
he must have been dreadfully actual to the inhabitants of Paris. The city
was almost totally destroyed; after the holocaust, we are told, only four
churches were left standing.

It was apparently after this brusque escapade that Björn Ironside and
his companion Hastein resolved upon an expedition that would make
history if nothing else. If they could sack the greatest city in northern
Europe, why not sack the greatest city in the world – Rome itself? And so,
with sixty-two ships, Björn and Hastein sailed back down the Seine on the
start of a spectacular adventure that would wreak a trail of havoc all round
the coasts of Europe and deep into the Mediterranean.

They seem to have had easy pickings as they beat round the coast of
Brittany and into the Bay of Biscay, for when they reached the shores of
Moorish Spain their ships were laden with prisoners, gold and silver,
according to Moorish sources. They fared indifferently in Spain; two of

77

their ships were captured in a skirmish off the mouth of the Guadalquivir, which was probably enough to deter them from making an attempt on Seville, as the earlier Viking fleet had done.

From the Guadalquivir they sailed through the Straits of Gibraltar, the fabled Pillars of Hercules, into the Mediterranean – probably the first Vikings to do so. Once there they plundered Algeciras, crossed to North Africa to pick up Negro prisoners, *blámenn* ('blue men'), who would end up as shivering slaves in Ireland, and then crossed back to the southern littoral of Spain and France. They ravaged the Balearics, Narbonne and the Camargue, sailing up the Rhône as far as Valence, 150 kilometres to the north, before being beaten back. On they went, prowling along the French Côte d'Azur and the Ligurian Riviera of northern Italy; they may also have sacked Pisa.

They sailed on until Hastein espied a great fortified city of gleaming white marble. Rome at last! But it was so strongly fortified that the Vikings doubted even their ability to take it by storm; and so, says the chronicler Dudo of St Quentin, 'the blasphemer Alstignus [Hastein], deciding that no force of arms could capture the city, devised a crafty plan of unspeakable treachery'. He sent messengers to the city to say that their chieftain was old and sick, and desired nothing more now than to be baptised into the true faith before he died. This pious plea was granted, and Hastein, feigning infirmity, was duly baptised and smeared with holy ointment and oil. Next day the messengers went back; their chieftain had died during the night, they said, and all they now desired was for the initiate to be given Christian burial in their cathedral. This plea, too, was granted:

A clamour of wailing is heard, and tumultuous mourning. The mountains reverberate, echoing the sound of deceitful grief. The bishop summons by bells the people throughout the whole city. The clergy came, dressed in monastic vestments. Similarly the chief men of the city came, soon to be crowned with martyrdom. The women came in throngs, soon to be led into exile. With one will they go to meet the monster laid on the bier. The scholars bear candles and crosses, walking before their seniors . . .

(Dudo of St Quentin)

And so the scene was set. As the body was about to be committed to the grave, the 'dead' Hastein sprang from his bier and cut down the officiating bishop with his sword. His men drew their concealed weapons from under their cloaks of mourning, opened the gates to their shipmates outside, and went on a merry riot of rape and pillage . . . It was a splendid Viking ploy, and one that would become a set-piece in other and equally unlikely yarns. There was a major snag, however – it turned out that the place was not the Eternal City after all, but a town called Luna, nearly three hundred kilometres to the north of Rome. All that ingenuity wasted! Hastein gave vent to his disappointment by massacring those of the in-

The Piraeus Lion at the old Arsenal in Venice; the runic inscription on the shoulders is now indecipherable.

habitants he did not want for slaves and burning the city to the ground.

There is one other snag to the story: by no stretch of the imagination could any Viking leader have confused Luna with Rome. That can only have been a chronicler's elaboration, to put it mildly. Luna had certainly been a large and important city in Roman times, but by the middle of the ninth century it was in serious economic decline and by 1200 it would be abandoned completely. By Hastein's time the impressive Roman buildings of Carrara marble from the quarries nearby were all in ruins, the magnificent amphitheatre and the forum lying derelict, the town reduced to a scattered settlement with a fortified nucleus round its cathedral.

Luna is now called Luni. It lies about two kilometres inland, just east of the headland of La Spezia, halfway between Pisa and Genoa. It is now under intensive archaeological excavation by the Centro di Studi Lunensi, which is gradually revealing the extent of the Roman city; but a small Anglo-Italian team, directed by Bryan Ward-Perkins, has recently started investigating the early medieval levels of the town for the first time – Hastein's 'Rome'. No trace of the destruction attributed to Hastein has been found so far – no ashes, no axe-heads, no discarded Viking spears.

However, the area where such evidence might be expected, around the remains of the church, has not yet been excavated.

Bryan Ward-Perkins himself thinks it very likely that Hastein's Vikings *did* sack Luna – but not under the foolish impression that it was Rome; after all, it is such an unlikely place for a chronicler to have invented. The coast was taking a battering from the Saracens at this date, and the sudden appearance of these alien Norsemen must have come as a shock to be remembered. But what Hastein actually did at Luna, and how he achieved it – that is probably a very different story.

Ironically, the only certain Viking 'visiting card' in the area is to be found in a city which we know the Vikings never molested at all. It is in the form of a runic inscription on the shoulders of a magnificent marble lion that now stands guard at the entrance to the old Arsenal in Venice. It is not a Venetian creation; it was looted from the Piraeus harbour of Athens during a Venetian military expedition to Greece late in the seventeenth century.

The inscription itself is now, alas, indecipherable, because it is so badly weathered. It was confided to the lion's shoulder late in the eleventh century, when the Viking surge was to all intents and purposes spent. It was done by a Swedish Viking, not very accomplished at rune-writing, who had reached the Mediterranean by the eastern route, down through Russia to Constantinople (*cf* Ch. 4). It is not inappropriate that his message should now be incomprehensible, because by then his occupation as a Viking was gone. He had become redundant, an anachronism. The Mediterranean had never really been for the Vikings. They were too far from their natural habitat. It is symbolic that the reason we cannot read these runes today is that they were not carved deeply enough on that proud lion from Classical Greece. Time and trouble have helped to erode them, and now only infra-red photography to divine the disturbed crystalline structure of the underlying marble might conceivably enable us to decipher them one day. But I doubt if we shall ever know. Like the runes on the Piraeus lion, the impact of the Vikings on the Mediterranean was simply too slight.

Hastein and his men seem to have realised this, too. There is a suggestion in the sources that they ventured even farther east, to Alexandria in Egypt; but eventually he turned for home, knowing that he would have to run the gauntlet of a lurking Moorish fleet with scores to settle off Gibraltar. In the ensuing battle the Vikings were badly mauled, but the survivors managed to slip through the Straits and head for home. They paused to land on the coast of Navarre, where they thrust inland to capture Pamplona and ransom its prince for a huge sum. Finally, in 862, they reached haven at the mouth of the Loire. Only twenty of the original sixty-two ships that had set sail four years earlier still survived. It had been, from one point of view, a spectacularly heroic adventure whose fame would never be forgotten; from another, a preposterous exercise in piracy that brought untold misery to those it affected, not least those wretched *blámenn* from North Africa.

Hastein's heroes returned to a Frankia even more deeply embroiled with the Viking menace. The scale of the depredations was constantly increasing; the second half of the ninth century was the heyday of Viking activity in northern Europe. Frankia was by now in something very close to anarchy, as the established political systems broke down. Unwittingly, the Vikings were helping to introduce a new kind of social order to France. Their assaults on abbeys and monasteries destroyed not only buildings but also the organisation of the extensive demesnes of the church. The old-style loyalties to State and Church were breaking down. In their place, rural seigneuries grew up, in which free men offered their services to the lords in return for protection; castles were built, ostensibly as a defence against Viking incursions; cities perforce developed their own defences and their own political structures. New men were taking over, men who owed allegiance only to themselves and their own districts. Self-interest and self-defence were the order of the day, requiring new obligations between lord and land-worker. The Vikings were the midwives of feudalism in France.

This is no doubt an over-simplification, but necessarily so in order to make some sense of the turmoil of the ninth century. From the confused clash of battles and burnings, routs and retreats, a pattern begins to emerge: the Franks were getting the measure of the Vikings. One turning-point was surely the heroic defence of Paris in the long and bitter siege of 885–6.

The Franks had realised for some years that the most effective way to check the Vikings was to block their motorways, the rivers, with fortified bridges – like sinking tank-traps and mines in more recent conflicts. The Seine was now thus fortified. Up the Seine, in November 885, came a huge Danish fleet of some seven hundred ships, according to the sources. For a whole year the defenders of the bridges and the walls held out against overwhelming odds. What had started, perhaps, as yet another plundering expedition became a symbolic trial of strength between Viking and Frank. Rather late in the day it dawned on the Frankish king (by now Charles the Fat) that Paris would prove to be the key to all France; if it fell, the Vikings would be free to roam at will south-east and north-east, devouring everything along the Seine, the Marne and the Yonne from Rheims to Burgundy. By the late summer of 886 he had gathered an army large enough to besiege the besiegers; and then, to the fury of the starved defenders of Paris, he actually paid the Vikings to go away in peace, with plenty of provisions and with seven hundred pounds of silver as a sweetener!

There was method in this apparent madness; for Charles the Fat also encouraged the Vikings to spend the winter in Burgundy, where he himself was having trouble with rebellious subjects. There is no mistaking the policy: for a large enough price the Vikings could not only be bought off, but used. They had become an undeniable factor in the political scene in Frankia. Viking war-bands, weary perhaps of the long years at the oar and sated with pillage, could now be induced to settle in the lands they had ravaged, there to form a new kind of bulwark against further attack. Viking dynasties would be formed on Frankish soil, flourish for a time, and then die out or be taken over. Only one would take root – the settlement of Northmen in Normandy in 911 (*cf* Ch. 10).

The story of events in the homeland of Denmark during this period is equally confusing, but much more obscure. Whereas there were plenty of chroniclers in Frankia to rehearse the misdeeds of the Vikings there, no contemporary source tells us anything about the history of Denmark itself. Occasional royal names emerge fleetingly, kings or would-be kings who lived briefly and died violently. It was an age of wars and rivalries and much piracy; and by the end of the ninth century we find Denmark ruled

Crucifixion scene on the massive Jelling Stone in Denmark. The runic inscription at the foot reads '*and made the Danes Christian*'.

The presumed double grave being excavated in the chancel of Jelling Church.

by a dynasty of Swedish kings. It is probably incorrect to think of Denmark as being a nation at all during this period; it seems to have been this that caused the appearance of so many 'royal' Danish fleets in Frankia: exiled kings or chieftains needed to vent their aggressions and recoup their losses somewhere!

It is not until the 930s or 940s that we reach firmer historical ground in Denmark, with the accession of King Gorm the Old. Gorm and his father seem to have wrested the throne of Denmark from the Swedes some time during these decades, and they established a royal seat at Jelling in Jutland. Later chroniclers were to be unkind, unjust or downright fanciful about him. Adam of Bremen in his monumental *History of the Archbishopric of Hamburg*, written *c.* 1075, would present him as a cantankerous old pagan, a malignant persecutor of Christians, when Archbishop Unni of Hamburg-Bremen renewed Anskar's mission to the Danes after an interval of nearly a century. Saxo Grammaticus, secretary to Archbishop Absolon of Roskilde late in the twelfth century and author of *Gesta Danorum* in sixteen books, and his contemporary chronicler Svend Aggesen, portrayed him as being slothful and incompetent, and very old. The Icelandic Saga-writers pay him the left-handed compliment of remembering him primarily as the husband of a remarkable queen, Thyri, and father of two remarkable offspring – Queen Gunnhild, wife of King Eirík Blood-Axe of Norway and York (cf Ch. 6), and Harald *blátönn*, King Harald Blue-Tooth of Denmark. In fact, Gorm the Old was the progenitor of a mighty Danish dynasty that would eventually conquer England, and, briefly, create a potent North Sea empire combining Denmark, England and Norway under his great-grandson, Knút (Canute) the Great (cf Ch. 9).

In addition to the erratic writings of later historians, we have more tangible evidence of Gorm the Old. We have a runic memorial stone he raised for his wife Thyri; we have a huge burial mound he built to hold her remains at Jelling; and now, sensationally, we may have the skeletons of Gorm and Thyri themselves, discovered in 1979 under the floor of Jelling Church – the first Viking Age dead we can actually identify. And thereby hangs a fascinating tale of archaeological detective work.

The modern town of Jelling (population 7000), to the north-west of Vejle, has always been one of the most celebrated Viking sites in all Scandinavia. The town is dominated by two immense burial mounds, one at the front and one at the back of a large, early twelfth-century church – the oldest surviving church in Denmark. In front of the church, in a direct line between the two mounds, stand two runic stones, the one erected by Gorm the Old, the other by his son Harald Blue-Tooth. The North Mound (behind the Church) was traditionally known as 'Thyri's Mound'; the South Mound was correspondingly called 'Gorm's Mound'.

In 1965, a district authority heating system was due to be installed in Jelling Church. Since it was a national monument, an expert from the National Museum of Denmark was called in: assistant curator Dr Knud Krogh, who had been trained as an architect. He noticed that the top-soil under the church floor was not the natural soil surface, but had been applied by human hands. He suspected that there might be more there than met the eye; ten years later he got the chance to find out, when he was put in sole charge of the restoration of Jelling Church in 1975.

It had previously been thought that there had been two earlier churches on the same site. Dr Krogh soon showed that there had in fact been three, all made of timber, which had burned down; the present church, built of stone, was erected on the same site around 1100. And then, in the area between nave and chancel, Dr Krogh came upon the remains of a large double grave. This grave, he proved by minute analysis and observation of the original ground surface, was contemporary with the building of the first church on the site.

The double grave was in a timber-lined compartment. Its size and the precision of its placing helped to confirm that the first church had been built round it and for it, as a kind of mausoleum. Inside the grave, Dr Krogh found what seemed to be the remains of two skeletons, one male

84

and one female. At the time of writing the anthropological examination of the skeleton material has not been completed. The bones were jumbled, as if the skeletons had already been disarticulated when they were laid to rest. The grave also contained a large quantity of gold thread from some long-vanished cloth, and two small and elaborately decorated strap-ends of silver-gilt and enamel, with double-headed animal motifs. It had clearly been a distinguished funeral – doubtless a royal one. And with these discoveries, a number of unresolved puzzles about the royal site of Jelling began to fall into place . . .

The two great burial mounds had always been rather an enigma. As early as 1607 the local farmers had tried to break into the North Mound – 'Thyri's Mound' – in search of treasure, but failed. Later, the villagers sank a well into the top of it. In 1820, when the summer was unusually hot, the well dried up. Thinking that it might simply be choked, the villagers climbed down to clean it; they dug deeper – and suddenly found themselves in a wooden chamber in the heart of the mound. They stopped working at once and informed the authorities, and Professor Finn Magnussen hurried from Copenhagen to take over.

The chamber was 2.6 metres wide, 6.75 metres long, and 1.4 metres high. The left-hand side had also been divided in two by a plank placed edgeways. It was obviously the mound's burial chamber – but there was no sign at all of any body or bodies. Instead, there were numerous well-preserved animal bones, proving that any human skeleton that might have been there had not decomposed without trace. In addition, the excavators found a small cross and a small silver-gilt beaker, only 4.2 centimetres high. It had been cast in two pieces, with the stem welded on, and was originally interpreted as a Christian communion vessel. It is now thought to have been part of a table set of small stoups or drinking vessels – the replica at the National Museum in Copenhagen holds exactly the same amount as a modern measure of *akvavit*! It is decorated with ribbon-like animals, elaborately intertwined, and it was this that gave the name to the well-known Jelling style of Viking art.

The finding of an empty burial chamber was puzzling. But the excavators also found tell-tale signs that the chamber had been broken into from above in antiquity, and it was assumed that grave-robbers must have forced their way in and carried off the coffin to examine their booty at leisure.

Some forty years later, in 1861, King Frederick VII, who was a keen amateur antiquarian, personally ordered the excavation of the South Mound ('Gorm's Mound'): he wanted his royal ancestor, Gorm, to be found 'with the reverence which both Gorm and science have a right to'. The excavation was entrusted to Denmark's great pioneer of archaeology, Jens Jacob Worsaae. Military engineers tunnelled into the mound at surface level and then, in response to a telegram from the impatient king, higher up. They found nothing at all; not even an empty burial chamber.

VIKINGS!

The tiny silver Jelling beaker, found in the empty grave-chamber in the North Mound at Jelling.

Another excavation was made in the early 1940s by Dr Einar Dyggve, in the belief that the grave might have been placed below ground surface, and that Worsaae's engineers might therefore have missed it. Once again, nothing was found. However, both Worsaae and Dyggve came across configurations of huge boulders that suggested that the mound might have been raised on the site of a much more ancient, perhaps Bronze Age, sacred area. Dyggve then re-excavated Thyri's Mound, and found that its burial chamber had in fact been sunk into the top of a Bronze Age grave-mound, which explained why it lay so high in the present mound.

Dyggve postulated the theory that Gorm and Thyri must have been removed from the North Mound and buried in the church at Jelling. In an attempt to prove it, he excavated inside the church itself, but found nothing. Knud Krogh's later excavation inside the church, and his discovery of the double grave, seems to prove that Dyggve's guess had been right. If, indeed, there is a couple in the grave they must surely be Gorm and Thyri, transferred there some years after they had been buried in the North Mound. And now the sequence of historical events became clearer.

Queen Thyri, 'Denmark's glory', had died before Gorm the Old, obviously – at a guess, say around 950. She must have been a memorable lady, because later tradition was to associate her with the building of the Danevirke! Gorm the Old laid her in a burial chamber on top of the Bronze Age mound at Jelling, and heaped a much larger mound over her; and he erected a small runic stone in her memory: 'King Gorm made this memorial to his wife Thyri, Denmark's glory.'

When Gorm himself died, his son, Harald Blue-Tooth, placed him in the same burial chamber as his beloved wife Thyri in the North Mound, and built the South Mound as a cenotaph to him, to give symmetry to the funerary site. And then, soon after his accession to the throne, Harald was converted to Christianity, around the year 960, by a missionary called Bishop Poppo. The occasion was recalled by Adam of Bremen, and graphically depicted in an early thirteenth-century gold-plated altar-piece in Tandrup Church, now in the National Museum in Copenhagen. In the course of a debate, Poppo offered to prove that Christ was more powerful than Óðin by undergoing ordeal: he would put on a red-hot iron glove without suffering injury. The relief panels from Tandrup show Poppo wearing the fearsome glove, to Harald Blue-Tooth's awe, and then Harald being immersed in a barrel of holy water at his baptism.

Harald now decreed that all Denmark should adopt Christianity and the Church in Denmark was organised as part of the arch-diocese of Hamburg-Bremen. To celebrate his conversion, Harald seems to have decided to give his parents a proper Christian burial. He would have exhumed their bodies from the North Mound in Jelling, and reinterred them in a church he built specially to receive them – Denmark's first church. Then, in front of the church door and on the spot exactly halfway on a direct line between the centre of the two mounds, he erected the

OPPOSITE Detail of Harald Blue-Tooth's baptism in a barrel by Bishop Poppo: from the golden altar-piece of Tandrup Church in Denmark.

famous Jelling Stone, a huge boulder that seems to have been left in the vicinity as part of the debris of the Ice Age.

Harald's Jelling Stone is a magnificent, three-sided monument. On the side facing worshippers as they approach the church there is a figure of Christ carved in relief – the earliest known Viking representation of Christ. It is usually interpreted as a crucifixion scene, but it could also be interpreted as Jesus with outstretched arms blessing the people entering the church. The second side is filled with a long runic inscription: 'King Harald had this memorial made for Gorm his father and Thyri his mother: that Harald who won for himself all Denmark . . .' The inscription is completed on the other sides: '. . . and Norway, and made the Danes Christian.'

Historians are unsure how seriously to take Harald's claim that he conquered Norway as well as winning Denmark; but there can be no doubt that the mighty Jelling Stone, and the conversion of Denmark to Christianity, represent a very real consolidation of royal power. Harald Blue-Tooth emerges from the past as the first major king *of* Denmark, rather than just a king *in* Denmark: a king with the resources and authority to undertake major and massive projects. Jelling was the birthplace of Denmark as a true Viking nation, and not just a land of Vikings.

The extent of Harald Blue-Tooth's public works are only now becoming apparent. A dendrochronological date of 968 from a section of the Danevirke suggests that not Thyri but Harald had a hand in at least refurbishing it. Even more recently, dendrochronology has produced a yet more sensational scientific coup: an absolute date for the great Viking Age 'barracks' of Trelleborg. In September 1979 it was announced by Dr Tage E. Christiansen of the National Museum of Copenhagen that timbers from Trelleborg had been dated by their tree-rings precisely to 980–1, i.e. within Harald Blue-Tooth's reign. It is sensational because it has overthrown all previous theories about the dating, and therefore the purpose, of the Viking Age Trelleborgs in Denmark.

'Trelleborg' (the name seems to mean something like 'slave fort') has become a generic term for a particular type of circular military-type encampment found in Denmark. There are four of them: Trelleborg itself, on the west coast of Zealand; Nonnebakken, under the city of Odense on the island of Fyn; Fyrkat, in east Jutland; and Aggersborg in north Jutland. They were all constructed with great precision: groups of barrack-like buildings surrounded by towering earthen ramparts, as perfectly laid out as any Roman legionary camp. They are all of different sizes, but all built to a similar blueprint. The largest by far was Aggersborg, three times the size of Trelleborg and Fyrkat. All had four gateways at the four points of the compass; two timber-paved streets, intersecting at right angles, divided the internal area of the 'camp' into four equal quadrants, each of which contained a regular number of four boat-shaped buildings arranged to form a hollow square.

Aerial view of Trelleborg. The configurations of the buildings have been marked in by archaeologists. On the far right, a full-scale reconstruction of one of the Trelleborg 'barrack-halls'.

What had been the point of these constructions? What had been their purpose? The archaeological evidence was equivocal. They had been in use for only one generation at most, and when they were excavated, hardly any artefacts were found – and particularly no discarded weapons. This could either mean that they had been barracks that had been kept scrupulously tidy by the soldiers; or that they had not been barracks at all.

Many scholars have concluded that they *must* have been barracks, built specifically for invasion purposes; and since the only major invasion undertaken by Denmark that we know about was the invasion of England by Harald Blue-Tooth's son, Svein Fork-Beard in 1013 (*cf* Ch. 9), it was assumed that they must have been built by Svein Fork-Beard for that purpose.

The new dendrochronological dating from Trelleborg has destroyed that assumption. Preliminary reports of dendro-dates from Fyrkat, suggesting the year 976, seem to confirm Trelleborg's dating. It is impossible to be certain yet, but it now looks very much as if all the four 'Trelleborgs' were built by Harald Blue-Tooth, and not during the reign of his son, King Svein Fork-Beard.

If this is so, it can only mean that Harald Blue-Tooth built them as

89

camps to house his own soldiery to consolidate his power over Denmark itself. Denmark was still volatile enough to require garrisoning against its own subjects.

The 'Trelleborgs' are now, more than ever, a matter of academic speculation: there are few certainties in history or archaeology. But at least we can be reasonably sure that the new dendro-dates for the 'Trelleborgs', like the new discoveries at Jelling, indicate the growth of royal power in Denmark under Harald Blue-Tooth, the king who made Denmark a Viking nation. It was Harald's son, Svein Fork-Beard, who invaded England, and his grandson, Knút, who consolidated that invasion into conquest; but it was Harald Blue-Tooth, it now seems, who made the enterprise possible.

4

'Hálfdan was here'

Throughout the Viking Age, one historic island can claim to have been the true centre of the Viking world – the Baltic island of Gotland, off the east coast of Sweden. Although it is now a province of Sweden, it has always prided itself on its independence of view and action. It is not a particularly large island, only 120 kilometres long and 55 kilometres wide, with a total area of just over 3000 square kilometres and a population of 55,000; but it occupies a strategic position in the Baltic, lying 90 kilometres from the mainland of Sweden to the west, 150 kilometres from Russia to the east, and 215 kilometres from the coast of Poland to the south.

It is this accident of geography that has made Gotland the 'archaeological deep-freeze' of the Viking Age, in the striking phrase of Professor Erik Nylén, the Director of the Antiquities Service in Gotland at Visby. There

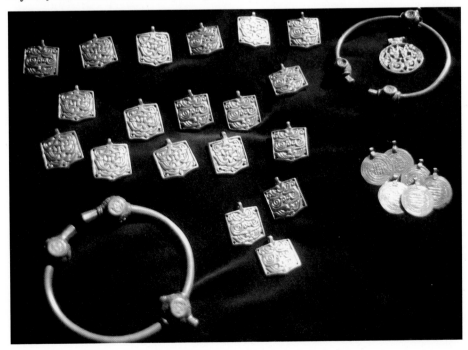

A Gotland hoard: Kufic coins, rings and silver plaques from a belt.

Penannular bronze
cloak-pin from Gotland
with gilt and silver
decoration.

are more Viking and pre-Viking antiquities on Gotland than in the whole of the rest of Sweden. It has provided a unique collection of some 370 picture-stones (*bildstenar*) dating from the fifth century onwards. It has also provided an astonishing wealth of silver coins and golden treasures: on Gotland, no fewer than 50,000 silver Arabic (Kufic) coins of the eighth to tenth centuries have been found, compared with only 35,000 in the whole of the rest of Scandinavia put together. Gotland lay at the crossroads of the world; it was the trade crucible of the Baltic, the *entrepôt* of east-west commerce.

It is not always the largest or the most impressive remains that tell the biggest story. Sometimes the most significant historical documents can look deceptively insignificant. My own favourite artefact from Gotland is a little whetstone that was found on the farm of Timans in the parish of Roma, dating from the late tenth century. It has a brief runic inscription scratched on it. It was not meant to be a momentous message for posterity – frankly, it was just a doodle done in an idle moment; but what it says is momentous enough: 'Ormiga: Ulfuair: krikiaR: iaursaliR: islat: serklat.' Transliterated, it reads: 'Ormiga, Ulfar: Greece, Jerusalem, Iceland, Serkland.' Which means, in effect, 'Ormiga and Ulfar have been to Greece [the Byzantine Empire], to Jerusalem, to Iceland, and to the land of the Saracens [probably Baghdad].'

The inscription may have been carved by the farmer father of two far-travelled Gotland boys; it may just have been Ormiga doing a draft of his expenses! But in that brief statement we have a veritable Cook's Tour of the trade routes of the Viking Age, crisscrossing from east to west and from north to south; it symbolises the enormous range of Gotland's mercantile interests just as effectively as a whole shelf full of books, in the same way that Gotland itself symbolises the essential cosmopolitanism of the Viking world.

The whetstone is one of the innumerable artefacts on display in Gotland's Historical Museum in the capital town, Visby, on the west coast. Visby is one great historical monument in itself, and to visit it is to be transported enchantingly back into the Middle Ages. The medieval town is surrounded by a massive turreted wall dating back to the late thirteenth century, when Visby was at the height of its prosperity as a Hanseatic trading town; the cobbled streets and lanes are lined with half-timbered houses leaning confidentially towards each other; there are towers and tall gable-stepped houses, arcades of tiny shops selling ancient handicrafts, high-walled cottage gardens and fine ruined churches, all topped by the majestic St Maria Cathedral.

Gotland's pre-Viking antiquities date back to the late Bronze Age, some 3000 years ago, with a huge number of graves marked by stone-settings in the form of ships, like the Viking graves at Lindholm Høje in Denmark (*cf* Ch. 3). But the Gotland ship-settings are 2000 years earlier. There are about 350 of them, some extremely large, like the grave at Gnisvärd, a few kilometres south of Visby, which measures forty-five metres in length and seven metres in width. These graves contained nothing but a small stone kist holding the remains of a cremation; but the proportions of the ship-settings, with a width to breadth ratio of about seven to one, are remarkably similar to the outlines of the later Viking Age longships.

These ship-settings afford us a very early glimpse of the concept of some kind of sea-voyage to the afterworld. The celebrated Gotland picture-stones give further glimpses of mythological beliefs leading us towards the Viking Age. The earliest stones, from the fifth and sixth centuries, feature a mystic symbol in the shape of a whirling wheel, which has been interpreted as a continuation of some Bronze Age cult of worship of the sun-disc. Viking Age stones make frequent pictorial allusions to Valhöll and the Valkyries who welcome the dead to Óðin's great palace of the slain; on some, the runic inscriptions beseech the gods to wreak vengeance for the fallen. At the other end of the time scale, when Thór had been driven from the field and Óðin had ridden his last ride on his eight-legged steed Sleipnir, the Cross has replaced the sun-disc and Thor's Hammer; the eleventh-century Hogrän Stone features a dead brother being commemorated in very practical fashion, by the building of a bridge both for the dead and the living. The runes now speak piety, seeking mercy and not the grim revenge of pagan times: 'Sigmund had this stone raised for his brother, and built a bridge for Sigbjörn. May the Archangel Michael help his soul . . . here stands this stone as a memorial, bright with colour at the bridge.' It was Sigmund's new passport to the next world, just as much as Sigbjörn's.

Scholarly interest in the stones has tended to focus most on those that portray ships, because they are an invaluable source of information for maritime historians; they afford a remarkably coherent picture of the evolution of ship technology from the rowing-boat to the sailing-boat and the kind of rigging that may have been used. The sixth-century Sanda Stone shows a boat being rowed by bearded oarsmen with a fine display of muscled vigour. Sails begin to be featured from the eighth or ninth century onwards; the earliest are depicted with a plaited or chequered pattern, presumably to make them stronger – there were no looms wide enough to weave a sail in one piece, so the strips had to be sewn together. Basically, the Gotland picture-stones show that the fully-fledged Viking ship was a Scandinavian rowing-boat that learned how to use sail; and this has been confirmed by the boats recovered by archaeology in recent years.

Oddly enough, despite the fact that many types of Viking and pre-Viking vessels are depicted on the stones, archaeology has not yet found the remains of an actual ship on Gotland. Perhaps they did not build their own ships? But in the Historical Museum in Visby there is a beautifully ornamented bronze wind-vane for a ship's mast, dated to around 1000, and decorated with a writhing serpent in what the Norwegians call the Ringerike style; and a lion stands on the top edge. This wind-vane was used for many

Viking ships from the Gotland stones, showing the transition from rowing-boat to sail-boat with very complicated rigging.

93

ABOVE Unique Gotland
'box-brooch'.

BELOW Gotland stone:
a dead warrior is
welcomed to Valhöll
by a Valkyrie. In the
lower panel, his fully-
rigged Viking ship.

centuries as a weather-cock on the fourteenth-century Källunge Church; some fifty years ago it was blown off, and only then was it recognised for what it actually was, a Viking Age artefact.

It is not surprising that the Gotlanders should have been so fascinated by ships, for ships were their economic mainstay. Gotland has no mineral or other natural resources of its own. Their craftsmen manufactured certain artefacts, including a unique form of decorated 'box-brooch', almost baroque in its elaborate ornamentation, which Gotlandic women wore as a single brooch on the middle of the chest – Viking women elsewhere usually wore brooches in pairs, to attach a cloak round their shoulders. But for the most part, Gotland's wealth came from the import-export trade. The Gotlanders were the quintessential middle-men, in every sense of the term.

There does not seem to have been any one major market centre on Gotland. There is some archaeological evidence that Visby itself dates back to a tenth-century Viking Age settlement, flanked to north and south by two satellite settlements at Gustavsvik and Kopparsvik whose grave-fields have been extensively excavated; and, more recently, indications of a port or lagoon-haven have been recognised at Pavik, near Västergarn on the west coast, and at Bogevik, near Slite, on the east coast. Dr Nylén thinks there were no highly specialised settlements based on organised professional trade on Gotland, like Helgö and Birka in Sweden; Gotland was one big trade centre, an island of farmers who all seemed to take part in trading as well.

Birka, on the other hand, certainly was a highly specialised settlement. It was located on the island of Björkö ('Birch Island') in Lake Mälar, in the heart of the extensive water-transport system of the east-central province of Uppland in Sweden. It was established around 800 as an apparent successor to the much earlier settlement at Helgö (*cf* Ch. 1), which seems to have run out of room for growth – and the need for growth was pressing. Sweden, like the other Scandinavian countries, seems to have experienced a very pronounced population expansion in the early 800s. This population explosion did not lead to massive emigration to add impetus to the Viking Age, as happened in Norway, because Sweden had vast reserves of virgin land waiting to be settled which absorbed the new numbers; it was accompanied by a considerable increase in local and international trade to satisfy this new and growing market. It has been estimated that there were something like 2000 farms scattered around Lake Mälar at this period.

Apart from its importance as a domestic mart exchanging food and small handicrafts for the farmers living in the neighbourhood, Birka was also one of the major international emporia of Viking Scandinavia, a clearing-place for world trade in the iron and furs of the northlands. It was a walled town guarded by a fortress, which is still visible as a commanding rocky outcrop

The site of Birka, on the island of Björkö in Lake Mälar.

defended on the landward side by a massive stone-and-earth bank. The town itself was on the low-lying land to the north, an area of eleven hectares enclosed by a defensive earthen rampart about two metres high. In the centre of this enclosure was the ancient settlement area, the so-called 'Black Earth' area whose soil is discoloured by a deep overburden of occupation detritus. A very small part of this Black Earth was excavated late last century by the pioneering Swedish archaeologist Hjalmar Stolpe. Stolpe concentrated his attention far more on the vast gravefields outside the town limits, which contained more than 2000 burials and which produced a mass of material of staggering wealth and quality from all over the known world: silver and silk from Arabia, pottery and glassware from the Rhineland, ornaments and weapons from England and Ireland, coins from western Europe worn as amulets, walrus ivory from the Arctic regions.

Today the site of Birka is a quiet and empty stretch of meadowland, dotted with birch trees and juniper, and it is hard to imagine it as it must have been in the Viking Age – a place teeming with activity, raucous with a babel of foreign tongues, buying and selling, wheeling and dealing, drinking and brawling, summer and winter alike. But we know a little about what it was like, from two visits made to Birka in the first half of the ninth century by the Christian missionary St Anskar, the 'Apostle of the North' (cf Ch. 3). According to his ninth-century biographer, Rimbert, Anskar's first mission to Birka was in 829. It almost ended in disaster before it had begun; on the way his ship was attacked by Viking pirates – piracy was endemic in the Baltic by this time. The ship was captured, but Anskar and his missionary companion, a monk called Witmar, managed to struggle ashore and make their way to Birka on foot; they lost all their possessions, however, including the gifts they were bringing for the local king, Björn, and their library of nearly forty holy books.

As an international port between east and west, Birka was full of people of many different religions, or none, and Anskar managed to establish a little church there, as at Hedeby in Denmark, for the benefit of the small community of resident or visiting Christians. This particular foundation, as at Hedeby, proved to be short-lived; but Anskar returned around 850, by which time he was Archbishop of Hamburg/Bremen, and was able to revive the mission, for a time at least.

From his two visits we are given an interesting glimpse of Birka society. Birka was governed by a *Ting* (local assembly) under the leadership of a royal prefect; but the king was by no means all-powerful. Rimbert says that when Anskar went to Birka on his second visit, the king told him so specifically: he could only speak in support of Anskar's mission at the assembly, 'and if they approve your desire and the gods consent, what you have asked for will come to pass, but if it should turn out otherwise I will let you know. It is the custom among them that the control of public business of every kind should rest with the whole people and not with the king.'

Anskar also found himself rubbing shoulders with two separate classes of people – the *populi*, who were the permanent residents, and the *negociatores*, who were foreign merchants. This social division appears to have been perpetuated into the next life, because there seem to have been two quite separate and distinctive burial areas: the vast fields of cremation graves in mounds for the *populi* outside the town walls, and much smaller fields of unburnt burials in an exclusive cemetery just inside and even under the walls of the town which were the preserve of the merchants. According to the latest excavator at Birka, Dr Björn Ambrosiani, Keeper of the Museum Department of the Museum of National Antiquities in Stockholm, these inhumation graves were quite un-Scandinavian in character and contained a disproportionate amount of foreign imported goods. Because of this, he believes that Birka itself was originally established by incoming merchants who remained a special class within the town.

Birka was primarily a port, rather than a manufacturing town. In 1969–71, Dr Ambrosiani conducted a small excavation in the Black Earth area in search of traces of a harbour. Two harbour areas were already known, but they were both outside the town walls; Dr Ambrosiani was looking for a harbour within the town defences, which he was sure must have existed. He knew that the water-level had been considerably higher during the Viking period, so he started digging a good way inland; and on the very first day, he struck stone. He had come across a stone-built jetty at a point that showed that the water had been five metres above the present level; in fact there were two jetties, one built on top of the other, which shows that the water-level was still rising at that time, only to fall sharply after Birka had declined early in the eleventh century. It was perhaps this drop in the water-level that influenced the decision to abandon it in favour of other trade centres, like Sigtuna to the north or Gotland itself.

Even though Birka, according to Rimbert's account, was not under the absolute authority of the Uppland kings, there can be little doubt that it must have enjoyed a large measure of royal protection. Birka lay not far from an important royal estate at Adelsø, and it is reasonable to assume that the king would be eager to develop Birka as a protected mart to centralise control of the trade that was already flowing past his doorstep, in order to exploit it with tolls and taxes.

Very little is known about the early evolution of kingship in Sweden, apart from Saga stories that are more legend than history. But there are many places in central Sweden which are still redolent of a time of great wealth and power stretching far back into antiquity. One such site is the impressive burial complex popularly known as *Anundshög*, just outside Västerås, at the western end of Lake Mälar. The site is dominated by an enormous burial mound known as 'Anund's Mound'.

It is at a site like this that one feels the early royal history of Sweden taking significant and formidable shape. This was one of the assembly sites (*Tingsteds*) where the king would meet his people and exchange mutual

Imported luxury goods excavated from merchants' graves at Birka.

oaths of allegiance, standing on the southern slope with the sun on his face. Alongside the mound there is a row of fifteen standing stones, which were discovered during excavations in the 1960s and re-erected in their original positions. The tallest stone, in the middle of the row, has a runic inscription which is dated to the eleventh century. It says: 'Folkvid raised all these stones in memory of his son, Anund's brother. Vred carved the runes.'

This Anund has been associated with a shadowy King Braut-Önund, who appears in Snorri Sturluson's *Ynglinga saga* as one of the early Yngling kings of Sweden (*cf* Ch. 2); if he ever existed, he would have lived in the eighth century. His nickname, 'Braut', means 'road', and according to Snorri he earned it by building a network of roads throughout Sweden for the first time. Snorri says that he was the most popular of kings, which may help to explain the association of his name with the huge mound at Västerås.

No one knows precisely when 'Anund's Mound' or its satellite mounds were made; they could date back to the Bronze Age, or be monuments from the Migration Period (AD 300–600) – they have not yet been excavated. But the significance of the site as a cult centre and/or political rallying arena for *some* early period is surely beyond dispute.

At the foot of the mound there are two spectacularly long stone ship-settings, placed end-on to each other, measuring fifty-four metres and fifty-one metres respectively. They seem to date from the Viking period, and may originally have been aristocratic burials, shaped into ships to symbolise both the earthly power of chieftains and their ceremonial voyage to the afterworld. But one great Swedish scholar, the late Sune Lindqvist, came up with a marvellously compelling notion about the real meaning of the ship-settings. He suggested that each stone in the setting might represent a warrior at his oar – and that every year, at the renewal of the oaths of allegiance, the districts that were required to provide a ship for the royal levy would send the crews to be inspected, weapons and all, standing by their stones, in a sort of Viking Trooping of the Colour. There is no documentary evidence at all for such a flight of fancy; but 'Anund's Mound' has the feel of that kind of history about it.

Elsewhere in the Uppland province, archaeologists have unearthed sensational evidence that the Swedes enjoyed a period of tremendous wealth and high culture for the three centuries that preceded the Viking Age. This was the so-called Vendel period (AD 500–800), named after a number of ship-burials in the district of Vendel, north of Stockholm. The first indications of this unsuspected Golden Age came in the 1880s, with the chance discovery of about a dozen of these ship-graves, which were crammed with rich grave-goods – magnificent helmets decorated with moulded bronze plates, costly double-edged swords with inlaid hilts and pommels, elegant animal ornaments and luxury goods imported from abroad. The superb art-work on them, and on very similar treasures from associated gravefields of the Vendel period at Valsgärde and Ultuna, is breathtaking in its flamboyant magnificence.

Superbly worked helmet from the Vendel period that preceded the Viking Age in Sweden.

And then, during the First World War, Professor Sune Lindqvist excavated an impressive mound, eight metres high, in the parish of Vendel which was popularly known as the 'Ottar Mound' (*Ottarshögen*). This Ottar was equated with another of Snorri Sturluson's shadowy Swedish kings in *Ynglinga saga*, King Óttar Vendel-Crow. Despite the somewhat haphazard nature of the Yngling genealogies in Snorri, one can be reasonably sure that King Óttar would have lived in the Vendel period.

When Sune Lindqvist investigated the mound, he found the remains of a funeral pyre in the centre of the grave. But his most sensational find was a Byzantine gold coin, used as a pendant, which had been struck for the Emperor Basiliscus (476–7); the presence of this gold coin dated the mound to around AD 500.

All this wealth, coupled with the remarkable homogeneity of style throughout, argues that for three centuries the Uppland province of Sweden enjoyed a remarkable social stability. The aristocratic burials were all those of equals; on the whole, no one grave was conspicuously more sumptuous than all the others. Any king who may have been buried at Vendel must have been *primus inter pares*.

There seems to be only one exception to this general rule: the monumental burial site at Old Uppsala. The early Yngling kings in Snorri Sturluson may be insubstantial figures, but there is nothing insubstantial about the three great royal burial mounds at Old Uppsala, which was for centuries the spiritual home and cult centre of the Yngling dynasty. They stand in an impressive row on top of a gravel ridge that emphasised their height, and are known locally as Óðin's Howe, Thór's Howe and Frey's Howe. Snorri in his *Ynglinga saga*, however, gives the names of three Yngling kings of the sixth century who were said to be buried there – Aun, Egil and Aðils. All three were men of relentless vigour and violence, according to Snorri. Aðils, for instance, was a magnificent horseman, but was thrown from his horse and killed at Uppsala while (or more likely after) attending a sacrificial feast; other sources simply say that he died of strong drink while celebrating 'with immoderate joviality' the death of an enemy. That is the kind of men they were in Snorri's eyes: hard-riding, hard-living, hard-dying – forceful men whose Yngling descendants would make the kingdom of central Sweden the main power in the land.

All three mounds have been archaeologically investigated, and were judged to belong to the Vendel period; the eastern mound was dug in the 1840s, the western mound in the 1870s, while the central mound was only excavated to the extent of a trial trench to clarify the method of construction of the funeral pyres which had been found inside the others. It seems that the pyre had been constructed on top of a stone foundation; it was a conical structure of huge logs, covered with a coating of clay and with a hole in the top to make it a furnace, in effect. The body had been placed inside the pyre with its grave goods; the heat generated by the pyre was so intense that the clay had burned into brick, which had gradually collapsed inside the mound that had afterwards been piled up over it. Although the grave goods were badly burned, Professor Bertil Almgren of Uppsala University thinks that the material from these three mounds was of even higher quality than that from the Vendel boat-graves. The dead had been equipped with magnificent helmets and swords, but also with ornaments of pure gold, which the Vendel graves had lacked. From this, Dr Almgren deduces that the Uppsala mounds were royal burials, whereas the Vendel boat-graves were those of a powerful aristocracy.

Uppsala is also famed in history as the site of the most notorious pagan cult centre in all Scandinavia. What people allegedly did at Uppsala during their rites was described in lurid detail to a German cleric, Adam of Bremen, who wrote it all down around 1075 in his *History of the Archbishopric of Hamburg:*

> It is customary also to solemnise in Uppsala, at nine-year intervals, a general feast of all the provinces of Sweden. No one is exempted from attendance at this festival. Kings and people, all and singly, send their gifts to Uppsala . . .
>
> The sacrifice is of this nature: of every thing that is male they offer nine heads, with the blood of which it is customary to placate gods of this sort. The bodies they hang in the sacred grove that adjoins the temple. This grove is so sacred in the eyes of the heathen that each and every tree in it is considered holy because of the death and putrefaction of the victims. Even dogs and horses hang there, along with men; a Christian told me that he had seen seventy-two bodies suspended there promiscuously. Furthermore, the songs customarily chanted in the ritual of a sacrifice of this kind are so manifold and unseemly that it is better to keep silence about them.

In a footnote, Adam of Bremen added that there was a large tree near this sacred grove, with wide-spreading branches that remained green all the year round. At its roots there was a spring, or well, in which human sacrifices were offered: if the victim sank without trace, it meant that the gods had accepted the sacrifice and would answer the devotees' prayers. By a tempting coincidence, a well with a ladder leading down it was found early in the 1970s at the roots of a single large tree that stands near the Uppsala mounds . . .

In another celebrated passage, Adam of Bremen also described a great golden temple that was said to stand at Uppsala:

> In this temple, entirely decked out in gold, the people worship the statues of three gods in such wise that the mightiest of them, Thor, occupies a throne in the middle of the chamber. Wodan [Óðin] and Fricco [Frey] have places on either side.
>
> The significance of these gods is as follows: Thor, they say, presides over the air, which governs the thunder and lightning, the winds and

The royal burial mounds at Old Uppsala in Sweden.

rains, fair weather and crops. The other, Wodan (that is, the Furious) carries on war and imparts to man strength against his enemies. The third is Fricco, who bestows peace and pleasure on mortals; and they fashion his likeness with an immense phallus. But Wodan they chisel armed, as our people are wont to represent Mars. Thor with his sceptre [hammer] apparently resembles Jove.

Now this sounds highly unlikely, not to say suspect: and not simply because the Vikings for the most part tended to wear their paganism lightly, without undue fanaticism. All the Germanic peoples, including the Vikings, worshipped their gods in the open air, at sanctuaries in groves or at mounds or beside springs. There is nothing anywhere else in the sources to suggest such an elaborate and dazzlingly ornate building for worship, which Adam of Bremen seems to have borrowed from classical, not Viking, mythology.

Yet there is one rather intriguing indication that there may have been some sort of pagan temple at Uppsala after all, and quite a substantial one at that, right on the site of the present twelfth-century church there. In the course of excavation by Sune Lindqvist of the church foundations, the post-holes for three exceptionally thick posts were found, as thick as the old pillars still to be seen in the bell-tower beside the church.

These post-holes indicated a rectangle about ten metres square, which bore no relationship at all to the architectural structure of the church. There was also an outer rectangle of much slimmer post-holes, which might conceivably have been the footings for any hoists required during the building of the church, because they ran along the inside of the transept. But the three thicker post-holes made a pattern *across* the base of the church tower, and were not an integral part of it.

So who knows? Professor Almgren, with a mischievous glint in his eye, suggests that Adam of Bremen may have been right after all, in this particular at least, and that there may have been an older pagan temple on the site of the present church. This would presuppose the existence of an organised, vocational priesthood, for which there is no other evidence anywhere in Viking literature or archaeology. But if there had been, it might well help to explain why Uppsala remained the last bastion of paganism in Scandinavia until well into the twelfth century, long after the rest of the Viking world had succumbed to Christianity. On the other hand, it could just as well be due to Sweden's relative remoteness from the major power-centres of European Christianity, and to the fact that the power of Swedish kings was not absolute; without the willing acceptance of the freeholder farmers of the local assembly they could not impose a new religion, unlike the kings of Norway, where the Conversion was carried out at sword-point (*cf* Ch. 10).

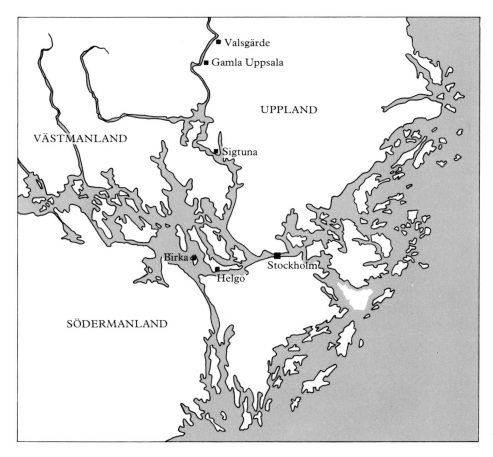

Sweden in the Viking Age.

VIKINGS!

One other historical source about Sweden in the Viking Age must be mentioned here – the runic inscriptions. Some 3000 of these inscriptions are known from Sweden, nearly four times as many as from the rest of the Germanic world put together. For the most part they are extremely brief, simply private memorial inscriptions carved in honour of dead relatives; they do not purport to be chronicles or annalistic entries. But they are contemporary documents, and taken together they plot the course of Swedish history and its developing interests and priorities throughout the Viking period.

For one thing, they show the evolving infrastructure of the kingdom in terms of road-building. Whatever Braut-Önund's alleged achievements may have been in this direction, it is clear from the rune stones that a land route called the 'Viking Road' (*Vikingavegen*) was built through Uppland in the ninth century to supplement the communications system based on water and ice. This route was punctuated by memorial stones, especially at bridges, where they were particularly useful as road-markers in deep snow. This extension of the transport system grew apace with the development of the internal structure of the state itself; by the first half of the eleventh century the growing farm population, which had started expanding very rapidly at the beginning of the Viking Age, was being harnessed into a formidable military organisation.

We see it happening through the rune stones at one particular stretch of the Viking Road in the district of Täby, just outside Stockholm. Early in the eleventh century, responsibility for the upkeep of that stretch belonged to a powerful local landowner called Jarlabanke. He took his duties seriously and put up about twenty inscribed stones along the way. Two magnificent pairs of matching stones are still to be seen *in situ* at a new causeway he built – Jarlabankesbro – which was 115 metres long and seven metres wide: 'Jarlabanke had these stones raised in memory of himself while he still lived. And he built this bridge for his soul. And alone he owned the whole of Täby. God help his soul.' Good works of this practical kind are evidence of the growing influence of the missionary Church in Sweden; converts were encouraged to provide roads that would be serviceable in all weathers to enable people to reach God's houses.

It was the Viking Road that led to the ends of the world. The runic inscriptions show that throughout the ninth and tenth centuries Sweden's external interests were mainly directed eastwards. But in the first half of the eleventh century – the last phase of the Viking Age – Swedish Vikings were turning their attention more and more towards England and the west; about one third of the extant inscriptions that refer to foreign trade and Viking expeditions are concerned with the British Isles and the western route, all dating from this late period. This matches the huge hoards of Anglo-Saxon coins of this date that have been found in Sweden.

In the rune stones, the name of England occurs almost as often as that of Greece (the Byzantine Empire) – more than twenty-five times, in fact.

Men 'died in Bath', men 'were buried in London', some died 'on the way to England', others 'took Danegeld in England'. All these were clearly connected with the renewed invasions of England by King Svein Fork-Beard of Denmark and his son Knút (*cf* Ch. 9), which the Swedes joined as enthusiastic mercenaries.

How extraordinarily far-flung these Swedish Vikings were, once they really got on the move! A memorial stone at a bridge at Broby ('Bridge Farm') in Täby on the Viking Road was erected as part of a set in memory of a farmer called Östen by his wife Estrid: *Es sotti IorsaliR ok andathis uppi i Grikkium* – 'He visited Jerusalem and died out in Greece'; presumably on a pilgrimage. Another inscription in bold verse says:

> They fared like men   far after gold,
>   And in the east   gave the eagles food.
> They died in the south,   in Saracenland.

The whole world was their oyster. But they paid for it dearly. Perhaps the most pointed and poignant of the inscriptions is a stone erected by a father in memory of his two sons. It says simply: 'One died in the west, the other in the east.'

There is one further stone I want to mention. It was found at Pilsgård, on the island of Gotland, in association with the harbour-lagoon at Boge-vik, near Slite. The runes are now blurred, but it is a memorial stone erected by four brothers in memory of a fifth brother, Hrafn, who had died far away in Russia: 'Hegbjörn and his brothers Röðvisl, Östen and Ámund had this stone painted in colours and erected; they have also raised stones for Hrafn south of Rufstein. *They went far into Aifur.*'

'They went far into Aifur.' The significance of that sentence is that 'Aifur' was the Norse name given to one of the frightening cataracts of the River Dnieper in southern Russia, where boats had either to shoot the rapids or be dragged overland to bypass them. It is a vivid glimpse of a family of five Gotland brothers on the make, carrying iron and furs and slaves, no doubt, to the markets of the East where they could exchange them for Arabic silver to be banked in buried caches at home on Gotland. One of them, Hrafn, died in the boulder-strewn torrents of the Dnieper; and the Pilsgård Stone immortalises not just him but the whole opening-up of the vast Russian hinterland by those Viking merchant adventurers from Sweden.

It is most unlikely that his brothers brought Hrafn's body back with them to Gotland. But if they did, they would have had it neatly processed and parcelled up first. Dr Nylén has found evidence in three or four graves of skeletons having been disarticulated before burial, and he thinks that the bodies were those of men who had died abroad. They had been taken to some monastery which specialised in supplying holy relics, where the corpses would be boiled to strip the flesh from the bones, and then the bones would be conveniently packed in boxes for suitable burial in the

homeland with all the other proper accoutrements of a Viking warrior's funeral.

For those whose bodies were not brought home for burial, there is a fascinating contemporary description of a Viking chieftain's funeral in the depths of Russia in the year 922. It was penned by an Arab diplomat called Ibn Fadlan, who was the secretary of an embassy from the Caliph of Baghdad to the ruler of the Bulgars of the Middle Volga. He wrote an account of his mission, called a *Risala*, in which he described his contacts with a tribe of armed merchants called *Rūs*, who are usually identified as Swedish Vikings settled in Russia. Not all Soviet scholars, it should be noted, accept this identification, however. One of the ceremonies Ibn Fadlan witnessed at first hand was a ship-cremation of a rich and important member of the tribe, which was preceded by some gruesome rituals of sacrifice for which no parallels can be found in Viking literature:

> I had heard that at the deaths of their chief personages they did many things, of which the least was cremation, and I was interested to learn more. At last I was told of the death of one of their outstanding men . . .

> When a great personage dies, his family asks his young women and men slaves, 'Who among you will die with him?' One answered, 'I' . . .

> When the day arrived on which the man was to be cremated, and the girl with him, I went to the river where his ship lay. I saw that they had

OPPOSITE Runic stone by a roadside at Broby in Sweden, commemorating a Viking farmer who had visited Jerusalem and died in Greece.

The Pilsgård Stone in Gotland, in memory of a trader who died in the cataracts of the Dnieper in Russia.

drawn the ship on to the shore . . . Then they brought a couch and put it in the ship, and covered it with a mattress of Greek brocade.

Then an old woman arrived whom they call the Angel of Death . . . It is she who has charge of arranging everything, and it is she who kills the slave girl. She was a strapping old woman, a stout and grim figure . . .

They carried the dead man into a tent which stood on the ship . . . The slave girl who had agreed to be sacrificed went to and fro from one tent to another, and the master of each tent had sexual intercourse with her and said, 'Tell your lord that I did this out of love for him.'

On the Friday afternoon they led the slave girl to a thing they had made that resembled a door-frame. She placed her feet on the hands of the men, who lifted her so that she could see over the frame. On the third time she was thus lifted, she said, 'I see my master seated in Paradise . . . he calls to me, so let me get to him.'

Now they took her to the ship. She took off the two bracelets she was wearing and gave them both to the old woman called the Angel of Death who was to kill her . . .

Men came with shields and staves. The old woman took her hand and made her enter the tent, and went in with her. Thereupon the men began to beat their shields with the sticks so that her cries would not be heard and the other girls would not be frightened and so refuse death with their master . . .

They laid her at her master's side. Two held her feet and two her hands. The old woman who was known as the Angel of Death . . . looped a cord round her neck, and gave the crossed ends to two of the men to pull. Then she came forward with a broad-bladed dagger and plunged it over and over again between her ribs, while the two men strangled her with the cord until she was dead.

Then the closest relative of the dead man came and took a piece of lighted wood. He was completely naked. He walked backwards towards the ship, holding the torch in his hand, and set fire to the pile of wood beneath the ship . . . Thereupon the flames engulfed the wood, then the ship, the tent, the man, the girl and everything in the ship.

One of the Rūs was at my side, and I heard him speak to the interpreter who was there. I asked the interpreter what he had said. He replied, 'He said that you Arabs are stupid.' 'Why?' I asked him. 'Because,' he said, 'you take the people you love and honour most and put them in the ground, where worms and insects eat them. But we burn them in a twinkling of an eye, so that they enter Paradise at that very moment.'

It is a spellbinding story. But there is considerable dispute in academic circles about how it should be interpreted. Was it a Viking burial? Was the tribe of Rūs described by Ibn Fadlan a community of Swedish Vikings settled on the Volga – or a tribe of Slavs who had been influenced towards Viking ways through contacts with Swedish traders in Russia?

It is a crucial question that takes us to the heart of what has been rather inelegantly termed the 'Normannist dispute'. Basically, what is at issue is the nature and extent of the Swedish Connection in the creation of the old Russian state. To put it simply, perhaps over simply, Western scholars have tended to believe that Russia was *created* by Vikings from Sweden, whereas Soviet archaeologists tend to argue that their effect on what was fundamentally a Slav state, which had been in existence for centuries before Scandinavian traders penetrated Russia, was negligible. Both sides have tended to adopt entrenched ethnic positions; they have used the rather meagre documentary sources to support their own theses; they have drawn essentially different conclusions from the available archaeological evidence. Today, happily, there are signs that the dogmatic attitudes of earlier generations of scholars are becoming more flexible.

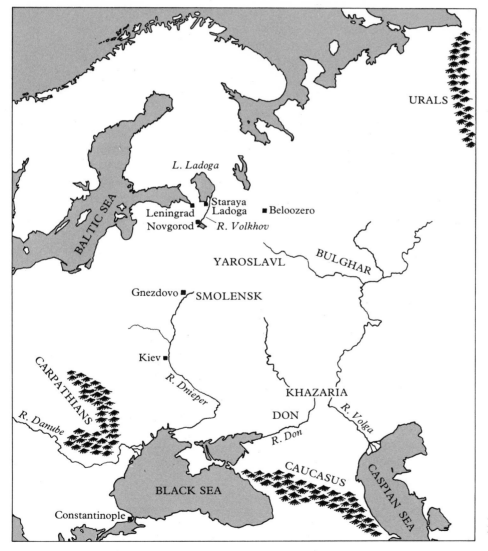

Russia in the
Viking Age.

Staraya Ladoga on the River Volkhov. In the background, where the river bends, is the site of 'Oleg's Mound'.

The conventional Western attitude has been based on documentary sources from Russia itself – the so-called *Russian Primary Chronicle* which, in the oldest of its extant forms, was compiled early in the twelfth century in the Cave Monastery outside Kiev, probably by a monk called Nestor (hence its secondary name, the *Nestor Chronicle*). It purports to tell how, just after the middle of the ninth century, the 'Varangians from beyond the sea' imposed tribute on the local Slav tribes and were thrown out by them, only to be invited back when law and order broke down:

> These are the narratives of bygone years regarding the origin of the land of the Rūs, the first princes of Kiev, and from what source the land of Rūs had its beginning . . .
>
> 6386–70 [AD 860–2]. The tributaries of the Varangians drove them back beyond the sea and, refusing them further tribute, set out to govern themselves. But there was no law amongst them, and tribe rose against tribe. There arose strife amongst them and they began to fight amongst themselves. And they said to themselves, 'Let us find a king to rule over us and make judgements according to the law.' And they crossed the sea to the Varangians, to the Rūs; for these Varangians were called Rūs as others were called Swedes, others again Norwegians or Angles or Goths. And to the Rūs [they] said, 'Our land is large and rich, but there is no order in it. So come and be king and rule over us.'
>
> And three brothers with their kinsfolk were chosen; they brought with them all the Rūs and came here. The eldest, Rurik, settled in

Novgorod; the second, Sineus, settled in Beloozero; and the third, Truvor, settled in Izborsk.

And from these Varangians the Russian land got its name, especially the district of Novgorod. The present inhabitants of Novgorod are descended from the Varangian race, but earlier they were Slavs.

After two years, Sineus and his brother Truvor died, and Rurik assumed sole authority. He distributed the towns to his men – Polotsk to one, Rostov to another, Beloozero to a third . . .

The *Russian Primary Chronicle*, it must be remembered, is not a contemporary source. Like the 'historical' Icelandic Sagas it was written down a long time after the event, and should therefore be treated with due caution. We should also note that there is a slightly divergent account in another version of the *Chronicle* known as the *Codex Hypatianus*:

They took with them all the Rūs and came first to the Slavs, and they built the city of Ladoga [modern Staraya Ladoga]. Rurik, the eldest, settled in Ladoga; Sineus, the second, settled at Beloozero; and Truvor, the third, settled at Izborsk. From these Varangians the land of Rūs received its name. After two years Sineus died, as well as his brother Truvor, and Rurik assumed sole authority. He then came to Lake Ilmen and founded on the River Volkhov a city they named Novgorod . . .

As if to corroborate this, there is the insistent Norse tradition that Russia was essentially a Swedish creation. In the Sagas, Russia was known as 'Greater Sweden'; and the Finnish name for Sweden, *Ruotsi*, is believed by many etymologists to be derived from the Old Norse word *róðr*, 'rowing waterway', which is still reflected in the name of a coastal area of Swedish Uppland called Roslagen. Scholarly opinion is by no means unanimous on this; but it fits very neatly the Western hypothesis that Russia was a dark and undeveloped continent until Swedish entrepreneurs arrived in their boats to exploit its huge market potential and link up with the trade routes to the Far East; and that it was these pioneers who founded the first towns from which the great Russian city-states of Novgorod and Kiev would grow.

Many distinguished Soviet scholars take a diametrically opposite view. When I visited Moscow I was privileged to be granted an interview with Academician B. A. Rybakov, doyen of Soviet archaeologists, who summed up for me that 'anti-Normannist' view as follows:

The role of the Vikings in the formation of the Russian state was rather small, because the Russian state had already been in existence for three hundred years before the arrival of the Vikings. A confederation of tribes had formed in the sixth century in the area of the middle Dnieper, and one of the eastern Chronicles mentions a 'People of Giants'. This 'People of Giants' formed, so to speak, the nucleus of the future Kiev state.

Later on this nucleus expanded further, and it may well be that

Vikings were attracted here by the glamour of the Kiev state, because the Kiev state traded actively with Constantinople [Byzantium].

There is a crucial difference between Eastern and Western Europe as far as the Vikings were concerned, because here in Russia the Vikings could not make the sudden smash-and-grab raids in which they specialised. The rivers were too fast-flowing, and they had to make long portages overland; if they wanted to join the trade convoys down the Dnieper to the Black Sea and Constantinople they had to apply for permission from the authorities in Kiev. Permission to join these convoys from Kiev depended entirely on the ruler of Kiev at the time.

It is not my intention to enter this 'Normannist' controversy here. I went to Russia to try to follow the Viking trade routes charted by the Sagas and the runic inscriptions in Sweden, along the mighty Russian rivers that led them arduously towards the exotic markets of Arabia and the Byzantine Empire. In the matter of who first founded the Russian state – Viking or Slav – there seemed to be a chicken-and-egg situation which is ultimately rather unimportant. I was curious to see at first hand the latest archaeological evidence, which is not readily accessible in Western publications yet, and to talk to the Soviet archaeologists who have been digging up the Russian past with frequently spectacular results.

The first port of call, logically, had to be Leningrad, the old capital of Russia. This was where the first questing Vikings would have nosed their prows towards the Russian hinterland. The Russian rivers like the Neva, which runs broad and purposeful through the heart of Leningrad, were the great arteries of trade from east to west, from north to south, that joined the Baltic to the Black Sea, the Atlantic to the Pacific: one half of the known world to the other. Did the Vikings *create* these trade routes? Did they *control* them? Or did they merely try to batten on them? From their activities elsewhere, it is clear that the Vikings were the super-technocrats of their time; they had a highly developed technology, in ship-building and metalwork, that gave them an advantage over their competitors; they were eager for wealth and success; they were natural entrepreneurial pioneers, men with a quick eye for potential profit. So what was their role in Russia?

Some of the evidence of their presence, at least, is to be found on the banks of the Neva in one of the greatest museums in the world – the Hermitage Museum, once better known as the Winter Palace. It is in the Hermitage that the classic conflict between hazy Saga evidence and hard archaeological fact begins to resolve itself.

There is a cornucopia of Viking finds to be seen in the Hermitage: a brooch which can only have come from Gotland; decorated combs which could have come straight from a workshop in Dublin (*cf* Ch. 6); a needle-case just like one found in Birka; a leather shoe – and I have handled one which could be for the other foot, in York (*cf* Ch. 5); gaming pieces, and the antler from which they were cut; the fragment of a brooch in a style familiar from Iceland and elsewhere; and unmistakably Viking runes, carved on a length of wood that looks as if it might have been part of a long-bow, but which may simply have been a rune-stick (*rúnakefl*) like the Bergen Stick (*cf* Ch. 2). It has been dated to the first half of the ninth century. The inscription seems to be a complicated skaldic verse, alliterative and esoteric; but the mythological allusions in it are so obscure that Soviet and Scandinavian runologists have come out with totally contradictory interpretations.[1]

Nearly all of the finds in the Hermitage were found at the site of Staraya Ladoga ('Old Ladoga'), where Rurik of the Rūs had first settled, according to the *Codex Hypatianus*. In the Icelandic Sagas it was called *Aldeigjuborg*, and is frequently mentioned as a target for attack or a convenient staging-post on the way to Kiev and the Black Sea. It lay on the left bank of the River Volkhov, some twelve kilometres from its outlet into the southern end of Lake Ladoga, in an easily defended position. The ancient settlement there was a very large one, some 9000 square metres, surrounded by a strong earthen rampart. It has been extensively excavated, most recently in a prolonged series of digs from 1945 to 1975.

There is no doubt that Staraya Ladoga was originally a Slav settlement, founded by some Finno-Ugrian tribe in the middle of the eighth century – a century *before* any traces of a Viking presence there. The earliest layers of house remains are non-Scandinavian, and Dr Anatoly Kirpichnikov of Leningrad thinks they were built by southern Slav peoples moving northwards from the Novgorod area to develop trade with the Baltic. Staraya Ladoga provided easy access to the Gulf of Finland along the River Neva. At Staraya Ladoga they created an early oasis of civilisation where they busied themselves not with agriculture but with trade and crafts. Dr Kirpichnikov, who thinks that the 'Normannist' controversy is now irrelevant, believes that the Vikings were simply immigrants who wanted to move in on Staraya Ladoga's growing prosperity; they came there, according to the archaeological record, in the middle of the ninth century. He thinks that the legend of the calling-in of Rurik and his brothers might well have a kernel of historical truth, except that the settlement was not actually *founded* by Rurik; but by the end of the ninth century the Rūs had helped to transform it into a prototype Russian town.

Soviet archaeologists believe that this process was in no way exceptional in Russia – simply that Staraya Ladoga, because of its ease of access from the Baltic, was the earliest example of it. But what part did the Vikings play there? Across the river from the settlement there was a cemetery of thirteen mounds which were excavated in 1938–40. They were cremation graves, and are considered to be uncompromisingly Scandinavian – in-

---

[1] The Soviet version runs, 'Scintillating elf, stay under the ground.' The Norwegian version reads, 'The tents of Velerido are enveloped with magic. Nibelung arrows will reap a terrible harvest of corpses.' Quite a difference!

RIGHT Silver ingots found in Gotland: on one of them the Slavic personal name 'Byleta' is engraved in Cyrillic script. An indication of the Russian Connection?

BELOW Uncompromisingly Viking finds from Staraya Ladoga, now in the Hermitage Museum in Leningrad. At the top, a rune-stick.

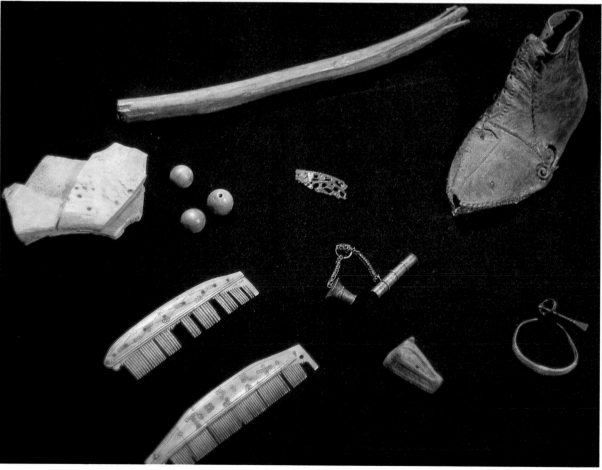

deed, Staraya Ladoga is the only early settlement in Russia which has a separate and distinct Viking cemetery; it is dated to the second half of the ninth century. Dr Kirpichnikov thinks that it was an exclusive burial ground for the court of the ruler of Staraya Ladoga, and that at the time the ruler was a Scandinavian, at the head of a compact group of resident Vikings.

This thesis is borne out by excavations at the fifteenth-century fortress of Staraya Ladoga, which Dr Kirpichnikov himself carried out from 1972–6. He discovered that there were two earlier sets of walls underlying the present walls, and that the earliest dated back to the 'Viking period' of the late ninth century. The site has now been handsomely restored, and there are replicas of the major finds in an excellent if somewhat dimly lit museum. But although the building of the first walls corresponds roughly with the date of Rurik's alleged arrival, the finds of pottery and weaponry and jewellery associated with it are decidedly *not* Scandinavian – they are all Slav.

Small gold head from the Gnëzdovo grave-field near Smolensk (Hermitage Museum).

Dr Kirpichnikov's interpretation of this apparent anomaly neatly reconciles the archaeological record with the literary sources. He thinks that the stone fort at Staraya Ladoga was built by Rurik's successor, a man with the hybrid Viking-Slav name of Count Oleg, who also took over the second town that Rurik had founded according to the *Chronicle* – Novgorod. Oleg had extended the Rūs territory he had inherited, by seizing Kiev as well, thus uniting the northern and southern Rūs; and in order to protect the northern frontiers of his huge realm, he had built the Staraya Ladoga fortress as a defence against pirates. By this time, however, the Scandinavians in Staraya Ladoga had become almost completely Slavicised themselves – hence the lack of any specifically Viking artefacts. According to this scenario, Oleg was trying to construct a coherent state of his own on the foundations of earlier Slav states – and he built the Staraya Ladoga fortress for his second-generation Scandinavians to stop any *new* Vikings trying to muscle in!

This matter of cultural assimilation and absorption is central to the 'Normannist' problem. Several huge gravefields have been extensively excavated by Soviet archaeologists – at Gnëzdovo near Smolensk, for instance, with its 5000 burial mounds – but there are major questions still to be resolved on dating and definition. The young Norwegian scholar, Anne Stalsberg of Trondheim University, has made a close comparative study of the masses of grave-goods that have been recovered from those cemeteries.[1] The Scandinavian finds are all concentrated on centres along the main rivers, as one would expect; but what constitutes a 'Scandinavian' find? So many of the artefacts show a hybrid culture; the proportion of 'pure' Scandinavian objects (that is to say, objects which would not have been casually acquired in normal trade exchange) is very small. The

[1] 'Skandinaviske Vikingetidsfunn fra det Gammel-Russiske Riket,' in *Fornvännen*, 1979.

115

number of Scandinavian graves in the cemeteries constitutes only about five per cent. Also, there is a dating problem, because some Soviet archaeologists tend to date to the tenth century artefacts that Scandinavian scholars date to the ninth, if found in a Scandinavian context. The two dating systems lead to some irreconcilable differences of historical interpretation.

Overall, however, Anne Stalsberg's conclusions are very close to the position of most leading Soviet scholars today: that the grave goods and other finds are evidence of normally peaceful relations between the Viking incomers and the native population of Slavs. She finds no evidence of Scandinavians as invaders who created a state where there had been none before; the Vikings clearly lived and moved in powerful circles of society in Russia, and certainly had an influence on the way the old Russian state developed, but their role in this was probably not as critical as the later literary sources would suggest.

Some kilometres to the north of Staraya Ladoga, at a bend of the River Volkhov, there is a huge burial mound dominating the landscape, called 'Oleg's Mound' – one can always rely on legend to enliven any archaeological site! It was excavated as long ago as 1823 with all the earnest enthusiasm of those days. All that was found in it was a broken spear-head; but this was apparently sufficient for it to be triumphantly identified with Rurik's successor, Count Oleg, the builder of the Staraya Ladoga fort, who is authoritatively reported in the *Chronicle* to have been buried there. It was a perfectly reasonable assumption to make, apart from one disagreeable little fact – in another version of the *Chronicle*, Oleg is also reported, with the same degree of authority and reliability, to have been buried in Kiev!

The archaeological evidence from Novgorod, the second city said to have been founded by Rurik, is less clear-cut than that of Staraya Ladoga, but it may well have followed a similar pattern of Slav settlement and temporary Viking takeover. Novgorod occupied an immensely important strategic position on the Russian trade routes; the Valdai Hills region, 150 kilometres to the south, was the great junction between the Volkhov via the Lovar, the western Dvina, the Dnieper and the Volga. This was where their head-waters rose; this was the area of the great portages or 'drags', where traders would haul their boats overland from one river to another: the western Dvina leading to the Gulf of Riga, the Lovar and Volkhov leading to the Gulf of Finland, the Volga leading to the Caspian and Central Asia – probably the most significant route of all, in terms of sheer wealth in silver – and the Dnieper leading to Kiev and the Black Sea.

In 880, according to the *Russian Primary Chronicle*, the formidable Oleg marched from Novgorod to Kiev with his army and seized it: 'Oleg set himself up as prince of Kiev, and declared that it should be the mother of Russian cities. The Varangians [Scandinavians], Slavs and others who accompanied him were called Rūs. Oleg began to build stockaded towns, and imposed tribute on neighbouring tribes.' This tribute would presumably have been paid in furs, in cash or in slaves.

The Arab geographer Ibn Rustah, writing around 920, compiled an account of how the Rūs of Kiev or Novgorod lived at the time:

> They have a leader called Khagan-Rūs. They fight with the Slavs and use ships to attack them; they take them captive and carry them to the Khazars and there sell them as slaves . . .
>
> They have no villages, estates or fields. Their only occupation is trading in sable and squirrel and other kinds of skins, which they sell to those who will buy from them. They take coins as payment and fasten them into their belts. They are clean in their clothing, and the men adorn themselves with gold arm-rings . . .
>
> They have many towns. They are generous with their possessions, treat guests honourably, and act handsomely towards strangers who take refuge with them, and all those who accept their hospitality . . .
>
> When a leading man amongst them dies, they dig a grave like a big house and put him inside it. With him they put his clothes and the gold bracelets he wore and also much food and drinking vessels and coins. They also put his favourite wife in the grave with him while she is still living; then the entrance to the grave is stopped up, and she dies there.

The description of Viking funerary practices sounds very familiar; so does the description of the appearance of the Rūs on the Volga, written by Ibn Fadlan:

> I have seen the Rūs as they come on their merchant journeys, and stay encamped on the Volga. I have never seen more perfect specimens, tall as date palms, blond and ruddy. Each man has an axe, a sword and a knife which he keeps by him at all times. Each woman wears neck rings of gold and silver, one for each thousand dinars her master owns.

From his stronghold in Kiev, Oleg now had control of the whole Dnieper trade route, from Staraya Ladoga to the Black Sea. But to achieve maximum value from it through customs duties, it had to be closely organised.

The Dnieper as it flows through Kiev looks calm and broad and serene, but appearances are deceptive; we know that the journey down to the Black Sea, the gateway to Constantinople, was an extremely hazardous one. Traders would congregate in Kiev in June, having waited for the spring floods to start to subside, and then set sail in huge convoys 'to face the perils of the voyage together', as one source puts it. The major hazard was a sixty-kilometre stretch of rapids and cataracts, where they were vulnerable not only to shipwreck but to ambush by local tribesmen, who would lie in wait for them where they had to come ashore to bypass the worst stretches.

We can read about these cataracts in a book called *De Administrando*

Viking finds from
Smolensk.

Imperio, written around 950 by no less a person than the Byzantine
Emperor Constantine Porphyrogenitus. He described how the merchants
would try to steer their boats between the rocks, jumping naked into the
water to feel the way with their bare feet, holding the boat steady and
straight with long poles. The emperor also gave the names by which the
individual cataracts were known, robust Viking names every one: *Essupi*
(Gulper), *Gelandri* (Yeller), *Leanti* (Seether), *Strukun* (Courser) – and
Aifur (Ferocious), the cataract recorded on the Pilsgård rune stone on
Gotland in memory of at least one Swedish trader who died in the fearsome rapids of the Dnieper.

Oleg's most significant political achievement, perhaps, in his own eyes
at least, was the treaty he was granted by the major European power of his
day, the Byzantine Empire based on Constantinople. Suddenly, in the year
907, he is said to have swept down the Dnieper with a huge fleet and over
the Black Sea. We are told that the defenders of Constantinople tried to
stop him by mooring heavy iron chains across the Bosphorus; but Oleg's
men, well schooled in the arduous portages of their native rivers, simply
dragged their ships ashore, put them on rollers, and trundled them
overland past the obstacle. And with Oleg at his gates, the emperor now
thought it prudent to start parleying.

The resultant treaty, as recorded in the *Russian Primary Chronicle*,
opens with a drum-roll of resounding Viking names, the fifteen envoys of
Oleg, Great Prince of Kiev: 'We the Rūs – Karli, Ingjald, Farúlf, Ver-
mund, Hróðleif . . .' The treaty gave Russian merchants highly advan-

OPPOSITE *Hálfdan*:
runic inscription on
the top surface of the
marble balustrade in
Hagia Sophia:
–A-L-F-T-A-N.

118

tageous terms as regards entry visas, customs duties, access to markets and supplies, ship's gear and so on. It also stipulated that they should be given as many free baths as they liked – they were a clean-living people, the Vikings, despite their unsavoury image!

With this one bold stroke, Oleg had put the Russia of Kiev and Novgorod, the Russia of the great Baltic–Black Sea trade route, on speaking terms with the greatest power in the western world, the successor to Rome, the Byzantine Empire.

The Norsemen called Constantinople *Mikligarður*, the 'Great City'. But that was an understatement. It was the *Greatest* City, Metropolis itself: a teeming polyglot city of half a million people that literally bridged the world of East and West across the waters of the Bosphorus. Today its population is 2,500,000, and although it is no longer the capital of Turkey it is still the largest and most cosmopolitan city in the country. Its name has been Istanbul ever since it was conquered by the Ottoman Turks more than five centuries ago; its original name was Byzantium, most magic of names, until the Roman Emperor Constantine moved the capital of the Roman Empire there early in the fourth century and renamed it in his own honour. They are all names that conjure up the greatness and majesty of past empires; but to me, the Viking Mikligarður sums it up best: the Great City.

Then as now it was a memorably beautiful place, with innumerable domes and basilicas and pinnacles and towers all gleaming in the sun. Here, power and piety sat enthroned, courtesy and cruelty walked hand in hand; here was wealth to be got beyond the dreams of peasant Viking avarice. Constantinople was the mecca, the magnet, for every merchant and mercenary from every known corner of the world. Constantinople was the Babylon of its time, and much more besides. It is not hard to imagine the overwhelming effect the city must have had on young men accustomed to rough living in their ships and trading settlements: the heady blend of luxury and corruption, of bartering and brawling, of West and East. No wonder it became such a legend for the Saga-writers in far-off places like Iceland, such an irresistible lure to the ambitious and the brave. No wonder it was considered such a signal honour to be picked for the élite Varangian Guard of Viking warriors, bodyguard to the emperor himself (*cf* Ch. 10).

The Vikings came here in their hundreds, perhaps even thousands, all drawn by the same things: money and power. And yet, as in so many other places, the Vikings left remarkably few traces of their substantial presence in Constantinople – nowhere, indeed, except in the most spectacular monument of all, the great cathedral of Hagia Sophia.

Hagia Sophia, which is now a vast and echoing museum, was built with unparalleled extravagance by the Emperor Justinian in 537 on the site where Constantine's cathedral had burned down. Inside, it is girt with deep galleries, reached by a paved but unstepped ramp. All the polished marble balustrades are now covered with scrawled graffiti, scored by countless visitors down the centuries.

A few years ago, in 1967, the great Swedish scholar Professor Sven B. F. Jansson, one of the world's leading authorities on runic inscriptions, recognised one of these casual graffiti as being runic. Most of it was indecipherable, but he managed to make out, in the opening letters, the ending of a personal name: – A – L – F – T – A – N, which in full would have read '*Hálfdan*', 'Half-Dane', both a royal and a common name in the Viking Age.

We do not know how the rest of the inscription reads. But I can easily imagine some bored young Viking up in the South Gallery a thousand years ago, having to stand through some interminable church service in a language he did not understand, and idly carving on the hallowed marble his own intimate message to posterity: *Hálfdan was here*.

5

England at Bay

While the most pious King Brihtric was reigning over Wessex [786–802] . . . a small fleet of Danes numbering three fast ships came unexpectedly to the coast; and this was their first coming. Hearing of this the king's official [*exactor*], then staying at the town of Dorchester, leapt on his horse with a small retinue and galloped to the port, thinking they were merchants rather than enemies; and commanding them imperiously he ordered them to be taken to the royal residence. But he and his men were promptly killed by them. The name of the official was Beaduheard.   (*Anglo-Saxon Chronicle*, Æthelweard version)

'*And this was their first coming*.' That was how a Latin version of the *Anglo-Saxon Chronicle* dating from the late tenth century reported the first remembered Viking raid on England two centuries earlier. It is thought to have taken place at the Channel haven of Portland harbour in Weymouth Bay in Dorset, now a terminal for Channel Islands ferries.

The *Anglo-Saxon Chronicle* was first compiled somewhere in Wessex, perhaps at Winchester, in the year 892, encouraged and possibly even directly instigated by King Alfred the Great of Wessex (871–99). In its initial form it was preoccupied exclusively with the political affairs of the West Saxons, and in particular with King Alfred's long struggle against the Viking invaders who threatened to overrun his kingdom. What was happening beyond the frontiers of Wessex interested the original Chronicler scarcely at all; for instance, he made no reference to the thunderbolt raid on Lindisfarne in Northumbria in 793 that heralded the start of the Viking Age for everyone else (*cf* Ch. 2). For him, the Viking Age began with the shock killing of an HM Customs and Excise officer at Portland harbour – because Portland was in Wessex, and Lindisfarne was not.

Personally I have always had a sneaking sympathy with the crews of those three Viking vessels (incidentally, they were probably Norwegian, not Danish – the *Chronicle* invariably calls all Vikings 'Danes'). Those men had voyaged hundreds of kilometres across the North Sea in open boats. All they wanted was a friendly welcome and a few beers in Weymouth. I think it likely that they *were* 'merchants rather than enemies' – at least until Beaduheard arrived.

They found themselves being pushed around by an officious bureaucrat who tried to order them to Dorchester, nine miles away. The result was inevitable: fists started flying, and then weapons started swinging. The Portland incident, to my mind, was probably not a 'Viking raid' at all but merely an ordinary quayside brawl that got out of hand, magnified by hindsight because Scandinavians had been involved.

It was an illuminating little episode in many ways. While the initial assaults against ecclesiastical centres by freelance Viking marauders made the world headlines, Portland suggests that the early Vikings were just as interested in trade and commerce, by fair means or foul. Casual piracy against coastal shipping was beginning to turn its attention landward, to the coastal or riverside marts which were the generating source of that mercantile wealth. Portland was remembered as the precursor not of the sporadic church raids of the 790s but of the determined and increasingly regular attacks by Danish expeditions on major trading settlements on the Continent from the 830s onwards (*cf* Ch. 3).

In Anglo-Saxon England the existence of a royal *exactor* like Beaduheard was in itself symptomatic of the growing importance of revenues from dues and tolls for the king's exchequer. It was his function to monitor the movements and transactions of itinerant traders and claim the appropriate taxes on the king's behalf. Throughout the eighth century there is both literary and archaeological evidence of the development of former Roman urban centres like London and York, and the foundation of specialised harbour emporia like Ipswich on the River Orwell and *Hamwih* (the forerunner of Southampton) on the west bank of the River Itchen in Hampshire. By the end of the eighth century, England offered an inviting prospect for anyone wanting to muscle in on European trade; and for the next two and a half centuries the British Isles would become a focal point of Viking activity – the earliest raids, the earliest settlements, the most widespread conquests all took place there. Britain was where the Norwegian and Danish thrusts to the west met and mingled.

In the latter half of the eighth century the dominant kingdom in England was Mercia, and the dominant political figure was Offa, King of the Mercians (757–96). By the time of his death he was the unchallenged ruler of all England as far north as the Humber: *rex Anglorum* (King of the English) or even, in one document, *rex totius Anglorum patriae* (King of all England). He was one of the most remarkable of all early English kings, and his command of England put him on an equal footing with the great Emperor Charlemagne himself. His reign is not nearly so well recorded as that of Alfred the Great, a century later; but it is clear that, like Alfred, he was a shrewd and wily statesman, a diligent legislator, and a notable patron of learning and the arts.

One index of his achievements can be found in his coinage. Throughout the eighth century, kings in England had been developing their own mints, which not only gave a literal stamp to their reign but also put a royal

A surviving section of Offa's Dyke at Llanfair Waterdine, Salop, looking north-west.

imprimatur on both domestic and foreign trade. Offa transformed English currency into a coinage acceptable throughout Europe. His silver penny (*sceatta*) became a weighty piece, solid and stable and elegantly designed; Offa's moneyers produced some of the finest coins ever minted in England, and set the course for English currency for the next five centuries. It also included one delightful aberration, a special-issue gold coin struck in imitation of an Arabic gold *dinar* and found in Rome. It seems that the moneyer did not realise that the 'scroll-work' on the coin he was copying was in fact an inscription in Arabic; as a result, the name of that Christian king of Mercia, *Offa rex*, appears (upside down) surrounded by the pious claim that 'There is no other God but Allah, and his apostle is Mohammed'! It is dated 157 AH, the Mohammedan equivalent of AD 774.

Offa is also traditionally associated with the most massive surviving monument from the Anglo-Saxon period, the most impressive feat of building work by any Anglo-Saxon king: Offa's Dyke.

Offa's Dyke is the longest of all the major frontier systems known in Britain, a bank-and-ditch earthwork that ran for about 180 kms from the Dee to the Severn to define the boundary between Mercia and Wales. There is no direct evidence to link it with Offa, apart from the ancient Welsh tradition that calls it *Clawdd Offa*, and a statement a century later by King Alfred's biographer, Asser, that Offa ordered a great *vallum* to be built from sea to sea between Mercia and Wales; but it is impossible to think of any other ruler of the period who had the authority and the resources to carry out such an undertaking. Not much of it remains today, and even what is left of the surviving sections is still being destroyed at a deplorable rate, despite being scheduled for preservation. But there is still enough of it visible to give a powerful impression of the royal authority and social organisation that its builder was able to command. Offa's Dyke was the English equivalent of the Danevirke of Denmark, whose earliest phases were built half a century earlier (*cf* Ch. 3).

The equivalence has a superficial neatness, at least: the Mercian builders of Offa's Dyke were kinsmen of the Danes who built the Danevirke, sharing a common ancestry with the tribes of Angles from 'Angeln' in the province of Schleswig-Holstein at the neck of the Danish peninsula – the precise area of the Danevirke. It was the Angles from Angeln, the Jutes from Jutland and the Saxons from Lower Saxony in north-west Germany who had taken over England in a series of massive migrations in the fifth century when the Roman legions were withdrawn to help defend the crumbling Roman empire nearer home. They had found a country ripe for the picking, a country on the verge of collapse, its towns abandoned, its internal administration tottering, its leaders at war with one another while under constant attack from north and west by tribes of Picts and Celts. The sense of desolation is eloquently expressed by the Anglo-Saxon poem called *The Ruin*, written by one of those Germanic invaders who gazed in awe and wonder at the great Roman cities and buildings which had fallen into decay:

> How wondrous this wall-stone, shattered by Fate;
> Burg-places broken, the work of giants crumbled.
> Ruined are the roofs, tumbled the towers,
> Broken the barred gate: frost in the plaster,
> Ceilings a-gaping, torn away, fallen,
> Eaten by age . . .
> Bright were the halls, lofty-gabled,
> Many the bath-house; cheerful the clamour
> In many a mead-hall, revelry rampant –
> Until mighty Fate put paid to all that . . .
>
> (*The Ruin, Exeter Book*)

And now, in the ninth century, history seemed to be repeating itself.

The map shows the British Isles with the following labels:

Shetland, St Ninian's I., Lerwick, Sumburgh, Birsay, Orkneys, Kirkwall, WESTERN ISLES, Iona, Rathlin I., STRATHCLYDE, NORTHUMBRIA, Lindisfarne, Jarrow, NORTH SEA, ULSTER, Sligo, Armagh, Isle of Man, Tynwald, York, Stamford Bridge, Riccall, CONNACHT, Clonmacnoise, Tara, Dublin, Clontarf, Sheffield, Lincoln, Clonfert, Chester, Nottingham, Newark, Derby, Leicester, Limerick, Arklow, Peterborough, MUNSTER, Waterford, Wexford, MERCIA, DANELAW, EAST ANGLIA, Cork, Maldon, Isle of Sheppey, Chippenham, London, Rochester, Isle of Thanet, Athelney, Edington, Winchester, Southampton, Hastings, WESSEX, Wareham, Portland, ENGLISH CHANNEL

The British Isles
in the Viking Age.

England was once more the target for attack from across the North Sea.

After the first sporadic Norwegian raids at the end of the eighth century, England enjoyed a respite from the attentions of the Vikings, though not from its own unending internecine battles; the Norwegians were more interested at that time in consolidating bases for themselves in the Northern Isles of Scotland (*cf* Ch. 9). When the next onslaught on England came, it came not from Norway but from Denmark, in the wake of the first Danish strikes against Dorestad and Continental Europe in 834 (*cf* Ch. 3).

126

In the following year, 835, 'the heathen devastated Sheppey', a small island in the Thames (*Anglo-Saxon Chronicle*). For the next fifteen years, Viking expeditions against targets on both sides of the English Channel went hand in hand, and attacks were reported on many places in the south-eastern quadrant: *Hamwih* (Southampton) and Portland in 840, London and Rochester in 842.

These raids were essentially summer activities. But in 850 an ominous new development occurred, when for the first time Danish Vikings over-wintered in England, on the island of Thanet in the Thames. Raiding was no longer a seasonal occupation; it was becoming a way of life, and an increasingly lucrative one. In 865 the *Anglo-Saxon Chronicle* records the first instance of the payment of *Danegeld* (Danes' Pay), when the men of Kent paid cash to a Danish band camped on Thanet to go away and leave them in peace – an agreement that the Danes, it is said, promptly betrayed.

But the autumn of the year 865 also saw a much more momentous development – a planned invasion by a Danish army intent on permanent conquest, not quick profits:

> 865 . . . And in this same year there came a great heathen host [*micel here*] to England and took up winter quarters in East Anglia; and there they were supplied with horses, and the East Anglians made peace with them.

(Anglo-Saxon Chronicle)

Anglo-Saxon coinage of the ninth century: silver pennies of Burgred of Mercia.

It is difficult to estimate accurately the size of this 'Great Heathen Host'. Professor Peter Sawyer of Leeds University has argued convincingly (*The Age of the Vikings*, 1971) that it should probably be numbered in hundreds rather than thousands. The main point is that the character of the Viking incursions had now changed drastically, and for the worse from the English point of view. The Danes had abandoned their ships as their major or sole means of transport and become a land force, well mounted and highly mobile. The significance of this new threat was not lost, it seems, upon the English; the archaeological record shows that during the next decade there was a dramatic, five-fold increase in the number of coin-hoards that were buried in the ground for safety and never recovered by their owners.

The story has to be pieced together from a welter of scattered sources. It seems that the invading army was led by three formidable Viking brothers: Hálfdan of the Wide Embrace, Ubbi and Ívar the Boneless, who had been making a bad name for himself in Ireland, according to the Irish sources (*cf* Ch. 6). These brothers were said to be the sons of a certain Ragnar – perhaps the Ragnar who attacked Paris in 845 (*cf* Ch. 3).

After wintering in East Anglia the army moved more than three hundred kilometres northwards towards their primary objective, the kingdom of Northumbria across the Humber. They rode into the city of York, capital of Northumbria, on All Saints Day, 1 November 866, when the city

Silver pennies of Alfred of Wessex.

Viking York was a centre for the manufacture of decorated combs made from antler. Plates of antler or bone would be sawn into teeth, and a curved back would be riveted on either side to hold the sections together.

was crowded with revellers, worshippers and chapmen from all over Yorkshire. They were apparently unopposed, because the Northumbrians were in the throes of yet another civil war at the time: King Osbert had been repudiated by his people in favour of King Ælla, 'a king not of royal birth' according to the *Chronicle*. The Vikings had an unerring nose for internal weakness in their potential targets, and they seem to have slipped into York almost unnoticed while the Northumbrians were busy fighting amongst themselves. Once inside the city, they patched up the old Roman fortifications and sat there throughout the winter to await the inevitable counter-attack once the natives had sorted out their own differences.

The expected attack came on 21 March 867. The two rivals, Osbert and Ælla, temporarily reconciled, made a joint attack on the city. Some of the Northumbrian army managed to break through the defences, but once inside the city they were slaughtered in great numbers, and both Osbert and Ælla were killed. To all intents and purposes Northumbria, one of the major kingdoms in England, was now a Viking possession.

That is the sober historical picture. But legend is never content to be as prosaic as that. According to late Saga traditions in Iceland and elsewhere, the capture of York by the Danes was a deliberate act of vengeance against King Ælla of Northumbria by the sons of one of the most picturesquely-named Vikings of all time – Ragnar *loðbrók*, Ragnar Hairy-Breeks. This Ragnar (apparently not the Ragnar of Paris fame) was the eponymous hero of a Legendary Saga which became immensely popular throughout Scandinavia. He was said to have been a famous king of Denmark, although there is no proper historical record of him. He earned his nickname from a special pair of trousers his wife had tailored for him, made of extra-thick fur, boiled in pitch and rolled in sand as a non-flammable protection against the fiery breath of a dragon he was required to slay.

It is said that in his old age Ragnar Hairy-Breeks grew jealous of the renown of his warrior sons, and set sail for Northumbria to make himself a bit of Saga-fame. But he was clearly over the hill by then; after a few brisk skirmishes he was defeated in battle by King Ælla and taken alive, and brought to York as a prisoner. He refused to divulge his name, and so, in order to loosen his tongue, Ælla had him thrown into a snake-pit.

That did the trick, but not in the way Ælla intended. As the snakes crawled over him, biting him with their poisonous fangs, Ragnar Hairy-Breeks chanted a heroic lay, the 'Death-Song of Ragnar *loðbrók*' (*Kráku-mál*), with its resounding refrain at the start of every stanza – 'Down we hewed them with our swords!' And with his dying breath, Ragnar uttered a cryptic prophecy: 'How the piglets would grunt if they knew the plight of the boar!'

And now, according to the Saga, the piglets were on the rampage in Northumbria, snorting and bristling to avenge their father. They captured the evil Ælla, and Ívar the Boneless is said to have devised a horribly cruel death for him: the brothers dedicated him to Óðin the All-Father by carving a 'blood-eagle' on his back. They hacked the ribs from his spine and pulled his lungs out, spreading them across his shoulder-blades like wings. This gruesome ritual (which is almost as grisly as the judicial execution practised in medieval England of hanging, drawing and quartering) has caught the imagination of everyone who has ever written or read about the Vikings. But it needs to be said that there is not a scrap of historical evidence that it ever happened outside the fevered imaginations of later Saga-writers.

Oddly enough, the Norse motif of revenge-for-Ragnar is transferred in

Anglo-Viking shoe – one of hundreds of pairs found in York in a perfect state of preservation.

129

English legend from Ælla of Northumberland to King Edmund of East Anglia. In the English version, it was Edmund, not Ælla, who was held responsible (mistakenly, as it turned out) for Ragnar's death; and Ragnar's sons put him to death in a manner so excruciating that he was instantly elevated to a martyr's sainthood. All we know for certain is that in 870 the Danish army descended on East Anglia and conquered it, and King Edmund died resisting the invasion.

The *Anglo-Saxon Chronicle*, little concerned as usual with the affairs of East Anglia, merely says, 'and they slew the king'; but the *Passio Sancti Edmundi*, written by Abbo of Fleury a century after the event, accords him a martyr's death strongly reminiscent of that of St Sebastian. He was placed with his back against a tree, as if on a rack (*eculeus*), and used for target practice in archery until he bristled with arrows like a hedgehog. When he was eventually wrenched away from the tree-trunk, half dead, his back was ripped open, exposing his rib-cage. There is an obvious consonance between the eagle (*aquila*) carved on Ælla's back and the rack (*eculeus*) against which Edmund's back was placed, as well as the 'blood-eagle' effect when his pierced body was torn from it.

Whatever the manner of Edmund's death, whether by torture, as legend insists, or in battle, as the *Anglo-Saxon Chronicle* implies (traditionally believed to have been fought near Hoxne in Suffolk), his fall marked the end of native Christian kingship in East Anglia. The East Anglians, who had meekly submitted five years earlier to Ívar the Boneless and his host and provided them with horses and safe passage, now found themselves firmly under the Danish yoke alongside the Northumbrians.

Two down (Northumbria and East Anglia), two to go (Mercia and Wessex). With the north and east of England in their grasp, the Danish invaders turned on Wessex. At the same time there was a change in the *dramatis personae* involved: Ívar the Boneless seems to have parted company with his army after the conquest of East Anglia, and gone north to join his friends from Ireland in the siege and destruction of the Strathclyde fortress of Dumbarton in Scotland in 870. From there he went on to Dublin, to take over the kingship of the Vikings in Ireland, where he died in 873 (*cf* Ch. 6). The Annals of Ulster refer to him as *rex Nordmannorum totius Hiberniae et Britanniae* – 'king of the Norsemen in Ireland and Britain'; that is to say, he was the effective ruler of the Viking enclaves in Ireland and England based on Dublin and York.

Ívar's return to his old stamping-grounds in Ireland was compensated for by the arrival of a new Danish army in 871 – the 'Great Summer Army' (*mycel sumer lida*) led by a king called Guthorm. This new invading army joined the resident 'Great Heathen Host' encamped in East Anglia, and together they mounted an assault on Wessex. For the whole year, Vikings and Saxons fought themselves to a stalemate in a series of indecisive running engagements; by the end of the season, in the autumn of 871, both sides were relieved to call it a day: the West Saxons, now led by the young

King Alfred, made peace, no doubt for a hefty payment of Danegeld, and the Vikings withdrew their forces to London.

Alfred had bought sorely needed time for himself and his kingdom of Wessex: time to consolidate, time to regroup, time to prepare defences in greater depth. Knowing what had happened to Northumbria and East Anglia, he must have realised that, sooner or later, Wessex was due for the same treatment. As it happened, he gained more time than expected, because of a series of political and military events elsewhere.

In 872 there was a revolt against Danish rule in Northumbria. The joint Danish army moved north the following year and crushed it, and then turned its full attention on Mercia, which had been despairingly trying to fend off the inevitable with annual payments of Danegeld. The end came in 874; the army moved in full force to Repton, drove the Mercian king, Burgred, overseas, 'and conquered the entire kingdom', putting in a puppet ruler, Ceolwulf, 'a foolish king's thane'.

But now the great army, apparently poised for a final descent on Wessex to complete the conquest of all England, separated into its component

Viking Age sword found at Abingdon.

parts: its leaders, Hálfdan of the Wide Embrace and Guthorm (there is no mention of Ubbi at this point), had clearly agreed to carve England up into two Viking realms, north and south of the Humber. Guthorm took his 'Great Summer Army' of 871 back to East Anglia, to Cambridge, to prepare for the reduction of Wessex; while Hálfdan took his Danish veterans of the 'Great Heathen Host' of 865 back north to Northumbria.

Hálfdan of the Wide Embrace, intent on justifying his nickname as a man of far-flung conquest, would have heard of the death of his brother, Ívar the Boneless, in Ireland, and was now wanting to establish his family claim to leadership of the Vikings in both Northumbria and Ireland. He set up winter quarters on the Tyne, and from there he raided deep into Strathclyde as far as Dumbarton, just as Ívar had done, to try to bring south-western Scotland into his embrace; and according to the Irish annals, he also made an abortive attempt to wrest control of Viking Dublin from the Norwegian Vikings who had taken over there after Ívar's death.

However, it seems that by now Hálfdan's war-weary men had had enough of campaigning. They had been ten years constantly in the field. Twice they had fought their way through the length of England. They were ready to settle down:

> 876 . . . And in this year Hálfdan shared out the lands of Northumbria, and they started to plough and to make a living for themselves.
>
> (*Anglo-Saxon Chronicle*)

Hálfdan himself, restless Viking to the last, made another attempt to recover Ívar's kingdom in Dublin, but his luck as well as most of his men had now left him and he was killed in a minor sea-battle off Ireland in 877. By now the bulk of the 'Great Heathen Host' of 865 were busy digging themselves in on their new holdings in Northumbria, having turned their swords into ploughshares. They and their descendants were to have a marked and enduring effect on the physical and social and cultural landscape of the north of England and especially on the Northumbrian capital, York, which the Vikings called *Jórvík*.

York was the first important English city to be captured and occupied by the Vikings, and they left a stamp on it that has lasted to this day. It had been the northern legionary base of Roman Britain from AD 71, under the name of *Eboracum* – a huge walled fortress on the north bank of the Ouse, some twenty hectares in size, sitting astride the major north-south land route where it crosses the navigable river eighty kilometres from the mouth of the Humber.

It seems that after the Roman legions were withdrawn in 410, the fortress and its civilian suburbs were occupied by squatters for a time. When the Angles from Angeln reached there, around 500, they used York as the capital of the kingdom they created 'north of the Humber' – Northumbria – and there is evidence of quite early activity by merchants from Frisia. It is now also clear – from recent archaeological excavations underneath the magnificent York Minster when the central tower of the minster showed signs of imminent collapse – that the great basilica of the Roman fortress was kept in good order by the Anglian kings in the pre-Viking period, presumably as a royal palace and administrative head-quarters. The Anglians kept the Roman fortifications in good repair as well; one can still see the substantial remains of a seventh-century Anglian tower that was built into a breach in the Roman fortress wall, and was covered over by later Viking ramparts until it was rediscovered in 1839.

What the Vikings liked about York was what the Romans had liked about it: it was a highly strategic and easily defended location on a spit of land between the Ouse and its tributary river winding down from the north, the Fosse. The Vikings broadened the bounds of the city considerably, towards the south-east; they built a new bridge over the Ouse, to take traffic swerving past the old Roman fort, approached by a street still called Micklegate – 'Great Street'. New fortifications were built to protect the new suburbs, extending and strengthening the Roman/Anglian defences – solid earthen banks topped by a timber palisade.

Under Viking rule, York doubled in size. It became the largest trading city in Britain, with an estimated population of some 30,000, and one of the most important mercantile cities in western Europe – the main Scandinavian trade outlet to the British Isles. The quaysides on the Ouse were lengthened, wooden houses and factories sprang up around and beyond the stone churches built by the Anglians. By the year 1000, according to a *Life of St Oswald*, 'York was enriched with the treasure of merchants who come from all quarters, particularly from the Danish people.'

It was now that the physical townscape of medieval York was established, the shape and lay-out of the heart of the city which later town-planners would follow without alteration. The street-names tell their own story, especially those ending in the suffix '-gate' (Old Norse *gata*, meaning 'street'). They commemorate Viking streets whose fundamental alignment has never changed in the huddled city centre: Walmgate, Skeldergate ('Shieldmakers Street' or 'Shelf Street'), Goodramgate ('Guthorm Street'), Hungate (originally *Hundagata*, 'Dogs Street'); and most especially Coppergate – 'Coopers Street', the Street of the Wood-workers.

Coppergate is particularly significant because it has been the scene since 1976 of one of the most prodigious Viking Age excavations ever undertaken outside Scandinavia, a large site of 1500 square metres right in the heart of the medieval city. The excavation has been sponsored by the York Archaeological Trust, whose director is Peter V. Addyman, with Richard A. Hall in charge of the site excavation. Because of its position near the confluence of the Ouse and the Fosse, the land there has always been waterlogged; successive generations built up the area to keep it above the water-level, and as a result the Coppergate site contained sealed and marvellously preserved occupation layers to a depth of up to ten metres.

Coppergate has thrown important new light on an aspect of the Viking world that has been largely ignored down the centuries – the urban Viking, the Viking as craftsman and artist, the Viking as trader not raider, the Viking as man not myth.

The earliest Viking settlers in Coppergate built houses of wattle-and-post – twigs and withies woven around posts driven into the ground and daubed with clay to make them weatherproof. But the next generation built in a much more substantial fashion: walls constructed of solid oaken planks laid horizontally on thick foundation beams, supported by squared internal uprights, with a roof of wooden shingles. These Coppergate houses, set end-on to the street-front, were the first well-preserved Viking timber buildings ever found in Britain. The walls were still standing to a height of one metre; one gable wall had collapsed like a pack of cards after the building fell into disuse, leaving a surviving structure of nearly two metres in height.

These houses, whose timbers have now been lifted and are undergoing conservation treatment in tanks of polyethylene glycol (PEG), will eventually, it is hoped, be reconstructed on or near the Coppergate site. They were combined dwellings and workshops, set deep into the ground like semi-basements, with rooms measuring on average about seven metres by three. One of the buildings was found with its floor covered with a mesh of willow twigs and brushwood, which has been interpreted as a kind of early cavity-wall insulation – a building technique used in Denmark until recent times, where the material is known as 'wood wool'. The buildings have been securely dated to the middle of the tenth century by the discovery in the floor debris of two silver coins from the mint of King Æthelred the Unready, issued around 980 (*cf* Ch. 9).

Viking York has proved an inexhaustible quarry for archaeologists. Several other gap-sites in the city centre have been excavated on a 'rescue' basis, all of which revealed evidence of a flourishing industrial and industrious community. There was a tannery for making Viking boots, a factory for making ice-skates of bone, and a workshop for making combs from bone or antler, many of them handsomely decorated. Indeed the Vikings, contrary to their scruffy, hairy image, seem to have been obsessed with personal hygiene. The thirteenth-century English chronicler, John of Wallingford, recorded complaints about it; he claimed that the Vikings had always been combing their hair and taking baths and changing their underwear, which gave them an unfair advantage over their Anglo-Saxon rivals for the affections of the local maidens! It has been claimed in the past that the living conditions in Viking *Jórvík* must have been distinctly uncomfortable, from the amount of insect-ridden putrefying waste which accumulated constantly within the city. Certainly, beetles and Viking Age fleas have been found and identified from microscopic analyses of soil samples at the Environmental Archaeology Unit at York University; but the picture of unrelieved filth and squalor conjured up by earlier com-

Viking bugs found in York: enlarged view of the bodies of two insects preserved amongst waterlogged organic debris – *Aglenus brunneus* (*above*) and *Cryptopleurum minutum*.

OPPOSITE The Viking site at Coppergate in York during excavation in 1979. Coppergate, the 'Street of the Wood-workers', runs past the far end of the site.

Moneyer's lead trial strip from York. On the left, *Eadwig rex*, on the right (inverted and upside down) *Frothric*.

mentators has now been modified by more recent environmental research. It is surely significant that the word for 'Saturday' in the Scandinavian languages is still based on the Old Norse form of *laugardagur*, 'hot-springs day' – in effect, 'bath-night'!

The finds from Viking York have been staggering in their quantity and quality. Already they have more than doubled the total number of Viking artefacts previously found in Britain. All the evidence so far points to a peaceable community of artisans and merchants. There was a hardware store that specialised in the making of metal artefacts; one of the finds was a broken mould for a fine trefoil brooch. Another find emphasises the mercantile importance of the city: a miniature set of bronze scales, complete with chain and pans, which could be folded up and placed in a pocket – essential equipment for a Viking merchant to weigh any precious metal he was being offered.

In Coppergate itself, the 'Street of the Woodworkers', one of the buildings turned out to have been the site of a little carpentry business; wood-shavings and chippings were found there, and some lathe-turned wooden bowls and platters, as well as the spoon-gouges and other tools required to make them. The back room of the house next door had been a jewellery workshop where pendants of jet, beads of amber, and various kinds of finger-rings were manufactured. The amber was probably imported, raw, from the Baltic, while the jet seems to have come from Whitby, some seventy kilometres away.

Two recent finds are strikingly illuminating, because they have a story to tell. One of them is a small strip of lead that had been used by a moneyer as a trial piece for testing the coin-dies being made by his apprentices. The moneyer was called Frothric, and he had been commissioned to strike coins for *Eadwig rex* (955–9). The lead strip found at Coppergate had on it the perfect impressions of both the obverse and the reverse side of the coin. It should be remembered that dies were quite tricky to make; they had to be made in mirror-image, in order that a coin could be correctly struck from them. When Frothric tried out the dies on his strip of lead, he would have seen that the obverse, with *Eadwig rex* and a cross, had been correctly made; but the reverse, bearing his own name, was inverted. In fury, I like to think, he bent the lead strip double and tossed it out of the window, to be found a thousand years later by the archaeologists at Coppergate.

The other recent find is sheer delight – a set of Viking pan-pipes. It was made from a single rectangular block of wood into which five holes had been bored. An accomplished musician can produce from it a clear five-note scale – A, B, C sharp, D, and E (or F – the fifth pipe is defective). Apart from the occasional contemporary bell that has been found, the Coppergate pan-pipes provide us with the only authentic Viking Age musical sound yet discovered.

The York finds have also helped to illuminate the profound influence that Viking artists had on the native art-styles of Anglo-Saxon England. More than five hundred pieces of sculptured stone labelled 'Anglo-Scandinavian' have been found in the north of England. Most of them have been associated with York and Yorkshire. Viking craftsmen in their homelands tended to work with wood, not stone; but once they came to England they were inspired by native stone-masons to transfer their skills to a new medium.

They brought with them an art-style known as the Jelling style (*cf* Ch. 3), which now energised and revitalised the current Anglo-Saxon art forms. A celebrated example of this cross-fertilisation of cultures is the Middleton Cross, which depicts a rather doleful-looking serpent on the back, and a Viking warrior on the front, properly accoutred with pointed conical helmet, spear and sword, axe and shield. It used to be thought that

Unique set of boxwood Viking pan-pipes discovered at Coppergate in York, here being tried out by site director Richard Hall.

137

this was a Viking warrior laid out for burial in his coffin – a Christian burial but with pagan grave-goods; but it is now thought that it depicts a warrior seated on his high-seat, which would explain why the legs look so fore-shortened. Across his lap he is wearing, or holding, a short-sword known as a *screamasax* – and from a site in York's Parliament Street, archaeologists have unearthed a superbly decorated leather scabbard for just such a *screamasax*, with fittings that show that it was not slung from the belt, but worn along it.

In this respect, one of the most significant finds from Coppergate, historically speaking, is a piece of carved decorative stone with an inter-laced animal design measuring about twenty-five centimetres square. It is decorated in the Yorkshire–Jelling style, and forms the unfinished corner of a grave-slab. Its significance is that it was found in a datable tenth-century context which helps to date all other Anglo-Viking sculptures found in Yorkshire.

The Coppergate excavation in York helps to modify the popular image of the Viking as a mindless barbarian thug. These finds emphasise the positive effects of the Viking impact on England. But it is only with the advantage of historical hindsight that we can celebrate the constructive aspects of the Viking incursions in the second half of the ninth century. They would not have been immediately apparent, or welcome, to the beleaguered King Alfred of Wessex.

Alfred had succeeded to the throne of Wessex in April 871, in the middle of the first Danish onslaught on Wessex led by Hálfdan of the Wide Embrace and his new ally of the 'Great Summer Army', King Guthorm. 871 was a hard year for the West Saxons. The Viking army, encamped at Reading, launched attack after attack. Some they won, some they lost. The *Anglo-Saxon Chronicle* is customarily laconic:

> And in the course of the year nine general engagements were fought against the host in the kingdom to the south of the Thames . . . And in the course of this year the West Saxons made peace with the host.

People tend to think of Alfred's kingdom of Wessex at that time as the last bastion of England, holding out for England's sake against foreign invasion. It was nothing of the sort. It was simply a kingdom *in* England, loosely organised and without a conspicuous identity, waiting apprehensively to be picked off as Northumbria, East Anglia and Mercia had been. The significant difference lay in the character and personality of its new king, King Alfred, as presented in the works of his propagandists – the compiler of the *Anglo-Saxon Chronicle*, and his biographer, Asser, an elderly Welsh priest from St David's, Pembrokeshire, who spent the last ten years of Alfred's life as his tutor, chaplain and confidant at court.

Alfred was the fifth and youngest son of Æthelwulf, King of Wessex (839–58). At the age of four he was sent on a ceremonial pilgrimage to Rome as a sort of hostage to divine fortune, where Pope Leo IV acted as the

boy's godfather at his confirmation and bestowed on him the honorary title and insignia of a Roman Consul. Two years later he was back in Rome, this time with his father, who had increasingly been leaving the defence of Wessex against Viking aggression in the hands of his eldest sons, Athelstan and Æthelbald. On the return journey they spent several months at the court of Charles the Bald, Emperor of the Franks. There was clear advantage to be gained from co-ordinating Frankish and West Saxon efforts to deal with the Viking threat on both sides of the English Channel, and this political alliance was sealed by the marriage of King Æthelwulf to Charles the Bald's twelve-year-old daughter, Judith. At the same time, young

Broken grave-cover of the early tenth century found in York, and decorated with an animal ornament in an Anglo-Viking version of Jelling style.

139

Seated Anglo-Viking warrior in full armour carved on the front of the shaft of the Middleton Cross, with a leather scabbard for a *screamasax* sword worn along the front of his belt. On the back of the shaft, a dragon-like animal echoing the Anglo-Jelling style.

Alfred was absorbing Frankish cultural influences that would colour his future governance of the kingdom of Wessex, for instance in the compilation of the *Anglo-Saxon Chronicle* in direct imitation of similar Frankish annals.

By the time Æthelwulf and Alfred returned to England, Wessex was sinking into trouble, politically amd militarily. The eldest son, Athelstan, was dead; the second son, Æthelbald, insisted on a division of the kingdom into East Wessex and West Wessex. Æthelwulf died in 858, Æthelbald two years later. The third son, Æthelbert, succeeded to the re-unified throne of Wessex. His reign was relatively untroubled by Viking sorties, but it was short; he died in 865 and was succeeded by the fourth son, Æthelred, in that ominous year when the 'Great Heathen Host' landed in East Anglia intent on conquest. Alfred, now a seasoned warrior at the age of sixteen, was appointed his *secondarius*, his second-in-command.

Alfred succeeded to the throne of Wessex when his brother died just after Easter, 871, the 'Year of Battles' when the combined Viking armies, from a fortified base at Reading, fought a series of engagements with the West Saxons for the control of Wessex. Even though King Æthelred had sons, they were still children, and Alfred was the obvious successor at this time of crisis, the last adult survivor of the Wessex dynasty.

By 876, King Guthorm of the 'Great Summer Army' of 871, now nesting in Cambridge, was ready for another assault on Wessex. What Alfred had been doing in the first five years of his reign we do not know, alas, but with the fall of Mercia exposing a vulnerable flank he cannot have been idle. The situation in Wessex must have been a little like that of England in 1940 after the fall of France and the retreat from Dunkirk.

Guthorm's advance into Wessex in 876 seems to have been deceptively leisurely. There was no frontal *blitzkrieg*. His army left Cambridge and slipped past the West Saxon defences in a series of lightning rides across the entire length of the kingdom to take up new quarters at Wareham, on the Dorset coast. Alfred followed the Viking movements warily, doing enough just to contain but not engage the Danish army. A peace treaty was patched up, and as quickly broken: the Danes burst out of Wareham and made a dash for Exeter, where they holed up again. Alfred followed, still wary; another peace treaty was arranged, and this time the Danes left Wessex after payment by Alfred of a large but unspecified amount of Danegeld. The Viking army returned to Mercia, where it wintered around Gloucester in 877–8. Some of its members seem to have gone further east and started settling in the eastern Midlands; it is from this period that the creation of the Danish 'Five Boroughs' is usually dated – Lincoln, Nottingham, Derby, Leicester and Stamford.

Guthorm's lunges through Wessex, as reported in the *Anglo-Saxon Chronicle*, might seem rather pointless. But the original plan seems to have been to link up with a Viking fleet sailing from the west – perhaps from Ireland or South Wales – which would rendezvous with the Wareham land force at Poole Harbour. The link-up was never effected, however; and when the Viking fleet tried to join the army in Exeter it was caught by a great storm off Swanage, and 120 ships, according to the *Chronicle*, were lost. However exaggerated this figure may be, it is clear that the combined operation against Wessex had failed.

Guthorm must now have decided that the key to success against Wessex lay in the person of King Alfred himself. Early in 878 – the year that was to prove the crucial year of Alfred's kingship and a watershed in the Viking Age history of England – Guthorm made his move. It was his third attempt on Wessex:

878. In this year, at midwinter after Twelfth Night, the enemy host came stealthily to Chippenham, and conquered and occupied the land of

The fenlands of Athelney in Somerset, now reclaimed, where Alfred took refuge from the Danes in 878.

the West Saxons and drove a great part of the people across the sea, and reduced to submission most of the others – except for King Alfred. Alfred, with a small band of followers, moved under difficulties through woods and inaccessible places into the fastnesses of the fens.

(*Anglo-Saxon Chronicle*)

It was a brilliant tactical coup, this midwinter invasion just after Christmas. The Saxon levies had been disbanded after the treaty of Exeter. Alfred was spending Christmas at his royal manor of Chippenham in Wiltshire, unprotected save for his personal bodyguard of picked followers. He seems to have been caught off-guard by Guthorm's 'stealthy' descent, but he managed to escape into the wilderness of the Somerset fenlands; and even though resistance in Wessex seems to have crumbled while the king was on the run, the failure to 'take out' Alfred, in the modern phrase, was to prove critical. As long as the charismatic Alfred was on the loose, there was always a chance that he could provide a rallying-point for renewed resistance against the Viking conquerors.

There seems to have been an early attempt to trap Alfred in a pincer movement. The *Chronicle* reports the arrival in North Devon of a fleet of twenty-three ships from South Wales, led by the shadowy Ubbi, brother of Ívar the Boneless and Hálfdan of the Wide Embrace. But Ubbi's force was unexpectedly mauled by a stout force of local militia besieged at the stronghold of Countisbury Hill, near Minehead: Wessex was not entirely crushed yet.

But the peril for Wessex, and King Alfred, was still very real:

At this time King Alfred was leading a hazardous life in great difficulties with a few of his nobles and some soldiers and vassals among the woods and marshlands of the county of Somerset. He had none of the necessities of life save for what he could take openly or by stealth, by raiding the heathens or even the Christians who had submitted to heathen rule.

(Asser's *Life of Alfred*)

In the late winter and spring of 878 Alfred was operating as a guerrilla leader, using the advantages of the terrain to make forays against the occupying forces from a base in the swamplands of the Somerset Levels in the vicinity of Athelney, on Sedgemoor. And it was from this area, and this period of his reign, that we get the celebrated story of the Burning of the Cakes. The purpose of the story was to illustrate the depths to which the young king had fallen at this nadir of his fortunes, and the humility and fortitude with which he faced his vicissitudes.

The story goes that Alfred had taken refuge in a herdsman's cottage, incognito of course. One day, while he was sitting by the fire, tending his weapons and no doubt brooding over his predicament, some cakes that were baking in the oven began to burn. The shrewish housewife, not realising that she was addressing her royal lord, scolded him sharply for letting them get scorched. It is a vivid little episode, and it has etched itself deeply on English folklore. But did it ever actually happen?

There is no way of knowing for sure, now; but in a fascinating monograph for the Historical Association, entitled *The Undergrowth of History* (1955), Professor Sir Robert Birley traced the literary development of the tale. It was formerly thought that it had originated from Alfred's biographer, Asser, but the Asser story is now recognised as a later interpolation. The earliest written form of it is now known to have first appeared in a lost *Life of St Neot* in the middle of the eleventh century, 150 years after Alfred's death. But this version, itself based on an older story in a homily on St Neot, incorporates a significant difference: it has the housewife ordering the king to watch the baking and to turn it when required, and the king actually doing it – 'He was at once obedient to that bad wife, because of necessity he had to be.' It was a parable of Alfred's royal humility, in effect.

The other significant difference in this earlier version is that it features not cakes but loaves. The Old English word for 'lord' (from which our modern word derives) was *hlāf-weard*, 'loaf-provider'; it epitomised the relationship between the head of the national household, as it were, and the subjects who ate his bread. The parable emphasised Alfred's royal duty to his people; and the original point it was making was not that Alfred burnt some cakes through his preoccupation with his own troubles, but that he turned the loaves, mindful of his responsibility as king.

143

Athelney and the Turning of the Loaves symbolised the turning-point in Alfred's fortunes. Some time in the spring of 878 he built himself a small fortress on the island of Athelney, a low swelling mound on the River Parrett, then surrounded by swamps, to provide a safe refuge and a base for guerrilla sorties. Later he was to express his gratitude to the place by founding a royal monastery there. Today, Athelney can show only a rather unprepossessing early nineteenth-century monument in the shape of a truncated obelisk, much defaced by graffiti and caged behind iron railings. The inscription on it reads:

> King Ælfred the Great . . . having been defeated by the Danes, fled for refuge to the forest of Athelney, where he lay concealed from his enemies for the space of a whole year [sic]. He soon after regained possession of his throne . . .

The manner in which Alfred 'regained his throne' was little short of miraculous. His position in March 878 must have seemed all but hopeless. But once the spring sowing was over, he was able to raise a big levy of local troops for a head-on confrontation with Guthorm. Guthorm's own army was depleted by warriors who were settling down in large numbers on the estates they had seized; the Viking and West Saxon roles had been reversed – it was now Alfred who was harrying the settlers.

Seven weeks after Easter, in early May 878, Alfred was joined by levies of men from Somerset, Wiltshire and Hampshire at an unidentified meeting-place known as 'Egbert's Stone' at the southern end of Selwood Forest:

> And when they saw the king they received him like one risen from the dead after such great tribulation, and they were filled with great joy.
>
> (Asser's *Life of Alfred*)

It was a formidable enough array that had assembled, and probably as strong numerically as Guthorm's own army. Alfred advanced north-eastwards along the western scarp of Salisbury Plain towards Guthorm's main encampment at Chippenham, where he himself had been caught so badly off-guard by the midwinter assault. Guthorm's army came out to meet him. The encounter took place somewhere on the downs near Edington (Anglo-Saxon *Ethandun*), a few miles south of Chippenham. And there, according to the *Chronicle*, 'he fought against the entire host and put it to flight'. The Danes retreated to their camp at Chippenham, hotly pursued by Alfred, and after a fortnight's siege they sued for peace.

In a paper delivered at the annual meeting of the Friends of Edington Priory Church in 1977, entitled *The Importance of the Battle of Edington*, Professor Dorothy Whitelock, distinguished doyenne of Anglo-Saxon scholars, argued cogently that Edington was one of the major turning-points in English history. It was this victory, epitomising Alfred's stubborn refusal to give in to the Vikings, that saved Wessex from Danish domination, and provided the platform for Alfred and his successors to reconquer the Viking-held East and North. Without Alfred and Edington, England would undoubtedly have become a Viking land.

The Danish surrender after Edington was formalised in a peace treaty that would have far-reaching political effects. Not only did the Danes swear to leave Wessex; but Guthorm and thirty of his foremost army leaders agreed to accept baptism as Christians. That autumn the Danish army withdrew as promised, to Cirencester in Mercia; and in the following year, 879, it moved farther east and proceeded to a systematic settlement of East Anglia. For the 'Great Summer Army' of 871, as for the 'Great Heathen Host' of 865 which settled in Northumbria, their Viking days were over.

Alfred had not so much 'defeated' the Danish invaders as come to an understanding with them. His treaty with them accepted their presence in England as a political fact of life; it was an agreement reached between two equal powers, now that Edington had given Alfred prestige and credibility as a king to be reckoned with. It even encouraged Alfred, in an excess of self-confidence, to strike a penny coin around 880 inscribed *Ælfred rex Anglorum* ('Alfred King of the English'). He certainly was not 'King of the English' in our sense of the term; but he had laid the foundations for the royal dynasty of Wessex eventually to assume the kingship of a united, Anglo-Scandinavian England *(cf* Ch. 6).

Before that, however, Alfred was realistic enough to recognise that England was now, in effect, two nations, one Saxon, one Viking. In a new treaty negotiated with Guthorm in 885–6, the partition of England was formalised; it was the first official definition of the limits of the Viking-controlled area of England which would come to be known as the Danelaw. The boundary between Viking England and English England would run 'up the Thames [to London] and then up the River Lea, along the Lea to its source and then in a straight line to Bedford, then up the River Ouse to Watling Street'.

This fundamental recognition and acceptance of the Viking presence in England did not bring any easement in Alfred's problems; it only helped to define them. It was by no means the end of recurring Viking attacks, but it gave him more room to manoeuvre, more time to plan a coherent strategy – a philosophy, even – for the kind of place he wanted England to be.

What shall I say of the cities and towns he restored, and of the others which he built where before there had never been any? Or of the works in gold and silver, incomparably made under his direction? Or of the halls and royal chambers, wonderfully made of stone and wood by his command? Or of the royal residences, built of stone, moved from their former positions, and most beautifully set up in more fitting places by the king's command?

(Asser's *Life of Alfred*)

ÆLFREDES LAGA CYNINGES

The treaty between Alfred and the Danish leader Guthorm that formalised the creation of the Danelaw. The first word of the sixth line is 'Thames', describing the start of the new boundary between West Saxons and Danes.

Asser's rhetorical questions can now be answered, in part at least; recent archaeological discoveries, combined with the evidence of contemporary documents, are providing an ever clearer picture of Alfred's achievements.

Of his palaces and royal residences we know nothing, as yet. But of his 'cities and towns' we now know a great deal. Alfred created a system of fortified strongholds called *burhs* (the forerunners of today's 'boroughs') to give his kingdom defence in depth. Some were custom-built, with an enclosing embankment and ditch; others, such as Bath, Exeter and Winchester, utilised the existing fortifications that dated from Roman times.

A record of Alfred's *burhs* is preserved in a remarkable document known as the *Burghal Hidage*, which was compiled shortly after Alfred's death and gives a list of those towns which had been fortified. A 'hide' was a unit of agricultural land sufficient for a peasant family to support itself, and each 'hide' of land had to contribute one adult male for the defence of the *burh*. Each man was allotted just over a metre of wall to defend at times of danger; so when the *Burghal Hidage* says that Winchester, for instance, was rated at 2400 'hides', we know that its perimeter defences must have measured about 3000 metres – and the Roman walls at Winchester confirm the accuracy of this figure.

The *Burghal Hidage* shows that the core of the kingdom of Wessex was defended by a ring of more than thirty of these *burhs*, and that no village was more than thirty kilometres from a *burh*. Archaeological excavations at

OPPOSITE ABOVE Edington, the site of the crucial battle of *Ethandun* near Chippenham, where Alfred won a victory against the Danes.

OPPOSITE BELOW Winchester: Alfred refurbished the old Roman walls here to create an Anglo-Saxon *burh*. The street on the right marks the course of a section of those walls. It was in Winchester that the first *Anglo-Saxon Chronicle* is thought to have been written, in Alfred's royal palace to the west (right) of the Cathedral.

Wareham, the Dorset town seized by Guthorm in his swoop on Wessex in 876, have revealed great earthen embankments built during Alfred's reign and measuring nearly 700 metres – corroborating the length specified in the *Burghal Hidage*.

The creation of the Wessex *burhs* meant that Alfred could rely on a local holding operation wherever his kingdom was under attack, until such time as he could send a relieving army, the levied *fyrd*, to its assistance. But because the *fyrd* tended to melt away when farming needs called, Alfred divided the organisation of the *fyrd* into two parts: one half would be in a state of mobilisation while the other half was free to return home and get on with the ploughing or reaping. It all sounds very obvious and simple now; but in Alfred's day it represented a revolutionary reform of a kingdom's defences, a lesson that had been learned from hard experience.

King Alfred's other major claim to greatness was that he inspired a tremendous renaissance of learning and literature in England – and in the native tongue, Anglo-Saxon. He himself, like practically everyone else in England at that time, had been illiterate during his childhood, according to Asser. Asser's pious narrative depicts Alfred as an eager student of learning all his life; and once he learned to read and write, there was no stopping him. The inspiration for the *Anglo-Saxon Chronicle* in all probability stemmed from Alfred, and its first compilation, in 892, is thought to have been written in a scriptorium in his royal palace at Winchester, whose archaeological remains are believed to lie in the area to the west of the present cathedral.

Not content with this exercise in royal Wessex propaganda, however, Alfred also started translating Latin works on his own account – edifying books for the benefit of clergy and laity alike. His first endeavour was a translation of a work called *Cura Pastoralis*, 'Pastoral Care', by Pope Gregory the First (590–604), a handbook on the duties of bishops and other clergy:

> When I remembered how the knowledge of the Latin language had previously decayed throughout England . . . I began in the midst of the other various cares of this kingdom to turn into English the book which is called in Latin *Pastoralis* and in English the *Shepherd-Book*; sometimes word for word, sometimes in paraphrase . . . And I will send a copy to every bishopric in my kingdom; and with each there shall go a costly pointer [*æstel*] . . .   (Alfred: Preface to *Cura Pastoralis*)

Some three hundred years ago a superb little jewel was found near Athelney in Somerset, where Alfred had built a fortress and thanksgiving monastery. It is perhaps the most celebrated artefact from Anglo-Saxon England, now kept in the Ashmolean Museum in Oxford and known as the 'Alfred Jewel'.

It is quite small. Behind a protective plate of rock-crystal there is a pear-shaped representation of a figure that has been interpreted either as Christ personifying Wisdom, or a personification of one of the Five Senses of Man – the sense of sight. Round the outside there is an Anglo-Saxon inscription cut in gold letters: AELFRED MEC HEHT GEWYRCAN – 'Alfred had me made'. The Jewel ends in a gold holder shaped and decorated like a boar's head. In the muzzle there is a socket with a broken rivet through it, a short open tube that clearly once held a little wand or rod of ivory or wood.

The style of decoration is right for Alfred's period, the language of the inscription is right for Alfred's period; and although there can be no absolute assurance that this Jewel was actually made for *King* Alfred, as opposed to some anonymous Wessex nobleman called Alfred, it is immensely tempting to associate the Jewel with one of the costly 'pointers' that Alfred distributed with every copy of the *Cura Pastoralis* that he sent to his bishops. Much depends on the interpretation of the Anglo-Saxon word *æstel* – 'pointer' or 'book-marker'. Costly it certainly was: in his Preface, Alfred declared that each one was worth fifty *mancuses*, and a *mancus* was a sum of gold worth thirty pennies, each *mancus* equivalent to the price of an ox.

If it was one of Alfred's *æstels*, as I like to believe it was, it would have been used during ceremonial occasions in church, both to impress the congregation and perhaps also to help bishops with failing eyesight to keep the place as they read aloud from the crabbed writing of the manuscript. This tradition of kingly gifts is attested by the visit to Alfred's court of the Norwegian merchant Óttar (Anglo-Saxon Ohthere) bearing exotic presents of walrus-ivory (*cf* Ch. 2).

By marvellous good fortune, one of the original copies of Alfred's translation of the *Cura Pastoralis* still survives: the book that was sent to Wærferth, Bishop of Worcester (889–99). It is now in the Bodleian Library in Oxford, familiarly known by its shelf number (Bodleian Hatton 20); and what a treasure it is.

In bold capitals at the top of the first page there is the legend: 'This Book is for Worcester'. And then the message:

> King Alfred bids greet Bishop Wærferth with these words of loving friendship. And I let it be known to you that it has often come to my mind what wise men there were formerly throughout England, both of sacred and secular orders, and what happy times there were then in England; and how the kings who had power over the nation in those days obeyed God and his ministers . . .

Alfred's work as a patron of learning and the arts, 'incomparably made under his direction', obviously endeared him to his encomiasts like Asser. He has become the nation's darling; but he is also one of the few people in history whose reputation has been not only confirmed but even enhanced by later historians. He was intelligent, skilful, far-sighted, energetic and profoundly complex.

The so-called 'Alfred Jewel', now in the Ashmolean Museum, Oxford. The lettering shown reads *Ælfred mec....*

He has also been called the 'father of the English navy', because he built a fleet to reinforce his land-defences, a fleet that could intercept Viking attacks before they had time to develop. Everything he did testifies to his outstanding qualities as a leader of a nation.

At Stouton in Wiltshire, near Bruton, there is a tall eighteenth-century tower that was built to commemorate his achievements. And no one, I think, would now quarrel seriously with the magnificent obituary written in the twelfth century by the English chronicler Henry of Huntingdon and interpolated into Asser's *Life*:

O Alfred, powerful in arms, thine innate nobility bestowed on thee the honour of probity and also the labour of probity; and labour has conferred on thee an everlasting name. Thy joys were ever mingled with pain. Thy hope was ever mingled with fear. If thou conquered, thou feared tomorrow's battle; if thou wert conquered, thou prepared for tomorrow's fight. Thy garments stained with constant sweat, thy sword stained with constant blood, prove how great was the burden of thy reign. Throughout the climes of this immense world, no one was ever permitted like thee scarcely to breathe in so many adversities . . .

Alfred died in October 899. In the last years of his reign he had a renewed Viking onslaught to deal with – a roving army that had been terrorising the Continent and was now looking for fresh fields to conquer. It sailed from Boulogne in the autumn of 892, heading for the River

Alfred's 'costly pointer': replica of the Alfred Jewel with a small ivory wand to show how it may have been used originally.

Lymne on the south Kentish coast, while another fleet, no doubt acting in concert, descended on the Thames estuary. The intention was clear – to 'do an East Anglia', whereby the eastern part of Wessex would be detached by a pincer movement and eventually settled. But Alfred's new defences by land and sea were equal to the thrust. In 896 the *Anglo-Saxon Chronicle* announced, not without relief, the outcome of this determined invasion by the new 'Great Heathen Host' of 892:

> In this summer the host dispersed, some to East Anglia and others to Northumbria; and those without money got themselves ships there and sailed south-over-sea to the Seine. By the mercy of God the Great Host had not utterly crushed the English people.

It was this 'Host' that would eventually take over Normandy as a permanent Viking conquest (*cf* Ch. 10). For the time being, however, England was safe – thanks to Alfred.

6

'Bitter is the wind...'

Bitter is the wind tonight,
White the tresses of the sea;
I have no fear the Viking hordes
Will sail the seas on such a night.

That evocative medieval Irish stanza, dating from the ninth century, was scribbled by a monk in the margin of a manuscript he was copying which is now preserved in the St Gall Library in Switzerland. The storm would bring respite from Viking raiders: no pirates would dare to brave the Irish Sea on such a night. It is an eloquent reflection of the reverse side of the picture – the fair-weather days when the seas swarmed with Viking ships – much more eloquent than the exaggerated rhetoric of the twelfth-century *War of the Irish with the Foreigners* (*Cogadh Gáedhel re Gallaibh*):

In a word, although there were an hundred hard-steeled iron heads on one neck, and an hundred sharp, ready, never-rusting brazen tongues in every head, and an hundred garrulous, loud, unceasing voices from every tongue, they could not recount nor narrate nor enumerate nor tell what all the people of Ireland suffered in common, both men and women, laymen and priests, old and young, noble and ignoble, of hardship and injury and oppression in every house from these ruthless, wrathful, foreign, purely pagan people.

More than a thousand years later the people of Ireland were up in arms again, metaphorically speaking, over those 'ruthless, wrathful, foreign, purely pagan people', the Vikings. In the summer of 1978 some 20,000 Irishmen marched through the streets of Dublin in pouring rain to protest against a new form of Viking 'vandalism' – but this time it was vandalism in reverse. They were demonstrating against a decision by Dublin Corporation to build four Civic Office blocks on an archaeological site called Wood Quay in what had been the heart of medieval Dublin. The site, which slopes down from the cathedral of Christ Church towards the River Liffey, had just been declared a National Monument after a three-day High Court hearing because of its significance as a *Viking* site: the 'foreign, purely pagan people' had been retrospectively naturalised, and were now accepted as an integral part of the Irish heritage. It all gave an intriguing new twist to the phrase *furore Normannorum*!

According to the Irish annals, Dublin was founded in 841 as a Viking *longphort* (ship fortress) at the ford of the River Liffey, at a place known to the Irish as Dubh-Linn, the Black Pool. In the early 1960s, excavations by Dr Breandán Ó Ríordáin, now the Director of the National Museum of Ireland, at a number of redevelopment sites in the shadow of Christ Church Cathedral began to reveal extensive and substantial traces of the tenth- and eleventh-century city that sprang up behind the original *longphort*, as well as a spectacular range of craft and trade artefacts.

Wood Quay, which has been excavated since 1974 by Patrick Wallace, an Assistant Keeper at the National Museum, is the latest of these urban Viking Age sites. The civic passions it has aroused are an index of the growing awareness of the significance of the earlier Dublin finds. Some 200,000 signatures were gathered for a petition to save the Wood Quay site from the developers. A 'Friends of Medieval Dublin' society was formed, led by a medieval historian, Professor F. X. Martin of University College, Dublin; they wanted the site to be left as a monument to the Viking Age in Ireland. They took out two successful injunctions in the High Court to stop the bulldozers; but ultimately the right to continue to develop the site was upheld by the Supreme Court in March 1979. However, the National Museum was at least granted access to complete the excavation and recording of the site.

Quite apart from its archaeological significance, the name itself – Wood Quay – is significant, because the site is more than a hundred metres away from the Liffey as it flows today. It sounds like a paradox, but it is a paradox that answers itself – when the Vikings founded Dublin in 841 the Liffey was very much broader than it is now. The Wood Quay excavations have revealed a Viking embankment that runs right across the site and was erected around 950 along the high-water line of the shore at that time. It was made up of earth and gravel bonded with estuarine mud, stabilised at its core by a wooden fence, and protected by a wattle-and-post breakwater.

This was not the original Viking *longphort* of 841, which probably lay a little farther downriver; but Wood Quay shows that within a century the Vikings of Dublin had started to reclaim land from the Liffey to make a stable waterfront, first with some low, clay flood-banks around 900 and then the embankment. But that was just the beginning. Around 1000 a second embankment was built farther out into the river, and a century later the incoming Normans built a third embankment, a really substantial structure of stone more than three metres high. Beyond this early city wall the Normans reclaimed more and more land behind a succession of timber quaysides, reaching almost as far as the present embankment and causeway along the south bank of the Liffey.

The rapid development of Dublin's waterfront illustrates very clearly the way in which the Vikings transformed Ireland's essentially pastoral

153

The Wood Quay site, to right of picture, stretching down towards the Liffey.

economy into a thriving mercantile economy, and made Dublin an important Viking Age mart. Dublin was the first, but by no means the last: the Vikings founded several other fortified trade ports whose names still echo their Scandinavian origins – Waterford, Wexford (*Veigsfjörður*), Wicklow (*Víkingaló*) and Limerick (*Hlymrekur*). Limerick in particular became for a time a royal Viking base to rival Dublin itself. With the coming of the Vikings, Ireland was brought into the mainstream of European trade, and the old Irish order changed – irrevocably.

The Ireland the Vikings found was a Celtic country. The Celts of Central Europe had started moving into the British Isles around the fifth century BC, or even earlier. They brought with them a new 'wonder product' – iron – which made much more effective weapons than the bronzework of the preceding age. In Ireland they built themselves thousands of fortified places like *crannógs* (artificial islands in lakes), small ring-forts (little more than defended homesteads), or vast and imposing hill-forts that would cover several acres of a hilltop within an enclosing wall and ditch. Socially and politically the incomers seem to have imposed a system of priest-kings, who combined secular and religious authority.

The most celebrated of these huge hill-forts is Tara – Tara of the Kings, *Teamhair na Ríogh* – in County Meath, north of Dublin. Even the name itself has a romantic ring to it; 'the harp that hung on Tara's walls' is a

OPPOSITE Illuminated page from the Book of Kells, now in Trinity College, Dublin.

The Ardagh Chalice.

tremendously evocative line, conjuring up all manner of magical images of Ireland's remote and legendary past, redolent of 'old forgotten far-off things and battles long ago'.

In pre-Christian times, Tara was the religious/royal seat of the priestly High Kings of Ireland, or men who claimed to be the High Kings of Ireland, exacting tribute and produce from the surrounding farmers. It is an impressive site, a low grass-grown hill rising to a height of a hundred metres with a magnificent view all around of the central plain of Ireland – some of the richest pasture-land in Western Europe.

The Hill of Tara is dotted with a number of earthworks and mounds, all with resounding traditional names such as the Mound of the Hostages, the Royal Enclosure, the Royal Seat, the *Lia Fáil* (the stone on which the High Kings were crowned, and which roared loudly under their feet if their inauguration was accepted), Cormac's House, and so on. All these names refer to legendary people and events from the heroic age of pre-Christian Ireland, around the third century AD. The archaeological evidence, however, suggests that the Hill of Tara had been a site of religious significance long before the arrival of the Celts, and that the priestly High Kings took it over in a conscious effort to impose their own new cult centres on the older burial cults of the indigenous population.

Whatever the reality of Tara, the *idea* of Tara has always been a potent symbol of Ireland's history and prehistory. It was from the Rath of the Synods on Tara that the High King Laoghaire is said to have seen a bright light shining on the Hill of Slane fifteen kilometres away, heralding the new religion kindled by St Patrick in AD 433. That light was to be the dawn of the Heroic Age of Celtic Christianity.

In St Patrick's wake, an extraordinary number of monasteries sprang up all over Ireland, self-contained and self-governing monastic establishments that soon became great centres of learning and culture. According to what little archaeological evidence there is, they tended to be surprisingly small: communities of beehive-shaped huts or cells (*clocháns*), enclosed within a circular wall – surprisingly, when one considers the enormous wealth of marvellous art-work that poured from them, like the superb Ardagh Chalice of the early eighth century or the great illuminated manuscripts like the Book of Kells (*c.* 800).

In their tiny, enclosed worlds, the monks of the early Christian Church in Ireland lived lives of exemplary discipline and asceticism. They studied and enriched the ancient learning salvaged from the destruction of the Roman Empire by the barbarian incursions of the fifth century. They encouraged the development of a vernacular literature by recording tales and legends of Ireland's pagan past. They copied out their gospels and psalters in beautiful manuscripts, sometimes adding in the margin little lyrics of nature poetry of great sweetness and intensity. Metal-smiths worked their matchless treasures, masons carved the legions of High Crosses that still enhance the Irish landscape.

It was all done in a spirit of penitential obsession. Their work was all for the glory of God and for forgiveness of sins. And in the same spirit of penance they would condemn themselves to exile from their homeland. The most extreme form of this was to set sail into unknown waters in their hide-covered *currachs*, looking for some empty island on which they could live out the rest of their lives as hermits. In this way, Irish hermits reached the Faroes and Iceland late in the eighth century, a hundred years before the Vikings did (*cf* Ch. 7) – and St Brendan, it is claimed, may even have crossed the North Atlantic. Other self-exiles elected to take the faith to the heathen, like St Columba in Scotland, preaching the Gospel all over Dark Age Europe, founding monasteries in England, France, Germany, Austria, even as far afield as Italy.

Such was the Heroic Age of Irish Christianity – a great cultural flowering that made Ireland the foremost centre of Christianity in Western Europe, an age of pious serenity and devout achievement. All this, we are conventionally told, the Vikings heedlessly and brutally shattered:

> The sea spewed forth such floods of foreigners over Erin that no harbour, no landing-place, no stronghold, no fastness might be found that was not submerged by waves of Vikings and pirates . . . so that they made spoil-land and sword-land and conquered land of her, throughout her breadth and generally; and they ravaged her chieftainries and her privileged churches and her sanctuaries; and they rent her shrines and her reliquaries and her books.

The first recorded Viking raid on Ireland took place in the year 795, with an attack on the island of *Rechru* – either Lambey Island north of Dublin or, more probably, Rathlin Island off the north-east coast. It seems to have been the work of a band of Norwegian 'Gentiles' (as the Irish annalists called them) that came prowling down the west coast of Scotland from lairs in the Orkneys or Hebrides (*cf* Ch. 9), attacking Skye and Iona on the way, and also the island monasteries of Inishmurray in County Sligo and Inishbofin in Donegal in Ireland.

For the next fifty years or so, the Irish annals record a number of raids on Irish monasteries and settlements, sporadic at first, but gradually escalating in frequency and intensity. They undoubtedly caused considerable disruption – but probably not as much as the tone of the later chroniclers would suggest. Throughout the eighth century, Irish society and politics had been undergoing change, as warring tribes and their petty kings fought one another to enlarge their territories. Cattle-rustling was endemic, as much a part of the pastoral scene as the spring sowing or the autumn reaping. Inevitably, the monasteries themselves became embroiled in these squabbles, for they were the community banks of their day, the repositories of lands and livestock and harvest wealth as well as church treasure. They were also becoming important political and economic factors in their own right, secular as well as ecclesiastical power-

The magnificently
ornate early twelfth-
century crozier of
the Abbots of
Clonmacnoise.

centres. Long before the first Vikings set foot on Irish soil, the Irish
themselves were busy burning the monasteries of rival tribes – the Irish
annals record at least thirty such desecrations before the raid on *Rechru* in
795. The churchmen themselves took part as lustily as the best of them: in
807, for instance, the monasteries of Cork and Clonfert fought a pitched
battle which resulted in 'an innumerable slaughter of the ecclesiastical
men and superiors of Cork'. As Dr A. T. Lucas, former Director of the
National Museum of Ireland, has noted, 'A short experience in the country would have taught even a freelance Viking band that a raid on an Irish
monastery was a sound economic proposition.'

It looks as if monastery-plunder may not always have been the primary
purpose of the Viking visitations, but merely a lucrative spin-off. There is
no doubt that the Vikings were also looking for land on which to settle,
either by conquest or purchase. Nor were they always considered un-
welcome visitors; Irish chieftains frequently used them as allies against
their own enemies or to further their own political ambitions, and there is
evidence of intermarriage and concubinage at every level of society.

Such is not the picture we get from the *War of the Irish with the*

Foreigners, which presents the Vikings as vicious invaders and predators and the Irish chieftains as noble-minded patriots defending their homeland with selfless courage. As a source, however, it is totally unreliable; it was written in the twelfth century as a nationalistic panegyric. But such is the spell of its rhetoric that it has imposed its view of the Vikings on all later generations, until now. Scholars today take a more objective view of that period of Ireland's history, and are recognising that the Vikings and the Irish had a great deal in common. Similarly, the facile assumption that any Irish 'treasure' found in a Viking grave must have been stolen from an Irish church is being reassessed. Some 'ecclesiastical' objects are now considered to have been secular in origin, and were not necessarily looted, either; while even those that are acknowledged to be ecclesiastical in origin may not have been plundered. A case in point is a small Irish casket-shrine, now in the National Museum in Copenhagen, which had been inscribed with a Norse runic inscription: 'Ranvaig owns this casket'. Had it been looted and given to a girl friend as a jewellery box? That is hardly likely, considering that when it was found it still contained holy relics and was reverently wrapped in silk cloth! In all probability it was a perfectly legitimate gift, perhaps even to a church in Scandinavia.

The Ranvaig Casket, now in the National Museum in Copenhagen.

One of the more celebrated fantasies elaborated by the *War of the Irish with the Foreigners* concerns the arrival in Ireland of a Norwegian sea-king called Turgeis or Turgesius with 'a great royal fleet' in the 830s. Once in Ireland, we are told that he proceeded to lay about him with more than usual gusto; he conquered Armagh, then Ulster; he raided Connacht and Meath; he declared himself King of all the Foreigners in Erin. For seven years he caused Ireland untold misery; and then, in response to some ancient prophecy, he was captured and put to death by drowning in Lough Owel. Stirring stuff – the very stuff of legend. And that is precisely what it is. Turgesius's career is, quite simply, largely fiction; his alleged exploits are not only ridiculous but also anachronistic. Nor was there any sea-king of Norway in the ninth century capable of mounting a great naval expedition in western waters before the time of King Harald Fine-Hair (*cf* Ch. 2).

The most preposterous of the allegations against him claimed that he was deliberately and virulently anti-Christian. He is said to have plundered Armagh Abbey and installed himself in place of the Abbot as a heathen High Priest; and after sacking the great monastery of Clonmacnoise in County Offaly, he is said to have placed his wife on the high altar, where she chanted heathen spells and devilish oracles. He is also charged with having tried, with some degree of success, to subvert the whole of Christian Ireland to the worship of the Norse god Thór; but this idea is so alien to the unfanatical Viking religious ethos that no one can possibly take it seriously now. The Vikings were entrepreneurs, not evangelists. The other side of the Clonmacnoise coin is the fact that, despite raids by Vikings and Irishmen alike, it became a great monastic university city-state which also emphasised the positive aspect of the Viking experience – the marriage of the art styles of Ireland and Scandinavia. One of the fruits of that fertile union of skills is the magnificent twelfth-century crozier of the Abbots of Clonmacnoise, with its interlace pattern and trailing tendrils in a development of the so-called Ringerike style of Scandinavia.

Irish craftsmen continued to adapt and embellish Viking art styles long after the end of the Viking Age proper. The final phase, the so-called Urnes style (*cf* Ch. 10), had its last flowering in Irish ornamental metal-work, particularly in the superb Cross of Cong, County Mayo. It is a processional cross, some seventy-five centimetres high, made as a reliquary for a fragment of the True Cross in the 1120s; ribbon-like animals writhe all over the decorated panels, looping and biting, while the shaft of the cross itself is gripped in the maw of a stylised animal-head.

But the real measure of the Viking effect on Ireland lies in the establishment of fortified sea-bases that grew into Ireland's first towns, especially Dublin in 841. It emphasises the proposition that the primary aim of the Vikings was not plunder but settlement. The prospect of trading in new markets was every bit as enticing as the incidental profits of raiding. There is clear archaeological evidence that even by the time of the establishment of the *longphort* at Dublin there were already distinctly Viking communities settled and resident in Ireland.

The main evidence for this comes from an extensive Viking cemetery on the western outskirts of Dublin at Kilmainham/Islandbridge. It dates from the middle of the ninth century; and although the graves came to light quite accidentally in the middle of the last century during construction work for the Great Southern and Western Railway, and were never systematically excavated or recorded, the amount of material from them indicates that it must have been the largest Viking necropolis yet found anywhere in the British Isles.

The grave goods from only one of the Islandbridge graves were properly recorded; they consisted of a sword, a spear, an axe, a shield-boss and a bronze pin – typical Viking warrior gear. But the National Museum of Ireland houses a rich collection of objects from the Islandbridge cemetery, which gives a good idea of the extent and nature of the settlement. There are forty swords of the ninth century, mostly of Norwegian manufacture but some of Frankish make – costly weapons, their pommels richly ornamented with silver. There are also thirty-five spear-heads and twenty-six shield-bosses, some of them made locally, and two iron axe-heads. The permanent nature of the settlement is proved by the fact that women were buried at Islandbridge, too, wearing characteristic Norse humped oval brooches, buckles and glass bead necklaces, and accompanied by domestic accoutrements like stone spindle-whorls, needle-cases and wooden linen-smoothers.

But it was not just warriors and their women who lived and died at Islandbridge. Many were craftsmen who had been buried with their

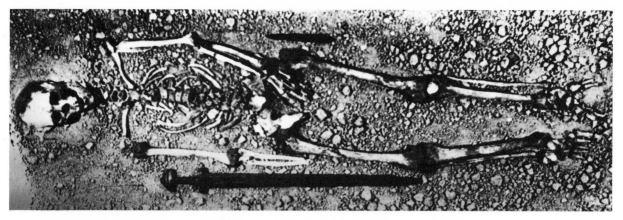

tools – forge-tongs, pincers, hammers, shears, sickles. Others had been merchants, for amongst the finds are sets of folding bronze scales, their pans brightly tinned on the inside, and with them a dozen handsomely fashioned weights with lead cores, sculpted and decorated with enamel and glass. Scales like these were used to weigh precious stones and metal, particularly silver. Silver from abroad was one of the staples of early Viking trade in Ireland (along with slaves), as evidenced by more than a hundred hoards and more than a hundred and fifty single finds of silver and gold in Ireland from the Viking period, as well as by the vastly increased use of silver in Irish ornaments of the ninth and tenth centuries.

Viking grave from Islandbridge.

The wealth generated by the Vikings in Ireland is also reflected in contemporary documents. When the Viking base at Limerick was raided by the Irish late in the tenth century, it is recorded that the victors looted from the Vikings 'their jewels, their saddles beautiful and foreign, their gold and silver, their beautifully woven cloth of all colours and all kinds, their satins and silks so pleasing and variegated, both scarlet and green'.

In 1962 the Corporation of Dublin embarked on a large-scale re-development scheme for the area around Christ Church Cathedral in the heart of what had been the medieval city. Occasional Viking material had already come to light during sewer-laying operations within the bounds of the medieval city, so when a block of old buildings on the south side of the High Street was demolished to make room for road-widening, the National Museum of Ireland was offered the chance of excavating in the cleared area. Dr Breandán Ó Ríordáin dug there from 1962–3, and again on a second, larger plot on the High Street from 1967–72. Meanwhile, in 1969, another cleared site became available on the east side of Winetavern Street running down towards the Liffey, which Dr Ó Ríordáin excavated simultaneously from 1969–73, and in 1972 yet another area was cleared and excavated south of the cathedral in Christ Church Place.

The cellars of the eighteenth-century buildings on the sites had disturbed the ground to an average depth of 2.5 metres below street level, obliterating all traces of previous occupation back to around 1300. But

Base of the Cross of Cong.

below that level there was a deep stratum of occupation debris, some two metres thick, in which were encapsulated some 30,000 artefacts and the remains of a large number of structures of various types dating back to the late ninth or early tenth centuries. They were all in a remarkable state of preservation, due to the high organic content of the debris (tannins and phosphates) and to the fact that the sites were permanently waterlogged – ideal archaeological conditions. From the lowest levels of these deposits, down at the original ground surface, a vivid picture has emerged of the earliest Viking settlements on the slopes around Christ Church Cathedral – the craftsmen's quarter during the heyday of Viking Dublin in the tenth and eleventh centuries.

Dr Ó Ríordáin's series of excavations revealed the ground plans of the houses and streets, as well as abundant evidence of the many trades and crafts that flourished in the city. Nearly all the houses and workshops were of wattle-and-post construction, with two spaced rows of paired upright posts with a weft of rods or wattles of hazel, ash or elm woven horizontally between them like basket-work, plastered with clay to make them weather-proof. They were rectangular single-storey buildings, varying in size from 3.8 metres by 3.2 metres to a spacious eight metres by six. The doorways had a wooden threshold with heavy oaken jambs on either side, slotted to receive the ends of the prefabricated wattlework walls. The stone-lined hearth, if there was one, was usually in the centre of the floor, and the floor itself would be strewn with rushes. The 'streets' in between the houses were exceptionally narrow pathways, no more than a metre wide, either stone-flagged or formed of short timber baulks laid transversely on parallel supporting beams of split tree-trunks, like a frontier-town boardwalk.

Here was where the craftsmen lived and worked. Generations of leather-workers had occupied one house, leaving a deep deposit of scrap leather and discarded soles and uppers. Another was a workshop for comb-makers and bone-workers, full of hundreds of discarded scraps and unfinished pieces. Woodworkers lived in another house, making lathe-turned bowls and platters. Metalwork was carried out in another house, as evidenced by a number of discarded moulds (including a soapstone matrix for casting Thór's Hammer amulets) and baked clay crucibles for smelting and casting bronze.

One highly significant group of discards amongst the debris consisted of a number of 'motif pieces' carved on bone as sketches and designs and finished patterns to be used later for casting metalwork. More than fifty of these motif pieces were found, covered with geometric or zoomorphic designs, all bearing a close affinity to the patterns of contemporary Irish metalwork and manuscript illuminations. They were found in late tenth-,

Bone 'motif pieces' from Dublin.

163

eleventh- and twelfth-century levels, and demonstrate the increasing in-fluence of Scandinavian art styles on native styles, fusing into a distinctive Hiberno-Viking style.

The Winetavern Street site, lower down the slope from the cathedral, provided one building that was significantly different in style from the High Street structures, and a good deal earlier. It seems to have been a workshop. Its floor, measuring 4.4 metres by 1.6 metres, was sunk deep into the boulder clay beneath the normal surface, about one metre below street level. Its walls were not of the wattle-and-post type, but were made of closely set vertical timber planks still standing to a height of about half a metre. In it was found an Anglo-Saxon decorated strap-tag of the late ninth century. The Winetavern Street site clearly indicated an earlier period of settlement than either of the High Street sites or Christ Church Place; it looks as if the Viking settlement of Dublin gradually spread up the slopes from the riverside.

Dr Ó Ríordáin's spectacular discoveries caused a tremendous stir in the world of Viking archaeology. They added hugely to our knowledge of the urban Viking, the Viking man-in-the-street, giving us an intimate picture of everyday life in the Viking Age that contemporary documents with their lurid emphasis on violence and destruction had always obscured. At the same time, Irish scholars like Dr A. T. Lucas and the historian Donnchadh Ó Corráin, to mention only two, were beginning to reassess the documentary 'evidence' and put it into more realistic perspective. And, gradually, the people of Dublin began to recognise more clearly the enormous contribution that the Vikings had made to their historical heritage.

In 1974 and 1975, three more plots were cleared by Dublin Corporation, to the east of the Winetavern Street site and almost adjacent to it. These plots, which comprised Wood Quay and Nos. 1 and 2 Fishamble Street, became known collectively as the Wood Quay site, and formed much the largest area that had yet been made available for archaeological excavation. By the summer of 1976, Patrick Wallace and Dr Ó Ríordáin had uncovered the various phases of the Norman wooden quays reaching down towards the Liffey, and the earliest Viking embankments – at which point the National Museum suddenly withdrew from the Wood Quay site.

This was the background to the 'Save Wood Quay' campaign, orches-trated by the Friends of Medieval Dublin with mass demonstrations and petitions, that culminated in the High Court hearing in June 1978. After taking evidence from eminent Irish, British, and Scandinavian scholars, Mr Justice Hamilton declared the whole of the Wood Quay site to the south of the City Wall a National Monument as defined by the National Monument Act of 1930.

As events turned out, this did not stop the redevelopment plans of Dublin Corporation; but it did gain valuable time for further excavation. Patrick Wallace started work again in November 1977, and although the

Supreme Court ruled in March 1979 that the Corporation could continue development work on the site, the archaeologists were given a series of extensions, until March 1980, to allow Wood Quay to be excavated and properly recorded at least. Provision was made for the stone wall of *c*.1100 to be preserved *in situ*, and for a new museum to be incorporated in the Civic Office complex so that the abundant finds from the site can be put on permanent display. They include a wide range of everyday domestic articles and ornaments decorated in the now-familiar Hiberno-Viking styles – and silver coins from the first Irish mint, established by the Norse King Sigtrygg Silk-Beard in Dublin in 997 in imitation of Anglo-Saxon coins.

This coinage seems to have been used to conduct trade with England, rather than with the native Irish. For a long time the Viking trade centres in Ireland, particularly Dublin, had closer ties with their Scandinavian homelands and with Scandinavian-held York (*cf* Ch. 5) than with their Irish neighbours, although they frequently became embroiled in the bewildering turmoil of dynastic and tribal feuds and battles that characterised Irish history of this period. Dublin remained the cockpit of Norse territorial ambitions not only for Ireland but also for the north of England and southern Scotland. A succession of Viking chieftains, both Norwegian and Danish, installed themselves as 'kings' of Dublin for longer or shorter periods; from Dublin, men like Ívar the Boneless attacked the Strathclyde fortress of Dumbarton in Scotland and dreamed ambitiously of a united Viking realm of Ireland and Northumbria (*cf* Ch. 5).

Occasionally, the Vikings would sally forth from Dublin in attempts to extend their territorial limits. But in 980 they were soundly defeated at the Battle of Tara by the Irish king, Maelschechnaill; and in 1014, in an epic encounter on Good Friday, they were defeated again at the Battle of Clontarf, outside Dublin – a battle which became part of the Saga tradition in both Ireland and Iceland. The victor, Brian Boru, who was killed in the hour of his triumph, was an Irish king who had long been jockeying for the position of High King of Ireland. He wanted Dublin as his own stronghold; the Vikings took up the challenge in what would be seen as a fight to the death for the soul and heart of Ireland.

Clontarf was the climax of the Viking Age in Ireland, but by no means the end of it. King Sigtrygg Silk-Beard of Dublin, who had gathered a great confederation of Viking allies from overseas for this confrontation, prudently watched the fighting from behind the walls of Dublin and would continue to reign there for several years despite the crushing of the Viking alliance. The days of the Vikings as a distinct and separate enclave on Irish soil were drawing to a close, however; yet there was no systematic attempt by Brian Boru's successors to extirpate the incomers or to drive them from Ireland for good. Dublin remained a Hiberno-Viking centre, and its wooden quaysides continued to be Ireland's major outlet to the mercantile world of which the Vikings had made it a part. Indeed, Clontarf was the

Excavation at the Wood Quay site in Dublin: woven wattle pathways and timber boardwalks being uncovered.

beginning of a new age of high prosperity for Dublin. The Vikings channelled their energies even more into commerce, as the Wood Quay excavation is so richly bearing out.

One of the Viking contingents in the alliance that supported Sigtrygg Silk-Beard at the Battle of Clontarf came, we are told in the Icelandic Sagas, from the Isle of Man. Two of their leaders are named – Bróðir and Óspak. Warned by omens of the slaughter to come, Óspak defected to Brian Boru's banner; but Bróðir stayed loyal to Sigtrygg, and even in defeat he carved himself a niche in history as the man who slew King Brian Boru. The Irish king had deliberately taken no part in the battle, because it took place on Good Friday; instead he had spent the day in prayer in a certain wood, protected only by the shield-wall of his personal retainers. Bróðir of Man, fleeing in the general Viking rout, came across this tableau in the wood, burst through the shield-wall, and hacked the king to death. He was quickly taken prisoner and put to a grisly death – his belly was slit open and his intestines pulled out of him as he was led round and round an oak tree, so the Sagas say. Brian Boru, on the other hand, achieved the instant immortality of legend.

The Isle of Man at the time was a kind of Ireland in miniature, a Viking kingdom in microcosm. We know very little about its early history at the

166

start of the Viking Age, except that it was inhabited by a native population of Christian Celts and that it lay in the path of the Viking surge to the west, in the middle of the Irish Sea basin. Like Ireland, it had a basically pastoral economy; and it can only be presumed, despite the lack of firm evidence either way, that it was subjected to the same pattern of raiding and settlement from 800 onwards by marauding Vikings in the western seas.

Coinage of Sigtrygg Silk-Beard of Dublin.

It is a very small island, only about 590 square kilometres in area. Geographically it occupies a pivotal position, very nearly equidistant from Ireland, Scotland, England and Wales, all of which can be clearly seen from the highest point of the island, the summit of Snaefell (620 metres). Local pride adds another realm to the list – the Kingdom of Heaven! To the north are flat glacial plains that provide excellent land for agriculture and long sandy beaches, ideal for beaching Viking ships; and it was in the north that the densest Viking settlement took place.

To the south-west lies Tynwald Hill at St John's. The name Tynwald is Norse in origin (*Thingvöllur*) and means, literally, 'Parliament Plain', like Dingwall in the north of Scotland and Tingwall in Shetland and, above all, Thingvellir in Iceland (*cf* Ch. 7). Traditionally, Tynwald Hill was the site of the Viking Assembly (*Thing*) which met in the open air every summer to govern and legislate and administer justice, like the *Althing* in Iceland; and every summer still, on Old Midsummer Day (5 July), the modern Parliament (known as the Tynwald) meets in open-air ceremony to promulgate the laws that have been passed during the year. The Isle of Man is still an independent sovereign country under the British Crown, a Crown dependency, in effect, but not part of the United Kingdom. It sends no MPs to Westminster, it is financially independent, and has a Governor appointed by the British Crown, because the British sovereign has had the title 'Lord of Mann' since 1765, when the 'regalities' of the island were sold to the Crown for £70,000. In 1828 the manorial rights were sold as well, for £417,000.

In July 1979, the Isle of Man celebrated the 'millennium' of the Tynwald, thereby claiming for it the distinction of being the oldest assembly in the world with unbroken traditions – the Icelandic *Althing*, established in 930, was suspended in 1798 and its proceedings transferred to the capital, Reykjavík. Everything was done with due pomp and panoply, in the presence of the 'Lord of Mann', Her Majesty Queen Elizabeth; and the sense of occasion was heightened by the arrival of *Ódin's Raven*, the millennium Viking ship, after its adventurous journey across the North Sea from Trondheim in Norway (*cf* Ch. 2).

There was no particular reason why the year 979 should have been chosen as the foundation year of the Tynwald by the Vikings. It was simply plucked from the empty air: the people of Man seem to have felt that it was time to have a millennium, so they just went ahead and had one! There are no historical records of any kind to corroborate the date; but it is not at all unlikely that the Tynwald, as a Viking assembly, was in existence

The terraced Tynwald Mound in the Isle of Man.

by the tenth century. The Viking settlement itself can certainly be dated to the late ninth.

Tynwald Hill itself and its associated ceremony may well be much older. It is now a tiered circular mound, some four metres high, standing at the end of a long processional way connecting it with the Royal Chapel of St John the Baptist. On ceremonial occasions, this processional way is strewn with rushes as the dignitaries walk from the church to take their places on the mound. The strewing of rushes is a practice that dates back to the Celtic Iron Age, much older than the Viking period; and it seems to hark back to a time when the islanders worshipped the mighty Celtic god Manannan Beg Mac y Lir, 'Little Manannan, the Son of the Sea', who was the guardian spirit of the island until he was banished by St Patrick. He seems to have been a very useful ally; according to one legend he once fended off a predatory Viking fleet by conjuring up a Manx fleet out of a handful of dead leaves.

The history of the mound itself stretches even further back into antiquity. It seems to have been, originally, a burial mound from the Bronze

168

Age, around 1500 BC. There is a matching mound just across the road to the north-west; and when the road was being built, it sliced right through this mound, exposing a massive stone cist-burial at its heart, in a textbook example of an archaeological section. So Tynwald Hill, too, is in all probability an ancient Bronze Age burial mound. That leaves open the question of the immaculate way in which the mound is now terraced. It is too regular, too classical, to be Viking – the Vikings tended to take things as they found them and put them to their own use, without any elaborate landscaping – and I suspect the tiers were probably made in the eighteenth century.

There has been considerable academic argument about the nature of the impact of the first Viking influx. Some place-name scholars, like Dr Margaret Gelling of Birmingham, past president of the Council for Name Studies in Great Britain and Ireland, have interpreted the lack of pre-Norse Celtic place-names as evidence that the Vikings more or less exterminated the native Manx population, and that the Gaelic language was only reintroduced after the end of the Norse kingdom in the thirteenth century when the last Scandinavian king of Man, Magnus (1252–66), finally came under the overlordship of King Alexander III of Scotland. Other scholars like Marshall Cubbon, the Director of the Manx Museum, dispute this interpretation; they think the place-name evidence is not compatible with the archaeological evidence, which suggests that there was in fact a substantial survival of the native population, with the Vikings moving in as a dominant social group.

Some twenty-five Viking graves or sites of gravefields are known on Man, and they suggest that the first arrivals married native Celtic women, who brought up their children or grandchildren as Christians and gave them Celtic names like Fiacc. Certainly the only unequivocally pagan Viking graves on Man date to the second half of the ninth century, like the splendid boat-burial at Balladoole in Arbory, in the south of the island, in which a man had been buried with his personal treasures and horse accoutrements (but no weapons, surprisingly) and a woman. The woman's skeleton showed no anatomical indications of the cause of her death; but its occurrence in the boat-burial is strongly suggestive of sacrifice.

One grave, however, does contain an unmistakable example of human sacrifice. It came from a burial mound in the farmyard of Ballateare in the north-western parish of Jurby, and has been dated to the second half of the ninth century. For many generations it stood undisturbed, despite its inconvenient location, because it was believed to be a 'fairy mound'. It was excavated in the late 1940s by the great German archaeologist Dr Gerhard Bersu, who had been interned on the Isle of Man during the war. In this mound a wealthy Viking farmer had been buried in a coffin with all his weapons – shield, three spears, and a richly ornamented sword still in its elaborate scabbard. This sword and one of the spears had been deliberately broken into three pieces before the interment – a ritual 'killing' of the

The Balladoole boat-burial: stone ship-setting at the left-hand edge of an Iron Age hill-fort.

weapons, designed either to warn off potential grave-robbers or to render them useless in case the dead man 'walked' after death to haunt the living. When the coffin had been lowered into the grave a circular mound of soil had been heaped over it; but before the mound had been completed, another body was laid to rest there. It was the body of a young woman in her twenties, lying face down with her arms raised above her head. The top of her head had been sliced off, very neatly, with an axe or a sword – perhaps the very sword found broken in the mound. The girl had obviously been a slave, a concubine perhaps, who had been chosen (or had chosen for herself) to accompany her master to the afterworld, along with an ox, a horse, a sheep and a dog. Her mutilated skull, carefully preserved in the Manx Museum in Douglas, is poignant evidence of the only fully authenticated case of a human Viking sacrifice yet found in these islands.

This period of 'high paganism' did not last long. By the tenth century the Vikings were burying their dead in Christian churchyards, but with some residual pagan burial customs like placing the dead man's sword in the grave as well. There are no signs of a religious crisis or forcible conversion such as happened in some of the other Scandinavian realms.

Nothing is known of the political position of the Isle of Man at this time. By the end of the ninth century it must be presumed that Man's strategic

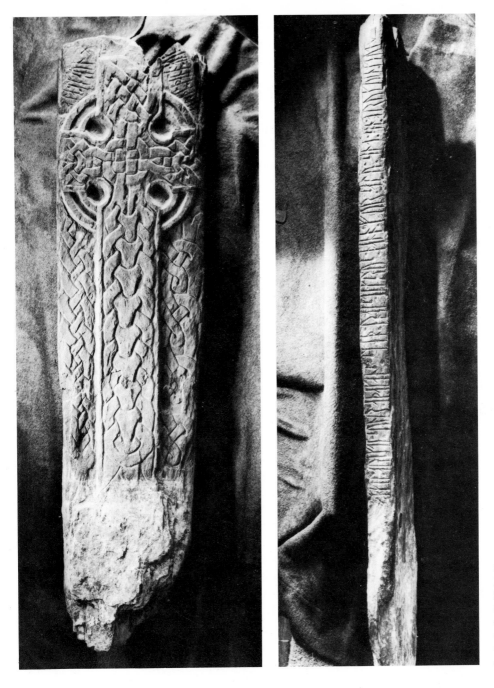

Gaut's Stone in Kirk Michael: the runic inscription runs up one edge of the stone, and is completed on the top corners of the front face – *'but Gaut made this and all in Man'*.

geographical importance in the continuing Norse struggle for the over-lordship of Ireland and the north of England was becoming recognised and exploited. Snorri Sturluson claims that King Harald Fine-Hair of Norway swooped on Man during his punitive expedition against the Viking nests west-over-sea (*cf* Ch. 2), only to find that all the Norsemen had fled at his approach. The documented history of Man does not start until 1066 with the *Chronicon Regum Manniae et Insularum* (*Chronicle of Mann*), which

171

opens with the arrival in 1066 of the Icelandic-born Godred Crovan, who had taken part, on the losing side, in the Battle of Stamford Bridge (*cf* Ch. 10). This Godred Crovan, who is undoubtedly a historical figure, managed to seize the kingdom by force of arms at his third attempt, at the Battle of Skyhill, near Ramsey on the north-east coast, in 1079; indeed, while the rest of Man was celebrating the Tynwald 'millennium' in 1979, the Manx Museum was more sedately celebrating the 900th anniversary of Skyhill with a special exhibition on the Norse heritage! Skyhill established the Norse dynastic rule of Godred Crovan and his descendants in Man for nearly two hundred years.

For the pre-1066 period we can only draw conclusions from the archaeological record, which is richer and more complete in Man than in any other Scandinavian colony in the west. One major source of information can be found in Man's collection of carved stone memorial crosses. They are the most striking of all the antiquities to be found on Man. Nearly two hundred of them have survived, standing huddled in churches and churchyards all over the island. They date from the Celtic early Christian period in the seventh century and through the period of the Viking settlement up to the early eleventh century.

The most interesting of them, historically speaking, is a tall grave-slab of dark local slate-stone which can now be found in a crowded corner of the transept of Kirk Michael, in the north-west of the island. There are no fewer than twelve of these crosses in Kirk Michael; but much the most celebrated of them is the so-called 'Gaut's Stone'. What singles it out is not the style of the carved ornamentation, which is robust and clear, but the runic inscription that runs the full length of one edge of the stone and continues on the front face above the cross-head: 'Maelbrigði, son of Athakan the smith, erected this cross for his own soul [saved from sin?]; *en Kaut kirthi : thano : auk ala : in Mann* – but Gaut made this and all in Man.'

Suddenly, out of the anonymous past, we have the name of the Viking sculptor who carved that memorial cross-slab: a man called Gaut. From another signed stone, at Kirk Andreas, we also know his surname: 'Gaut made [this], son of Björn from Kuli' (probably the Hebridean island of Coll). And so, because he claimed on the Kirk Michael stone that he himself had made 'all' the Norse runic crosses in Man at that time, around AD 950, we know that this Viking immigrant, Gaut Björnsson, was the founder of a whole industry in Man, a school of monumental sculpture that would flourish on the island for nearly a century and culminate in a rich flowering of artistic achievement. In his island 'studio' he fused traditional Celtic art motifs with the familiar decorative forms of Scandinavia, to create a distinctive interlacing style of his own that later sculptors of his school would develop and embellish. Gaut's own style was plain and simple, and so recognisable that several other unsigned stones have been attributed to him. His carvings represent a wheel-headed cross standing

out in low relief, decorated with plain interlacing bands. The shaft is decorated with a 'ring-chain' pattern formed of three interlacing chains, which would become a common feature of many later Manx crosses.

Other Manx stones are equally interesting from another point of view, because they show how the newly Christianised Viking sculptors decorated their stones with memories of their pagan mythology and heroic legends. Four picture-stones, at Jurby, Andreas, Maughold and Malew,

The 'Ragnarök Stone' at Kirk Andreas: Óðin being devoured by the wolf Fenrir.

173

show scenes from the legend of Sigurð the Dragon-Slayer, the hero who slew the dragon Fáfnir to rescue the Treasure of the Nibelungs; another, in Kirk Andreas, depicts Óðin the All-Father, naked and with a raven on his shoulder, gripped in the jaws of the ferocious wolf Fenrir which was destined to kill him in the Norse version of Armageddon, the Ragnarök (Doom of the Gods). The reverse shows a belted figure bearing aloft the Cross and the Book, trampling on a serpent and attended by a large fish (*ichthus*), an early Christian symbol. The juxtaposition of the two scenes represents most effectively the concept of Christ reigning in Óðin's stead.

There is a marked similarity in decorative style between the tenth-century Manx crosses and the Anglo-Scandinavian crosses found in the north of England; and it has been suggested that Gaut Björnsson may have learned the rudiments of his craft there. Despite the likely identification of his birthplace, *Kuli*, as the Hebridean island of Coll, some commentators think he may have been brought up in the north of England, in Cumberland, say, or Westmorland, where we know there was heavy infiltration and colonisation by Norsemen from Ireland and the Scottish islands early in the tenth century. Some think he may even have reached the Isle of Man as a fugitive after the Battle of *Brunanburh* in 937.

Brunanburh was a crucial battle. It ended in a devastating defeat for a major alliance of northern and western Vikings at the hands of the most charismatic of the tenth-century Anglo-Saxon warrior-kings, Athelstan of Wessex, grandson of Alfred the Great (*cf* Ch. 5).

After King Alfred's death in October 899, his children – his son King Edward the Elder of Wessex (899–924) and his daughter Æthelflaed, wife of the doughty Æthelred, ealdorman of Mercia – continued their father's strategy of containing and squeezing the Danes of the Danelaw by energetic attrition. After a decisive victory at the Battle of Tettenhall, near Wednesbury, in 910, they established fortified boroughs deeper and deeper into Danish-held territory, to consolidate every forward movement. By 918, the year of Æthelflaed's death, the whole of the Danelaw south of the Humber had been brought back under English rule. In 920 King Edward the Elder also received the formal submission of the Scots under King Constantine, the Britons of Strathclyde under King Owen, all the people of Northumbria, and the Viking Rögnvald from Dublin, newly installed as the Norse ruler of York. It was a remarkable achievement. By 918, the year of Æthelflaed's death, the whole of the Danelaw the Athelney marshes in Somerset, his son was established and accepted as the most powerful ruler in Britain.

Meanwhile, however, in the north of England, the Dublin–York axis had been growing stronger as waves of settlers from across the Irish Sea began to colonise the north-west and link up with the Norse residents in eastern Northumbria. A huge treasure-hoard of more than 7000 silver coins and pieces of hack-silver, weighing forty kilograms in all – much the largest Viking hoard ever found – was buried in Lancashire on the banks of the River Ribble at a place called Cuerdale around 903; the Cuerdale Hoard, now in the British Museum, was accidentally discovered by workmen in 1840, and must have been the pay-chest for a band of incomers from the Irish Sea. There was invasion of the Wirral by Norsemen from Ireland in the first decade of the tenth century, and the coastal areas of Lancashire were overrun. The Norse presence in the north-west is amply evidenced to this day by the huge number of Scandinavian place-names, and the vast quantities of Viking-style stone crosses, like the Gosforth Cross in Cumberland.

This was the major problem that had to be tackled by Edward the Elder's successor, his son Athelstan (924–39). He was a vigorous, flaxen-haired man who had inherited not only his father's strategic sagacity but also his grandfather's humanity and interest in the arts and devotion to the Church. He had been brought up in his aunt's court in Mercia, and was therefore more than acceptable to the Mercians, traditionally hostile to Wessex kings. He assiduously cultivated good relations with foreign rulers; he was on the warmest terms with the veteran King Harald Fine-Hair of Norway, who even sent his youngest son, Hákon, to be fostered at Athelstan's court – Hákon Athelstan's-*fóstri*, as history would call him. But when Athelstan came to deal with the Viking menace in the north, it was another sort of ally that he cultivated, as Professor Peter Sawyer of Leeds University has emphasised in his book *From Roman Britain to Norman England* (1978) – St Cuthbert of Lindisfarne.

St Cuthbert (d.687), prior and patron saint of the Holy Island of Lindisfarne, had been the posthumous victim of the first Viking raids on England (*cf* Ch. 2). His *Life* by the Venerable Bede had spread his fame throughout England and the Continent. His relics had survived unscathed that first assault on Lindisfarne in 793; later, however, they were taken to the mainland for safety, first to Norham on the Tweed, then to Carlisle, and then, after seven years of wandering, to Chester-le-Street, before finding a permanent resting-place in Durham Cathedral.

It did not take Athelstan long to make his first moves towards the north. In 926 he gave one of his sisters in marriage to Sigtrygg, Rögnvald's successor as Norse ruler of York. The arrangement did not last, for Sigtrygg died the following year, whereupon his son by a former wife, Ólaf Sigtryggsson, supported by his uncle Guthfrith, the Norse king of Dublin, tried to claim his inheritance by force. Athelstan promptly invaded and expelled them both from York, razed its defences, and assumed the over-lordship of Northumbria. Seven years later he consolidated his northern position by a sweeping invasion of Scotland; his army harried unopposed as far as Kincardineshire, north of the Firth of Forth, while his fleet ravaged the eastern coast all the way north to Caithness.

It was on this northern expedition that Athelstan went out of his way to patronise and encourage Northumbrian cults, including that of the potent English saint, Cuthbert. St Cuthbert's shrine at Chester-le-Street had lost

Coinage of Sigtrygg One-Eye of York, King Athelstan's brother-in-law.

estates to the Vikings, seized by the pagan Rögnvald of York and distributed amongst his followers; so Cuthbert afforded a powerful patriotic rallying-point against the heathen invaders. To the shrine of St Cuthbert Athelstan gave the most magnificent gifts; apart from church plate, money and the royal estate of Wearmouth, he gave several books, including Bede's metrical and prose *Life of St Cuthbert* complete with an illumination depicting Athelstan making the presentation (this copy still survives at Corpus Christi College, Cambridge), and some valuable vestments, including a stole and maniple of silk and gold thread that are now preserved in the Treasury of Durham Cathedral. According to inscriptions on both vestments, they had been made at the behest of Athelstan's aunt, Æthelflaed of Mercia.

Also in 934, Ólaf Guthfrithsson, son of that Guthfrith whom Athelstan had expelled from York in 927, succeeded to the leadership of the Dublin Vikings. Soon after he came to power he raised a great alliance against Athelstan. He set sail from Ireland with a large fleet and landed in the north-east of England, where he was joined by King Constantine of the Scots, still smarting from the 934 invasion, and the Britons of Strathclyde under King Owen. Thus reinforced, the Viking army swept through York and headed for the Midlands.

Athelstan responded by raising all his Mercian and West Saxon levies and marching out to meet them, his half-brother Prince Edmund at his side. The armies met at a place the English called *Brunanburh*, which would be commemorated in verse and folk-memory as the bloodiest encounter yet fought on English soil:

> Athelstan the king,   lord of earls,
> And ring-giver to men,   his brother beside him,
> Edmund the Ætheling,   won undying glory
> In furious battle   with the blades of their swords
> At Brunanburh: burst through the shield-wall,
> Hewed at the bucklers   with well-forged swords,
> The sons of Edward . . .
>
>   . . . Many a man lay there,
> Spreadeagled by spears,   northern warriors
> Pierced through shields;   Scotsmen too,
> Wearied with war. . . .
> And so the brothers,   both together,
> King and Ætheling,   returned to their home,
> The land of Wessex,   triumphant in war.
> They left behind them,   to enjoy the corpses,
> The horn-beaked raven,   black of plumage,
> The white-tailed eagle,   garbed in grey,
> The hungry war-hawk,   and that dark beast
> The forest wolf.   Never before
> In all this island,   as ancient sages

'BITTER IS THE WIND'

Tell us in books,   was an army put
To greater slaughter . . .   (*Anglo-Saxon Chronicle*)

Unusually, that contemporary poem, *The Battle of Brunanburh*, was incorporated directly into the *Chronicle* for 937, an indication of the great importance that the Anglo-Saxons attached to Athelstan's crushing victory. Apart from that, we know very little about the battle itself. Five kings and seven earls from Ireland died, although Ólaf Guthfrithsson survived and made good his escape back to Dublin. Constantine of the Scots survived, but his son did not. But no one has the faintest idea *where* the battle took place. The name *Brunanburh* has disappeared, its location totally forgotten, and scholars have attempted to locate it in various ingenious places anywhere between the Solway Firth and Derby or Birmingham.

But out of the mists of uncertainty that shroud the circumstances of the battle there looms one great figure, a towering crag of a man, larger than life and twice as ugly. His name was Egil Skallagrímsson, warrior and poet from Iceland.

Egil is the eponymous hero of a magnificent Icelandic Saga, *Egil's Saga*, written, it is generally believed, by Snorri Sturluson. According to the Saga, Egil Skallagrímsson fought on the winning side, on Athelstan's side, as a Viking mercenary in the battle at *Brunanburh*. Egil Skallagrímsson stayed on in England long enough to collect rich gifts (and compensation for his brother, who was killed in the battle) from the victorious Athelstan, and then returned to Iceland; but later he would make a spectacular re-entry on to the English scene, in the royal hall of the Viking kings of York.

Egil's Saga is a great literary epic, an archetypal story of Viking derring-do and heroic passion set against the backcloth of tenth-century Anglo-Scandinavian history. It tells how Egil's father and grandfather had been hounded from Norway for defying the growing power of King Harald Fine-Hair, and emigrated to Iceland, to the manor-farm they founded at Borg, in Borgafjörður. Egil himself had later gone out to Norway to seek fame and fortune; but he in turn had fallen foul of royal authority there, this time in the person of Harald Fine-Hair's eldest son who had succeeded him, King Eirík Blood-Axe (*blóðöxi*) and his imperious consort, Queen Gunnhild. In a flurry of violent raids on royal estates, Egil killed many of the king's men, one of the king's sons and one of Queen Gunnhild's brothers, and then left Norway, an outlaw, after delivering a final, mortal insult: he erected a 'scorn-pole' on which he carved runic curses against Eirík Blood-Axe and all his kin, and called on the land-spirits of Norway to drive him from his throne.

He was a compelling, complex character, Egil Skallagrímsson: a man of great violence and greed, yet capable of deep and abiding love, a crude peasant with an extraordinary genius for poetry – poetry that could be as tender as his battle-rage was furious, as when he lamented the death of his sons by drowning and railed against his god, Óðin:

VIKINGS!

For my line now	has reached its end,
Felled to the ground	like windblown wood;
Who else so bold,	what other thane,
Shall stand by me	in time of need?
If only my wrongs	I could right with the sword,
The ocean god	would drown in his blood;
Bare now I know	and open stands
That breach in my sons	the sea won in me.
Me has the ocean	sadly plundered,
Cruel to tell	of fallen kinsfolk.
My boy is come	to Óðin's homestead,
My wife's own son	to seek his kin.
Friends I was	with the Lord of Spears;
Trusting I was,	and kept my faith.
But now the All-Father,	God of Battle,
Has turned his face	away from me . . .

(*Egil's Saga*: from *Sonatorrek*)

Egil Skallagrímsson: seventeenth-century manuscript illumination from a collection of Sagas of Icelanders.

In Norway, Eirík Blood-Axe's reign proved troubled, and short. Before his accession, he had justified his nickname by killing off as many of his half-brothers and potential rivals for the throne as possible. He made enemies of every noble family in the land. In 947 a claimant arrived to challenge him for the crown: Harald Fine-Hair's youngest son, Hákon Athelstan's-*fóstri*. Without friends to turn to, Eirík Blood-Axe fled the land and made his way to Northumbria and York.

Despite the defeat at *Brunanburh*, the Northumbrian Vikings were still at large, York still the centre of their ambitions. After Athelstan's death in 939, Norse kings ruled in York again, precariously and chaotically; to the Norsemen of Northumbria the arrival of a 'real' king of the royal house of Norway gave promise of security and independence from Wessex, and they immediately accepted Eirík as their king.

And then, suddenly, Egil Skallagrímsson of Borg arrived from nowhere, it seemed, and walked into the royal hall in York, straight into the clutches of his arch-enemy, Eirík Blood-Axe. He had sailed from Iceland to rejoin his former patron, King Athelstan, apparently unaware of the fact that Athelstan had been dead by then for nearly ten years. On the way south his ship had been wrecked at the mouth of the Humber, eighty kilometres away from York. But Egil's pride would not allow him to go skulking through Eirík's kingdom like a craven; and besides, he felt a strange compulsion to meet his adversary again in a last clash of wills, the ultimate confrontation between commoner and king.

Queen Gunnhild wanted him put to death at once: 'Have you forgotten, king, what Egil has done? Killed your friends and kinsmen, yes, and more than that, your own son? And heaped scorn upon your person? Was there ever such an insult to a king?'

But Eirík Blood-Axe wavered, and granted him a night's reprieve. Egil spent the night, we are told, labouring for dear life itself to compose a twenty-verse eulogy, a *drápa* of praise to assuage the king's wrath. And next morning, in the king's hall, he delivered the poem he had prepared, the *Höfuðlausn* (*Head-Ransom*):

> Heed now, O king,   what honour I bring;
> Silence I pray   while I speak my lay,
> Your exploits to tell   which all men know well.
> Only Óðin can say   where the dead lay.
>
> Sword-metal pealed   on rim of shield,
> The king advanced   while axes danced.
> Distant shore   heard clamour of war;
> Blood ran free   beyond the sea.
>
> I praise the king   throughout his land,
> And keenly sing   his open hand –
> His hand so free   with golden spoil
> But vice-like, he   grips his own soil . . .
>
> To praise my lord   this tight mouth broke,
> The word-floods poured,   the still tongue spoke;
> From my poet's breast   these words took wing:
> Now all the rest   may learn to sing.
>
> (*Egil's Saga*: from *Höfuðlausn*)

In English translation it cannot help sounding like doggerel, because the intricate metaphors and kennings of Viking skaldic poetry have to be reduced to banality to make the sense intelligible. But as stanza followed clashing stanza in the original, it became clear that the poem represented a revolutionary technical innovation in Old Norse poetry. In addition to the internal rhyme and assonance within the lines, and the alliteration that welded the half-lines together, Egil had introduced to Viking poetry, for the first time, end-rhyme as well – a technique he may have learned from Latin hymns in Anglo-Saxon churches during his service with King Athelstan. It was striking evidence of the way in which Anglo-Saxon and Scandinavian cultures could fertilise one another, and the effect of this virtuoso, close-clenched performance must have electrified the listeners.

It certainly had its effect on Eirík Blood-Axe. He sat bolt upright throughout, glaring at Egil. He must have realised that the eulogistic phrasing was perfunctory, a flowery composition lacking conviction or particularity. Yet as he listened to this *tour de force* of skaldic ingenuity, he must also have realised that his own immortality was now assured through that one poem by his enemy. And in return he gave Egil his life.

Coinage of Eirík Blood-Axe of York.

179

Eirík's own life had not long to run by then. In 948 he was expelled from York at the instigation of Athelstan's brother, King Eadred. Four years later he was back, only to be expelled again in 954. As he left his land, he was ambushed at Stainmore in Yorkshire and killed after a valiant defence. With his death, the line of Norse kings of York came to an end, and with it an end to Norse ambitions for an independent Viking kingdom based on York and Dublin. It was the end of one Viking era – but not the last one.

After Eirík's expulsion, Northumbria was governed by a succession of earls ruling nominally as deputies of the kings of England. England was a single united kingdom at last, and for a quarter of a century, under strong kings like the young King Edgar, Athelstan's nephew (959–75), the country enjoyed a long period of relative internal peace and respite from attacks from abroad.

In 978, however, a child came to the throne, Edgar's ten-year-old son Æthelred, whom history would know as Æthelred the Unready (*unraed*, the Rede-less, the No-Counsel). Within two years of his accession, Vikings were on the prowl again across the North Sea, and England would be treated to nearly four decades of mounting pressure from Scandinavia again, culminating in total conquest and subjection under a foreign king – Knút (Canute) the Great of Denmark (*cf* Ch. 9).

7

'An island called Thule'

Iceland is the youngest country in the world. Formed during a succession of titanic volcanic eruptions only twenty million years ago, it is a mere stripling in geological terms. It was still uninhabited when it was 'discovered' in the ninth century AD, first by occasional Irish monks and then, more purposefully, by the Vikings. Colonists from Norway created in Iceland a microcosm of the Viking world: the only independent Viking nation, built on virgin territory, that has survived to this day.

It must always have seemed a rather unstable place, in the literal sense of the term. The first settlers found that it tended to move disconcertingly beneath their feet because it was still in the process of creation, with an earthquake or a volcanic eruption every five years or so. It has been rightly called nature's geological laboratory. The whole vast island fumed with raw energy: spouting hot-springs, bubbling mud-pools, dormant volcanoes under a dome of ice waiting to unleash their power. Iceland must have presented an alarming chaos of fire and frost, a somewhat dubious prospect for settlers; but it also gave their mythology, their understanding of Creation, a new relevance and immediacy:

> In the beginning of Time
> There was nothing,
> Neither sand, nor sea,
> Nor cooling surf.
> There was no Earth,
> No Upper Heaven,
> No blade of grass,
> Only the Great Void –
>
> Until the gods
> Lifted up land,
> Made Middle Earth
> A matchless place.
> Sun shone from the south
> On a world of rock;
> From the ground there grew
> Green fields.
>
> (*Völuspá – The Sibyl's Prophecy*)

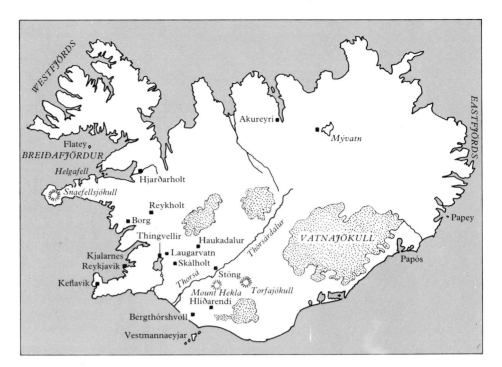

Iceland in the Viking Age.

Iceland also tended to move around the northern oceans in the inventory of geographical knowledge amongst the ancients. It used to be thought of as a place called Thule, *ultima Thule* indeed. The name first cropped up as long ago as 330 BC, when a resourceful navigator, Pytheas of Marseilles, was commissioned by his local city fathers to reconnoitre a new trade-route to the tin and amber markets of northern Europe, not overland but by sea. His report on his voyage only survives in fragmentary references in later geographical works, especially in the massive *Geographica* of Strabo of Pontus, who called Pytheas 'a man upon whom no reliance can be placed'. According to Pytheas, 'Thule' lay six days' sail north of Britain; it was a sunless place in winter, whose inhabitants lived off millet, herbs, berries and roots. Further north there were volcanoes erupting under glaciers, and the sea congealed into a primeval jelly.

Pytheas seems to have been describing the arctic regions of Norway, not Iceland, which was uninhabited at the time. But the name of Thule stuck to Iceland. It looks as if the Romans knew of it, because four copper Roman coins from the period AD 270–305 have been found at scattered sites in the south of Iceland; this was a time of peak Roman naval power in Britain under the command of Carausius (AD 286–293), and the most likely explanation of the presence of these coins in Iceland is that they were left or lost from a Roman ship on long-range patrol, and then hoarded as souvenirs by the first Viking settlers.

The Venerable Bede, writing in England in the early eighth century, applied the name Thule to Iceland, and mentioned actual sailings to and from it in his time. A century later, in AD 825, the Irish cleric Dicuil in his geographical treatise *De mensura orbis terrae* reported that Irish monks in

182

search of solitude had been to Iceland/Thule, and returned to tell the tale:

It is now thirty years since priests who lived in that island from the first of February to the first of August told me that not only at the summer solstice but on the days to either side of it the setting sun hides itself at the evening hour as if behind a little hill, so that no darkness occurs during that very brief period; but whatever task a man wishes to perform, even to picking the lice from his shirt, he can manage as precisely as in broad daylight . . .

These Irish hermits were known to the early Icelandic historians as *papar* − 'little fathers'. Ari the Learned in his *Íslendingabók*, written around 1130, reports that they departed the country when the Vikings arrived − in some haste, it appears, because they left behind them 'Irish books and bells and croziers', from which it could be deduced where they had come from. There are also place-names in the south-east of Iceland that seem to commemorate their presence, like Papey and Papós, although no archaeological traces of their lonely vigils on the coasts of Iceland have yet been found.

The renaming of Thule as 'Iceland' did not happen until the Viking Age. *Landnámabók* (*Book of Settlements*) records two early explorers: a Norwegian Viking called Naddod who named the country *Snæland*

Glaciers on the south coast: a first glimpse of Iceland for the seafarer.

('Snowland'), and a man of Swedish stock, Garðar Svafarsson, who re-named it *Garðarshólm* ('Garðar's Isle'). Neither new name caught on; but word went quickly round the Northlands that there was land for the taking if anyone had need of it.

One of the men who took up the challenge, according to *Landnámabók*, was a Norwegian called Flóki Vilgerðarson, 'a great Viking', around the year 860. He took livestock with him, for he planned to settle permanently. Like a latter-day Noah he also took three birds, three ravens dedicated to Óðin, to help him find the way, 'because in those days ocean-going mariners in the Northlands had no lodestone'. For that reason he became known as *Hrafna-Flóki* (Ravens-Flóki).

He headed first for Shetland, where an almost unrecognisable place-name still enshrines a poignant memory of his visit: Girlsta Loch, just north of Lerwick, the deepest in Shetland. In the dark waters of this loch, Flóki lost a daughter in a drowning accident; her name was Geirhild, and she is still remembered in the name of the loch, now reduced by custom and corruption to Girlsta. From Shetland, Flóki sailed to the Faroes, some 300 kilometres away, a voyage for which he required neither lodestone nor ravens. Here he lost another daughter, this time by the happier accident of marriage; 'from her was descended Thránd of Gata' (modern Syðrugöta), according to *Landnámabók*.

Today the Faroes are a self-governing state within the kingdom of Denmark, still peopled by the pure-bred descendants of Ravens-Flóki and Thránd of Gata and other Viking settlers. It is a marvellous place to visit, strong and self-reliant in its traditions. The small inshore Faroese fishing boats, elegant and seaworthy, still echo their Viking origins. The colourful ballad-dances, intricate ring-dances performed to the accompaniment of sung folk-ballads, keep alive the memories of stirring events from a heroic past. The capital, Tórshavn, makes mercifully few concessions to the demands of modern packaged tourism. The Faroese are their own people.

We do not have any very clear idea of what the Faroes were like when Ravens-Flóki cast anchor there around 860. The archaeological evidence is thin, and the documentary evidence insubstantial. In his *De mensura orbis terrae*, Dicuil claimed that 'a certain holy man' had informed him that Irish anchorites had lived there for about a hundred years before the arrival of the Vikings drove them out:

> But even as they have been constantly uninhabited since the world's beginning, so now because of Norse pirates they are empty of an-chorites, but full of innumerable sheep and a great many different kinds of sea-birds.

The sea-birds are still there in their millions, making the Faroes an ornithologist's paradise. And the sheep are still there – approximately 70,000 of them, compared with a human population today of about 40,000; indeed, the very name of 'Faroes' bestowed by the Vikings (*Færeyjar*) means 'Sheep Islands'. These sheep may have been introduced by Dicuil's *papar*, but it is impossible to be certain; the most recent research suggests that farming activity in the Faroes started before 700, and on a scale that indicates deliberate settlement rather than casual habitation; perhaps the Norsemen were migrating west across the North Sea very much earlier than we are led to believe by the documentary sources.

Systematic archaeological excavations in the Faroes only began as recently as 1940, but already several important farm-sites of unmistakably Norse character have been unearthed. The first major site to be investigated was at Kvívík on the western side of the main island, Streymoy, in 1942. It was a very large one-roomed long-house measuring some 22 metres by 5.5, with curving cavity walls of stone infilled with soil and gravel: a classic example of a Viking hall, with raised platforms along the side, a floor of stamped clay and sand on a flagstone base, and a long-fire down the middle with a sunken stone-lined ember pit. Beside it was another building in the form of a mini long-house, measuring 10 metres by 3.5, which served as a cow-byre and barn; there was a stone dung-channel running down the middle, with stalls on both sides to accommodate up to twelve cows. The foundations of these buildings are now carefully conserved with a covering of turf, and the hundreds of finds are on display in the Føroya Fornminnisavn (Faroese Ethnological Museum) in Tórshavn. These finds prove that Kvívík was a busy and self-sufficient homestead: there were stone sinkers for fishing-lines (fishing is still the mainstay of the Faroese economy); there were spindle whorls and loom-weights to work wool into textiles (there is an old saying that 'Wool is the gold of the Faroes'); there were sewing-needles and leather shoes and wooden toys, and also some objects that had been imported – beads of amber and silver-foiled glass, evidence of trade and cultural contacts with the rest of the Viking world.

Other equally significant Viking Age excavations have followed since then. In 1956, the first Viking cemetery to be found in the Faroes was excavated at Tjørnuvík, the most northerly village on Streymoy. At least twelve people lay buried there, including a grown woman whose skull is labelled in the museum in Tórshavn as 'the oldest person found in the Faroes'; her grave has been dated to the tenth century. One of the grave-finds was a ring-headed bronze pin with an ornamented head, with a shred of cloth still adhering to it.

Other Viking Age habitations have now been excavated at Fuglafjørður on Eysturoy, at Sandur on Sandoy, at Sandavágur and Sørvágur on the island of Vágar (where the airport is located), and at Syðrugöta on Eysturoy – which reminds us of Thránd of Gata. One outstanding feature of all these dwellings was the liberal use of wood for the internal structure, in a country where not a single tree grows; such lavish importing of building-timber betokens a level of domestic prosperity one would hardly expect in the forbidding environment of the Faroes.

But the most impressive monument of past times in the Faroes is of stone – the unfinished cathedral intended for the bishopric at Kirkjubøur, at the southern end of Streymoy. It was built, or rather begun, late in the thirteenth century by the most formidable of the early Faroese bishops, Bishop Erlendur (1268–1308). It is an unaisled rectangular structure, with a two-storeyed annexe which is commonly interpreted as a lady chapel but which may have been simply a chapter house for the use of the canons. The architecture of the whole building, in early Gothic style, is of the highest standard, as befitted a bishop of whom it was recorded that 'more than all his predecessors, he enriched the Faroese church with privileges, lands, and worldly goods'. But he was also a man of controversy and conflict, constantly embroiled in feuds, and the same records report that 'in his time the episcopal church and palace were destroyed by a treacherously raised fire'. Perhaps all this feuding explains why the building of the Kirkjubøur cathedral came to an abrupt end before it was completed – there is no evidence of flooring or altars, it is uncertain whether it was ever roofed, and although there are eight consecration crosses on the walls, the church itself was never consecrated, according to the eminent Faroese archaeologist Sverri Dahl. But even though it was never used, it is a magnificent memorial to the power and drive of the Medieval Church in the Faroes.

These material remains tend to match – very roughly – the kind of

Ring-dancing in the Faroes, to the accompaniment of sung ballads.

OPPOSITE ABOVE Colt Island, opposite Kirkjubøur in the Faroes.

OPPOSITE BELOW The excavated Viking long-house at Kvívík in the Faroes.

picture presented by the limited documentary sources. The main source is an Icelandic Saga written early in the thirteenth century called *Færeyinga saga* (*Saga of the Faroemen*), which is not so much a history as a historical romance.

Færeyinga saga is essentially a dramatised story of a power struggle between two prominent Faroese landowners late in the tenth century: the hero Sigmund Brestisson of Skúvoy and the shrewd and ruthless opponent who eventually destroyed him – none other than Thránd of Gata. The author does not seem to have known the Faroes personally – his geography is woeful – but to have relied entirely on oral traditions. One of these traditions was that the first settler, around AD 825, had been a man called Grím Kamban, of whom nothing is known; another was that the most important dynasty in the Faroes was the Gata family of Syðrugöta, and that its most celebrated scion was Thránd of Gata, descendant of the daughter of Ravens-Flóki.

After his daughter's wedding, Ravens-Flóki sailed off from the Faroes. He knew that his course should be north-west, but he did not know how far away his destination lay. It was time to use his ravens. Soon after leaving the Faroes he released the first bird; it flew straight back the way they had come. A little later he released the second bird; it flew high into the air, took a good look round, and returned to the ship. When he released the third raven, however, it flew straight ahead and disappeared over the horizon. Much encouraged, Flóki set course in the same direction, and soon they sighted land, 400 kilometres from the Faroes:

> They made land at Vatnsfjörður on Barðaströnd [on the west coast]. The fjord teemed with fish of all kinds, and they were so busy fishing that they paid no heed to gathering hay for the winter; and that winter, all their livestock died. The following spring was an extremely cold one. Flóki climbed a high mountain and looked north towards the coast, and saw a fjord choked with drift-ice; and so they called the country *Ísland* [Iceland], and that has been its name ever since.
>
> (*Landnámabók*)

So severe was that spring and summer that it was not until the following year that he was able to return to Norway, disgusted with the country he had tried to settle in – 'he did not have a good word to say of it', according to *Landnámabók*. But he had two companions with him who redressed the balance. One of them, a man called Herjólf, said it had advantages as well as disadvantages; while the other, Thórólf, said that in the land they had found 'butter dripped from every blade of grass'.

Thórólf Butter, as he came to be called, was no doubt exaggerating somewhat to make up for Flóki's surly disillusionment. But Iceland in the ninth century was a more inviting place than it seems now at first glance. The climate was appreciably warmer, by an average of 1° Centigrade, which makes quite a difference at those northern latitudes. And although the highlands in the heart of the country, then as now, were barren and uninhabitable, the coastal plains and valleys were covered with birch trees and scrub willow: 'In those days, Iceland was wooded between mountain and shore,' says Ari the Learned in *Íslendingabók*. Modern botanical research suggests that twenty-five per cent of the land was tree-covered in those days; today, the figure is only one per cent.

Within a very few years of Flóki's abortive attempt at colonisation, new settlers were streaming across the ocean to take land in Iceland. According to the early Icelandic historians, the main reason was political: they were refugees from the growing power of the crown in Norway, where King Harald Fine-Hair was relentlessly subjugating the local chieftains to his rule (*cf* Ch. 2). Men who prided themselves on their noble birth and independent spirit resented this new royal despotism; and rather than knuckle under, they sold up their ancestral lands, loaded their ships with family and friends, slaves and dependants, livestock and farming gear, and set sail for a land where they could be free and independent once again. It is no doubt an idealised picture; their motives must sometimes have been less high-minded. But that was their story, and today's Icelanders are sticking to it!

The ships these early settlers used for the voyages to the west, to the Faroes and Iceland, were not the classic Viking longships like the Gokstad ship. Despite the epic achievements of Captain Magnus Andersen's voyage across the Atlantic in a Gokstad replica in 1893, and the North Sea crossing by the Isle of Man millennium boat in 1979, longships of the Gokstad type were not designed to be deep-sea boats. They were not the merchantmen, the all-purpose cargo ships that tramped the Viking trade routes; they were built to prowl in coastal waters.

The maid-of-all-work of the northern seas was a buxom, swan-breasted cargo boat called a *knörr*, much more bulky than the lean-lined longships. For centuries, the *knörr* was only a word in the dictionary, and a vivid metaphor (in its genetival form) for a generously-endowed woman: *knarrar-bringja*, '*knörr*-breasted'. But in 1962, the dictionary word became actual when a Viking Age *knörr* was salvaged, almost entire, from the waters of Roskilde Fjord in Denmark.

Artist's impression of the deep-sea *knörr*, the kind of cargo vessel the Vikings used for their Atlantic voyages.

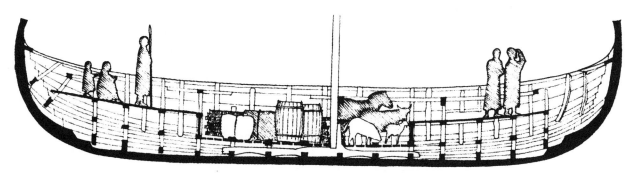

The unfinished cathedral at Kirkjubøur in the Faroes.

This *knörr* was one of five Viking ships that had been scuttled to block the fjord against enemy attack in the middle of the eleventh century (*cf* Ch. 10) – a veritable underwater ships' cemetery. In a brilliant salvage operation directed by Dr Ole Crumlin-Pedersen of Denmark, all five ships were retrieved – or what was left of them, at least. A magnificent new museum was built at Roskilde to receive, conserve, reconstruct and display them. The first ship to be restored there was the *knörr*.

She is not a beautiful boat, like Gokstad; she is plain and functional. But every time I visit Roskilde Museum, it gives me a great thrill to see and stroke her, to touch the chisel-marks of the Viking shipwrights who fashioned her, to experience the very feel of Viking history in her battered timbers. She is unexpectedly short and stubby, only 16.5 metres long compared with the 23.3 metres of Gokstad; she was built of pine with a keel of oak, with a fixed half-deck at prow and stern and an open hold amidships where the mast stood firmly in its socket in the keelson. Stranded in the Viking Ship Museum at Roskilde, she looks clumsy and cumbersome; in the water, it would have been a different story.

How did the Vikings find their way across uncharted oceans? That has been a matter of great argument among scholars. Much has been made of a so-called 'bearing-dial' found in a Norse ruin in Greenland in 1948; this was a part of a notched oaken disc with a hole in the centre. It was published by a Danish mariner, C.V. Sølver, with a drawing of a plausible-looking reconstruction, complete with thirty-two points of the compass, a handle-shaft, a shadow-pin (like a sun-dial), and a course indicator. But scholars no longer accept this as a possible representation of a Viking navigational aid.

Much has also been made of the supposed properties of the Icelandic 'sun-stone' (*sólarsteinn*), a translucent piece of calcite (Iceland spar) whose crystalline structure polarises the light and can theoretically pinpoint the position of the sun in overcast or even foggy conditions. There is a striking reference to its use in Snorri Sturluson's *St Ólaf's Saga* (one of the Sagas in *Heimskringla*); it tells how St Ólaf, King of Norway (1014–30), was sailing one day in fog and heavy snow. The mate told him there was nothing to worry about, since he could locate the sun with his sun-stone – 'And then the king picked up the sun-stone and saw how the sun was radiating, and from that he concluded that this was true.' Unfortunately, today's scholars do not rate the so-called sun-stone as a Viking Age navigational aid either, any more than the so-called 'bearing-dial'; nothing is sacrosanct in the severe world of scholarship. So we have to fall back on the age-old wisdom garnered by men of the sea: visual observation of the sun and the stars when possible, the flight of birds, the appearance of seaweed, the smell and feel of the sea – and blind faith. All we can be sure of is that it was never easy, usually hazardous, and quite often fatal.

Early in the 870s, the man celebrated by Icelandic historical tradition as Iceland's First Settler approached his appointed land, sailing in a small

Restoration experts at the Roskilde Ship Museum rebuilding the *knörr* salvaged from Roskilde Fjord in 1962.

191

knörr crammed with his family, his farm-hands, and a cargo of seasick sheep and cattle; everyone cold, wet and uncomfortable, but filled none the less with a sense of mission. His name was Ingólf Arnarson, and he came from western Norway. He and his family had fallen foul of powerful men in their district, so they decided to get out while the going was good and emigrate to the newly-discovered island of which they had heard such mixed reports.

Ingólf Arnarson was not the sort of man to tackle an enterprise of this kind lightly. He and his brother-in-law, Hjörleif, made a preliminary reconnaissance to Flóki's Iceland, and decided that they liked what they saw. On his return to Norway he made sacrifice to the gods to discover what the future held in store for him, and the oracles told him that his destiny lay in Iceland. When he and his loaded *knörr* caught sight of the south-eastern coast, he observed another prudent ritual; he cast overboard the sacred carved pillars of his high-seat from his home in Norway, vowing that he would make his home wherever the pillars happened to be washed ashore. He was sending them ahead as hostages to fortune, as ambassadors, to ask the natural guardian spirits of the country to indicate where they would find his landing acceptable.

It took Ingólf three years to find the pillars, moving slowly westwards along the south coast, searching all the time. Eventually they were discovered lying on the shore of a wide sheltered bay on the south-west coast, ringed by distant mountains and carpeted with rolling meadows that steamed with the vapour of innumerable natural hot-springs. So he named the place *Reykjavík* – 'Steamy Bay' – and there he built his homestead.

It was the start of an enterprise that was astonishing in retrospect: the translation of a whole European society with all its deep-rooted traditions, its culture, its technology, its social customs, hundreds of kilometres across an almost unknown ocean into an empty and not always inviting island.

A statue of Ingólf Arnarson now stands on a grassy hillock, *Arnarhóll* (Eagle's Knoll), overlooking Reykjavík's bustling modern harbour. It commemorates the precise spot where his high-seat pillars were found on the shore. But it was not a city or a town that Ingólf founded at Reykjavík – that would come much later, almost a thousand years later, in fact, by a casual accident of history that would turn the manor-lands of Reykjavík into Iceland's capital.

Archaeological excavations at gap-sites in the city centre in the 1960s and 1970s by the National Museum of Iceland have now found traces of a very early settlement farm, dating from the late ninth century, which are consistent with the documentary accounts of Ingólf's arrival. It now seems certain that Ingólf's home-field, where he grew his hay, was the present city-centre square, Austurvöllur, fronted by the Cathedral and the Parliament House building beside the Tjörn (Pond). His homestead was sited under the southern end of Aðalstraeti ('Main Street'), which runs from Austurvöllur down towards the harbour. The traces that have been found

OPPOSITE City-centre excavations in Reykjavík, the capital of Iceland, looking for traces of the earliest settlement farm founded by Ingólf Arnarson. On the far left, tell-tale shadows in the soil indicate the remains of turf walls in which were found traces of volcanic ash that helped to date the site.

are insubstantial enough – shadows in the soil, a riddle of crumbling artefacts, an arrangement of rough stones, a hint of an ancient hearth, a midden of old animal bones, an indication of a floor of stamped earth. They were contained within an archaeological 'time-seal' that enables us to date it precisely. Among the grass-roots of the remains of a turf wall were found traces of volcanic ash (tephra) which have been identified as the fall-out from a volcano in the Torfajökull area, in southern Iceland, shortly before AD 900. Vulcanologists call it, familiarly, the Settlement

193

Age tephra, layer VII ab, a wafer-thin layer of dark basaltic ash under a light-coloured spread of rhyolitic ash. Such are the microscopic scraps of evidence on which modern archaeologists can now build their conclusions.

These excavations tell us almost nothing about the kind of buildings that Ingólf erected, or the kind of life-style he enjoyed. But we know from the sources that Ingólf staked out a claim to enormous tracts of land round Reykjavík, which he shared out amongst his family and friends. As the First Settler, he and his descendants enjoyed great prestige and political power, and the original homestead at Reykjavík acquired an aura of national importance for later generations. *Landnámabók*, written at least two and a half centuries afterwards, reads almost like a tourist guidebook:

> He made his home at the place where his high-seat pillars had been washed ashore, and lived at Reykjavík. Those high-seat pillars are still to be seen in the hall there.

We are told by the sources that the early settlers lived in considerable style. Some of the literary descriptions may well be exaggerated, like the sumptuous residence said to have been built by Ólaf the Peacock at Hjarðarholt in Laxárdalur which, according to *Laxdæla saga*, could accommodate more than a thousand guests. But there are many other references to great halls with panelled walls on which were carved scenes from myth and legend; and the oldest surviving relics of wood-panelling, now preserved in the National Museum, which date from the tenth and eleventh centuries, all suggest considerable generosity of scale.

A great number of Viking Age house sites in Iceland have now been excavated, enough to make it clear that the houses built by the early settlers were of the classic Norse long-house type: a single hall. Later, this might be partitioned, and other rooms would be added to it for specialised purposes – a weaving-room for the women, a larder, and so on – in addition to the farm out-houses nearby. The overwhelming impression one gets is of sheer size; long-houses of forty metres were not uncommon. The houses of the Viking Age Icelanders were roomy and capacious, and extremely effective for their environment. Although they had walls of turf and stone, they were essentially timber-framed houses with those thick outer walls for insulation.

The most impressive Viking Age house yet discovered by archaeology anywhere is to be found in Iceland: a farm called Stöng, near the head of the valley of Thjórsárdalur in the south of Iceland. It has been called, somewhat fancifully, 'Iceland's Pompeii', because its preservation was due to a volcanic eruption; in the year 1104 it was smothered under a tremendous outpouring of tephra from Iceland's most notorious volcano, Mount Hekla. It was excavated in 1939 by a team of Scandinavian archaeologists led by the late Dr Aage Roussell, former curator of medieval antiquities at the National Museum of Denmark.

Thjórsárdalur ('Bull River Dale') is a remarkable valley. Its bedrock

was formed by the most prodigious lava-flow the world has known since the last Ice Age – a huge river of lava covering some 800 square kilometres that swept for 130 kilometres south to the sea. That was 8000 years ago. Time and erosion gradually mellowed the unyielding lava; the minerals helped to create fertile grasslands, and a new river – Thjórsá – gnawed its way down to the coast. But it has remained an intensively volcanic area; away to the east broods the majestic hog-backed outline of Hekla, queening it over the southlands in a perpetual ermine mantle of snow, always ready to erupt yet again.

Hekla is a very beautiful volcano, but also a very violent one. She has erupted no fewer than fifteen times since the first settlers came to Iceland. Throughout the Middle Ages, Hekla was held in superstitious awe by European clerics as a gateway to Hell itself and a terrible premonition of the torments of damnation; to the Icelanders who lived in her vicinity, she represented a greater hazard for this life than for the next.

In the year 1104 Hekla had a major eruption. At that time there were at least twenty farmsteads in the upper reaches of Thjórsárdalur. Millions of tons of tephra shrouded the green pastures. All the farms died. Now, through archaeology, one of them at least has come to life again: the farm of Stöng. And through Stöng we can experience what domestic conditions in Iceland in the Viking Age were really like.

The modern full-scale reconstruction of the farmhouse of Stöng, known as the 'Commonwealth Farm'. It stands a few kilometres down Thjórsárdalur from the original site.

195

Stöng has its own saga. The first known settler there was a tenth-century champion called Gauk Trandilsson; we are told that he was killed in a duel by his foster-brother, Ásgrím Elliða-Grímsson, who figures largely in *Njál's Saga*, mightiest of all the Icelandic Sagas. Folk-tradition supplies the reason: Gauk had been having an affair with the housewife in the neighbouring farm of Steinastaðir who was a kinswoman of Ásgrím's, so honour was at stake. A snatch of a surviving ballad provides the clue:

> Those were the days,
> When Gauk lived at Stöng;
> Then the way to Steinastaðir
> Wasn't long.

Oddly enough his name crops up again in the most unlikely place imaginable, two hundred years later and six hundred kilometres away, in the magnificent Neolithic burial mound of Maeshowe, in the Orkneys, acclaimed as the finest chambered tomb in Europe. It is a great, grass-grown conical mound; inside, a low entry-passage leads to a lofty central chamber, beautifully built of Orkney flagstones and corbelled in overlapping courses, dated to around 2700 BC. When Maeshowe was first excavated in 1861, it was apparent to the antiquarians who went into it that they were not the first 'moderns' to have broken into the tomb; other men had broken in, some seven hundred years earlier, and had left runic graffiti on the walls. There are twenty-four of these runic inscriptions. Two of them refer explicitly to the fact that 'Jerusalem-farers' (Crusaders) broke into Maeshowe in the twelfth century in search of treasure – which they did not find.

Most of the inscriptions are ordinary and commonplace, which gives them a special value. These are not the epics of kings and heroes that you find in the Sagas, but the authentic voices of the ordinary folk who are usually as anonymous as a flock of birds. In Maeshowe they had their brief say, recorded for ever on stone, because the old burial chamber seems to have become a popular venue for Viking courtship. One inscription states, rather smugly: 'Thorný bedded; Helgi writes it.' Another, with engaging simplicity, says, 'Ingigerð is the sweetest woman there is.' Another refers obliquely to the activities of the local *femme fatale*: 'Ingibjörg the fair widow; many a woman has had to lower herself to come in here, despite her airs and graces. Erlingr.' (When you bump your head creeping along that entrance passage, you realise what a neat pun it is.) But the most intriguing of these spidery runic inscriptions is in the form of a four-lined stanza, which starts on a stone to the left of the burial cell in the south wall of the chamber (to the right as you go in) and continues on the lintel above it:

> THESE RUNES
> Were carved
> By the greatest runester west-over-sea,
> With the axe once owned by Gauk
> Trandilsson in the southlands of Iceland.

What was Gauk Trandilsson's axe from Stöng doing in Maeshowe? The riddle has now been brilliantly solved by Hermann Pálsson, Reader in Old Icelandic at Edinburgh University. Using the Saga sources, he showed how Gauk Trandilsson's axe became an heirloom in the family of his killer, Ásgrím Elliða-Grímsson, and that in the year 1153 a direct descendant of that family, Thórhall Ásgrímsson, was the captain of a ship docked in Norway that carried an Orkney Earl, Rögnvald Kali (*cf* Ch. 9), back to the Orkneys on the last homeward lap of a Crusade to Jerusalem. We can now imagine the scene. When the Orcadian Jerusalem-farers reached home they boisterously suggested a night out – in Maeshowe. Thórhall went with them. In Maeshowe, a boastful runester wanted to show off his prowess and asked for an implement. Thórhall volunteered his axe, and told him its story. And thus an immortal runic inscription was born.

It is a fascinating tale. But what intrigues me most is the way in which, in that ancient place, time and story have come together to produce something unique: Maeshowe, the prehistoric burial mound that the Vikings of the Orkneys made their own.

At Stöng in Iceland, Gauk Trandilsson had made a good life for himself. His farm was too far up the valley, too close to the line between vegetation and desert in the Icelandic highlands, to be really prosperous. But the excavated remains of Stöng, maintained as a covered showpiece for the public, give a very good impression of what life was like in Viking Age Iceland on an ordinary farm settlement. This impression is now vividly reinforced by a full-scale reconstruction of the Stöng farmhouse that has recently been built nearby, known as the 'Commonwealth Farm'. Some of the details are, necessarily, speculative; but the building as a whole has a fine feel about it.

Stöng was built in the traditional Icelandic fashion with thick walls of turves laid on two foundation-courses of rough stones, and with a turf roof. It was a medium-sized farm, with a working household of about twenty people. The single doorway led into a vestibule which contained a storage room for dried fish, it is now thought – one can imagine the smell in the house! This vestibule led in turn to the main room, the typical Viking long-hall (*skáli*), which was used for working and sleeping. It was seventeen metres long and six metres in breadth. Down either side there were raised platforms on which members of the household sat at work and slept. In the centre of the hall there was a lockable bed-closet for the head of the family and his wife. It was a bit cramped, but at least it was private; the rest of the household had to get on with their love-lives as best they could in public. It does not seem to have inhibited them. At the far end of the hall, a doorway leads into another room which had been added on. This was a living-room (*stofa*), which was primarily a work-room for the women, with the weaving loom set up at the far end, and a special dais called the *kvennapallur* (women's platform) under which the textiles were stored as they were made. This room also doubled as a dining-room, with family

The great Neolithic burial mound of Maeshowe, in the Orkneys, where an axe from Iceland was used to incise a memorable runic stanza.

and friends on one side, work-people on the other. When parties and dances were held at Stöng, the dining-tables in this room would be hoisted up to the rafters to make more space.

Life at Stöng seems to have been good – until Hekla erupted in 1104. At least the inhabitants had warning of the disaster, for they had time to evacuate the farm with all their valuables – all they left behind were the casual bric-à-brac of any household at a flitting. As the shroud of tephra from Hekla began to accumulate on their land, they would have recognised the danger they were in. Thjórsárdalur was obviously dying, so they made their escape. And they made it on horseback.

The Icelandic pony (*equus scandinavicus*), sturdy, docile and sure-footed, was just as important a catalyst for settlement by land as the *knörr* was by sea. It was the pony, imported from Norway, that conquered distance and difficulty and made the birth of the Icelandic nation possible; it was the pony that helped to create out of scattered settlements a coherent society. Iceland was a terribly difficult country to colonise, a land of mountains, lakes, glaciers, massive waters thundering towards the sea – all potent barriers to communication when the Viking settlers wanted to form a nation. It was the pony that conquered this formidable terrain, carrying everything and everyone on its back. And it continued to do so for a thousand years; indeed, the first road for wheeled vehicles was not built in

Iceland until 1874, on the occasion of a royal visit from Denmark to celebrate Iceland's millennium. Today, roads have everywhere replaced the bridle-paths of old, the aeroplane has taken over from the pony; but the pure-bred Viking horse still abounds in Iceland, now as a playmate rather than a beast of burden. There are some 60,000 of them in Iceland today, adding glamour to the landscape as they range free in the upland pastures, and Icelanders regard them with pride and profound affection. They have a unique range of gaits – step, trot, canter, pace and rack – and they are wonderfully handsome creatures in their own right. To own a herd of ponies has become something of a status symbol in Iceland; the herd represents, I think, an instinctive folk-memory of the time when these friendly, unassuming animals made possible the achievements of medieval Iceland.

One of the most enduring of these achievements was the creation of a parliamentary commonwealth in the year 930. The early settlers had soon established their own district assemblies (*Things*) to create local laws and settle local disputes, on the old Norwegian model. The *Thing* was where political power was evolved: an assembly of free-born farmers meeting under the presidency of the local priest-chieftain (*goði*), who had both secular and religious duties. These chieftains (*goðar*) were the dominant political force in Iceland, and many of them exercised their power just as ruthlessly as the older petty princelings of Norway, collecting chieftaincies into private empires through marriage, inheritance, even purchase and extortion.

The earliest recorded *Thing* to be established was at Kjalarnes, just across the bay from Reykjavík, soon after 900; not surprisingly the leading figure seems to have been Ingólf Arnarson's son, Thorstein, exercising his authority as chieftain of the First Settler's dynasty. To start with, these local assemblies were enough; the huge land-takes of the original settlers

199

had been parcelled out amongst kinsmen, friends and followers, creating close-knit clan communities of which the family head became natural leader by dint of wealth, personal authority and patronage. His title of *goði*, priest-chieftain, gave him temporal power that was bolstered by his spiritual function as the pagan priest responsible for local religious observances, which were conducted at the chieftain's home and not, as was previously thought, in specially built temples.

The so-called 'Settlement Age' in Iceland is dated to about 870–930. By the end of that period it was becoming obvious that some sort of national authority was required, some sort of *modus vivendi* to enable neighbouring communities to deal with problems that spilled across their boundaries – straying sheep, runaway slaves, brawls, killings.

The lead in the political initiative seems to have been taken by the Reykjavík family. In the 920s a man called Grím Goat-Shoe (*geitskór*) was commissioned to reconnoitre Iceland to hold a kind of opinion poll on proposals for a National Assembly (*Althing*), and choose the most convenient site for it; meanwhile his foster-brother, Úlfljót, was sent to Norway to prepare a suitable code of laws – not for a monarchy, but for a republic.

And so, on a June day in the year 930, the people of Iceland gathered at a place called Thingvellir (Parliament Plains), fifty kilometres to the east of Reykjavík and just outside the boundaries of Ingólf's original land-take. Thingvellir is a great natural arena of lava that was formed as the earth cracked and lurched in a geological subsidence thousands of years earlier; this convulsion has left a depression forty kilometres long and ten kilometres broad, with a wall of riven lava at one side that made a splendid sounding-board for speakers' voices in those days before microphones and amplifiers were invented.

Thingvellir is a spectacular place; but it was also a spectacular enterprise that these Icelanders were embarking upon. They were meeting to create a state the like of which had not been seen before in Europe – a state without a king. A republic. What they were doing was entirely logical and consistent. They had left their homelands to get away from the power of kings. Now they formed an oligarchic commonwealth, a country without a king at a time in history when the idea of kingship, of royal authority, was becoming politically paramount.

The system was not always successful. The *Althing* had no executive powers – no army to enforce its will, no police force to carry out its judicial or legislative decisions. It depended entirely on a willing acceptance of the concept of law and order in an age of violence, on a willing suspension of the prevailing belief that only might was right and effective.

At Thingvellir there was founded a unique social and political experiment long before its time, long before Simon de Montfort's parliament in England in the thirteenth century. If Westminster is the mother of parliaments, then Thingvellir is the grandmother of parliaments.

The *Althing* was held in midsummer, either in June or July, for a fortnight. It had both a judicial and a legislative function. Basically, it was the central institution of a federation of the thirteen district *Things*, which in turn were grouped into four provincial (Quarter) *Things*. The *Althing* was the common legislative authority, with a legislature consisting of all the chieftains, each accompanied by two legal advisers. The president of the legislature was the Law-Speaker, who was elected for a period of three years and whose title reflected the fact that he was required to recite the laws publicly, from memory; until the law-code was written down for the first time in 1119, the Law-Speaker was the living repository of the nation's laws: 'With law shall the land be built up, and with lawlessness laid waste.'

Court cases were held in the four Quarter Courts, with jurymen nominated by the chieftains, although litigants could challenge the inclusion of individual jurymen. Later, in 1005, a Fifth Court, a supreme Court of Appeal, was instituted. It was in these courts that the great family feuds that figure so largely in the Icelandic Sagas were argued and eventually settled. It was not a perfect system; too often, the quality of justice depended on the power of individual chieftains who set themselves above the law, and became progressively more powerful as landed wealth became more and more concentrated into fewer hands, and the political rights of the farmers became correspondingly eroded.

Today, Thingvellir is a National Park, blessedly empty of monuments; it is a monument in itself, Iceland's Parthenon and Runnymede combined. It is now a centre of stillness where visitors can imagine for themselves what it must have been like to attend the *Althing* in the old days. It was the great annual moot for people from all walks of life, and from all parts of Iceland – it took seventeen days for the men of the Eastfjords to reach Thingvellir on their ponies, but that just added to the holiday atmosphere. The plain below the so-called Law Rock, where the laws were recited, became a temporary town of tents and booths. It was the social event of the year for farmers and farm-hands, chieftains and churls, friends and enemies, boys and girls. Thingvellir was as much a fairground as a parliament, a place where gossip flew while news was made, where stories and poems were told, where plots were hatched and marriages arranged, and occasional heads broken. It was boisterous, vivid, animated.

There are very few material relics left of those stirring times, apart from a small bronze crozier-head, shaped like the letter T, lost by some bishop in the eleventh century and found at Thingvellir accidentally a few years ago. It symbolises the most significant event in the early history of the Viking parliament: the Conversion of Iceland to Christianity in the year 1000, not by the sword as happened so often elsewhere, but by parliamentary decree.

We are told that King Ólaf Tryggvason of Norway (995–1000) had been putting strong pressure on the Icelanders to accept Christianity, sending

Thingvellir: the wall of riven lava to the left; in the centre of the picture, the Law Rock from which the Law-Speaker announced judgements and recited the laws.

missionaries and holding chieftains' sons hostage in Norway. There were far-reaching implications for both Iceland and Norway, implications that were more political than religious. Paganism in Iceland had always been rather easy-going, and some at least of the earliest settlers were already Christian, in their own way; it is said of one of them, Helgi the Lean, that he had a mixed faith – 'He believed in Christ, but invoked Thór for sea-voyages and in times of emergency.' And there is a charming story in *Landnámabók* about Ingólf Arnarson's grandson, Thorkel *máni* (Moon), who was Law-Speaker at the *Althing*: 'When he was lying on his death-bed, he had himself carried out to a shaft of sunlight, and commended himself to the god who had created the sun. He had led a life as blameless as the best of Christians.'

By the year 1000, political opinion about the potentially divisive issue of the Church had polarised into two bitterly opposed factions. They met at the *Althing* – the new and militant Christian party who wanted to bring Iceland into the orbit of Christian Europe, and the old, conservative pagan party. Both sides were armed and prepared for a showdown. Civil war seemed imminent, with the political partition of Iceland the only possible resolution. And then, in the interests of peace, the leader of the Christian party, Hall of Síða, went to the Law-Speaker – who was a pagan – and asked him to arbitrate; and everyone at the *Althing* swore to abide by his

202

sole decision. The Law-Speaker, Thorgeir Thorkelsson, retired to his tented booth, where he lay meditating for a day and a night under a fur cloak. On Monday, 24 June 1000, he emerged and summoned everyone to the Law Rock to announce his momentous decision:

He said he thought an impossible situation would arise if men did not all have one and the same law in Iceland, and urged people not to let that happen, and said that it would lead to such divisions that fighting would most certainly break out that would destroy the nation.

'It seems to me good sense,' he said, 'that we do not let those who wish conflict decide the issue, but that we should seek a middle course, so that we all have one law and one custom; because if we divide the law, we will divide the peace.'

Then Thorgeir declared the law, that all unbaptised people in the land should become Christian and be baptised.   (*Íslendingabók*)

It was a momentous and statesmanlike speech, finding compromise in the midst of imminent conflict, for certain pagan practices were not to be banned, as long as they were carried out privately to avoid giving offence to Christian neighbours. The actual mass baptism did not go quite so well; many people felt that the water of the river Öxará (Axe River) that meanders through Thingvellir was too cold, and the Northerners insisted on waiting until they were on their way home, when they could be

Skálholt, site of the first native bishopric in Iceland.

203

immersed in the lake of Laugarvatn, which has a hot-spring warming it!

But, to me, one of the most telling moments in the historic confrontation at the *Althing* had come a little earlier, before the Law-Speaker's decision. During the passionate arguments that were raging in the parliament, a breathless messenger came running into the arena with the news that a volcano was erupting near the home of one of the leading Christians. 'Aha!' said the pagans. 'That proves that the gods are angry at all the blasphemies they have been hearing.' Whereupon a wise old chieftain, Snorri Thorgrímsson, one of the leading pagans, turned and looked at the great volcanic cliff behind him and remarked wryly, 'At what were the gods angry when *that* lava flowed?' There was no answer to that; and so realism, political pragmatism, and downright common sense won the day, and Iceland remained a united nation.

The Conversion to Christianity had a profound effect on Iceland, socially, politically and culturally. Chieftains who had been in charge of pagan ceremonies now built churches whose tithes would add to their wealth and power. Within no more than fifty years, the Church established itself as a potent new power factor, trafficking not just in men's souls but also in their lands and ancient authorities.

In 1056, a native Icelandic bishopric was established at Skálholt, a manor-farm in the south-west that had belonged to one of the leaders of the Christian party, Gissur the White; it was his son, Ísleif Gissurarson, who now returned from lengthy education abroad in Westphalia to become Iceland's first bishop. But the really important impact of the Church was that it made Iceland literate; it brought her into the mainstream of European culture and learning. The Vikings in Iceland had their runes, of course, for inscriptions, but by 'literate' I am referring specifically to the use of the Roman alphabet, which was brought to Iceland by English missionary bishops early in the eleventh century. The *lingua franca* of Europe at that time was Latin; but through its church schools, the Icelandic Church also encouraged the use of Icelandic, translating edifying books into the vernacular so that the rural folk in their remote and scattered farmsteads could read the good news. And thus the Icelanders learned to write for themselves as well.

The first great scholar of the early Icelandic Church we know of was Sæmund the Learned (1054–1133), who wrote a Latin history (now lost) of the kings of Norway. He was followed by Iceland's first vernacular historian, Ari the Learned, who wrote *Íslendingabók* (*Book of Icelanders*) around 1130. Simultaneously, he and other erudite scholars were busy compiling the first version of Iceland's Domesday Book – *Landnámabók*, the *Book of Settlements*, a systematic account of the first four hundred settlers in Iceland, their land-takes and their descendants. *Landnámabók* reflected the decisive break that Iceland had already made by opting for a republic: the history of Iceland was not the story of a single royal line, but the story of *all* Icelanders. And with that, a latent national genius for story-telling was unleashed, and the literature of the Icelandic Sagas was born.

Saga-writing became a great industry in Iceland. Sagas were regarded as 'serious entertainment', not only immensely popular but functionally important as well, for they enshrined genealogical memories that had peculiar significance in a country whose social fabric was woven on the loom of family kinships. They were written on calfskin (vellum), penned by the sharpened quill-feathers of swans or ravens, using a glossy ink distilled from bear-berry plants. The vellums were expensive to make, yet Sagas and other learned works poured out in their thousands. What is more, they never became the exclusive possession of any one social class; they were available to all, and treasured by all. Even after Saga-writing had reached its apogee in the thirteenth century, the old Sagas were cherished as family heirlooms.

Quantities of these manuscripts were collected by antiquarians in the seventeenth century and found their way to libraries abroad, especially to Denmark, for Iceland was at that time a Danish colony. Then, on 21 April 1971, the manuscripts started coming back to their homeland after the Danish Parliament, in a gesture of unparalleled magnanimity, agreed to return the majority of them. On that memorable day a Danish frigate came into Reykjavík harbour bearing the first two, and the whole population of Iceland, it seemed, turned out to welcome them. Since then the manuscripts have been coming back in regular consignments.

They are now kept under lock and key in a vault in the basement of the Manuscript Institute of Iceland, behind a massive two-ton door – purely for safety reasons, because they are priceless and irreplaceable. But they are not inaccessible, any more than they ever have been; the manuscripts, and what they contain, have always been the common and shared property of the whole nation, expressing as they do a deep love of history and learning and literature, and a deep need for them.

They are not particularly beautiful books, like the Lindisfarne Gospels in the British Museum or the Book of Kells in Trinity College, Dublin; the pages are worn and yellow, the writing crabbed and faded. That is because they were always being used and read, copied and re-copied. Nineteenth-century travellers to Iceland marvelled at the continuing tradition of reading and reciting the Sagas even in the poorest hovels, as immortalised in a celebrated painting of a typical Saga-reading scene by H. Schiett, now in the National Museum of Iceland. And for that reason the most telling manuscript at the Institute, to my mind, is not so much one of the great codices like *Flateyjarbók*, all 226 pages of it, which was one of the first two books to be returned in 1971, but one single page: a page of a fourteenth-century vellum book that some anonymous tailor in the seventeenth century trimmed to use as a pattern for making a waistcoat. It was not because he had no respect for what it contained, but because it had already been copied out on paper (which was cheaper and more legible), and therefore it was no longer required as reading matter.

Nineteenth-century oil painting by H. Schiett, now in the National Museum of Iceland, of a typical Saga-reading scene in an Icelandic farmhouse.

The Sagas were Iceland's greatest cultural achievement, perhaps the greatest achievement of European medieval literature. Now they are no longer thought of as pure history, but as historical novels based on many different sources. One reason they used to be considered to be verbatim orally-transmitted history is because they are so vivid and circumstantial. Part of their charm, indeed, is that one can visit the sites where the Saga-events are said to have taken place and savour the landscapes that helped to create them in the Saga-writer's mind.

Take, for instance, that great heroine of *Laxdœla saga*, the beautiful and imperious Guðrún Ósvífursdóttir. Her grave lies under the slopes of Helgafell (Holy Fell), on Snæfellsnes. She was a lady who loved not wisely but too well, and at least once too often: she had four husbands and a lover – a lover whom she forced one of her husbands to kill, out of jealousy and spite.

Towards the end of her life, when she was old and blind and had become a nun at the convent at Helgafell, her son once asked her a pointed and searching question. 'There is something I have always wanted to know,

206

Whale-catching in Iceland; an illumination from a fourteenth-century copy of the Icelandic law book, *Jónsbók*, now in the Royal Library, Copenhagen.

Icelandic ponies, pure-bred descendants of the original Viking horse, *equus scandinavicus*.

mother,' he said. 'Which of your men did you love the most?' And Guðrún answered, with one of those laconic replies so characteristic of the Sagas: 'I was worst to the one I loved the most.' I still do not know which one she meant: the lover she had had killed, or the husband who killed him at her behest and forfeited his own life in the inevitable blood-feud that ensued. It was her secret – a profound secret of human behaviour – and she took it with her to that grave at Helgafell.

In the light of the Sagas, it is clear that women played an unusually positive role in society for those medieval days. They were frontiers-women in action and spirit; they also had 'liberated' legal rights far in advance of the times, like the right to divorce and a claim to half the marital property. They made their presence felt – at times, quite literally, with a vengeance.

Njál's Saga, written in the second half of the thirteenth century, is the greatest of the Sagas. It tells the story of two men and their violent destinies – and their forceful wives: the hero Gunnar of Hlíðarendi, and his close friend Njál of Bergthórshvoll. Gunnar was the sort of man who attracted trouble not because he was a trouble-maker but because he represented a challenge to all the young lions in the district (the 'fastest gun in the West' syndrome). Eventually he was sentenced to exile for three years because his prowess provoked so much aggressive envy, and the district wanted peace. Gunnar dutifully prepared to leave Iceland for exile in Norway; but as he left his home at Hlíðarendi, his horse stumbled. Gunnar was thrown, but managed to land on his feet, facing back towards the way he had come. He looked at his farm of Hlíðarendi, and realised that he simply could not, and would not, leave it, especially under duress.

He knew it might cost him dear, because by refusing to accept the sentence of exile he could now be attacked with impunity by his enemies. And attack they did. One night they gathered at Hlíðarendi and besieged him in his home. For a long time he fought them off with his bow and arrows, until his bow-string snapped. Gunnar turned to his wife, Hall-gerð, and asked her for a lock of her long, beautiful hair to plait into a bow-string for him. But Hallgerð, with her husband's life at stake, refused; there had been a time once, she said, when Gunnar had slapped her on the face, and she would just remind him of that fact now. 'To each his own way of earning fame,' said Gunnar. 'You shall not be asked again.' He knew that without his bow he was doomed, but he would not ask for his wife's help twice. In that sort of situation, in those retorts, lies the essence of the Sagas.

South from Hlíðarendi, across the broad expanse of the Land-Isles, Gunnar's friend Njál was helpless to prevent the tragedy that enveloped Gunnar and was now about to envelop himself and his family. Njál was a man of peace; his sons were not. Soon, with an awful inevitability, the violence of the times reached his house at Bergthórshvoll . . .

It was the evening of Monday, 23 August 1011. A hundred men had gathered with vengeful intent to attack Njál's sons, and now they came

208

riding deliberately over the plain. The Njálssons and their farm-hands lined up in front of the door, armed to the teeth, a formidable crew, waiting to make a fight of it. But now their father, old Njál, made a strange decision; he asked his violent sons, hard men all of them, not to wait outside but to go inside the house. The Saga-writer knew, Njál knew, his sons knew, that it was courting disaster: inside the house they would be much more vulnerable, especially to fire. And yet they did it, to grant the old man his last request, and because the inexorable logic of events demanded it. So they went inside, their enemies set fire to Bergthórshvoll, and they all burned to their deaths.

There was one moment of great grandeur at that terrible scene. As the house blazed, the leader of the Burners urged Njál's wife, Bergthóra, to come outside and save herself; to which Bergthóra replied, with magnificent dignity: 'I was married to Njál young, and promised him then that we would share the same fate.' And with that she went back inside the house to die with her husband.

We do not know who it was who wrote this masterpiece. It was not the custom in those days for an author to sign his work. But there is one writer we *do* know of, because he played such a major part in the politics of his age as well: Snorri Sturluson of Reykholt – poet, historian, politician, statesman, Saga-writer and Saga-maker, the man who gave the world his monumental history of the Viking Age in *Heimskringla*, his vision of the world of the old pagan gods in *Snorri's Edda*, and, in all probability, *Egil's Saga* as well.

His own life reads like that of a Saga hero, full of promise and early fulfilment but ending in tragedy. He was born to wealth and authority in 1179, descendant of some of the most influential figures in Iceland's early history. His life was conditioned by the traits he inherited – ambition, pride, love of power, artistic creativeness. He became the friend of kings abroad, but at home his rivals were suspicious and resentful of his success. Iceland in the thirteenth century was racked with vicious power struggles between warring chieftains, and on the night of 23 September 1241 his enemies attacked him at his home at Reykholt. For some reason the house was unguarded, and his assailants, seventy of them in all, went unchallenged through the defensive stockade that Snorri had built against just such an eventuality. They chased him down to the cellar, and there they hacked him to death – a squalid way for Iceland's most distinguished man of letters to die. Today the physical memory of Snorri Sturluson is kept vivid at Reykholt by an unusual monument – a circular stone open-air bath built by him, which was fed from a natural hot-spring nearby, and in which we know Snorri used to sit and discuss politics and literature with his cronies. Part of the underground passage leading from his house to the bath has now been excavated and restored by the National Museum of Iceland. At the other end, it once opened into the cellar in which he was murdered.

erfingi ſkal rett taka at konu huͤre eꝛ
hu er ſegin. karl maðr en eigi kona. þo
at hu ſie erfingi. ⁊ ſa ſin ſomeigð e ſin
puſtida ⁊ taki ubods mann þꜱ. huit
hꜹða⸱ nea hu eigi ſi bꜹda. þa tekur h
rett at konu hure· Kona ſkalp at rett at
ker eꝛ hu e borð ⁊ at hu ſi eigi bonda·
h̶uuetna þ ſin koa uðr barſ harꜹði
þa ſk ſa e þ tin at yra þu ⁊ koſt e kou
anꜹðigt með hu u ſ þu ſiukleika ⁊ ſo
þ buꝛioſti· Hu eꝛ ſa man e andað e ko
nu heꝛ legit· þa ſk erfingi ſua þn ſe
tti ⁊ koſtnaði ſ ulu ſin hu heꝛ þe tek
ept h en e menſa· Gu augu at þn at
ſua þar ſin þu erþiſ edr

huͤi iſſꝛ uꝑ
þu þorda hlut langbok· ag ſei
ger byꝛſt u kueia giptuig ⁊ hu
gip u ſe ſk ua

ſldom eꝛð
madeꝛ ſku raſ
gipting dꜹt ſin
na· eꝛ þau eu
Gu eꝛ þra miller· þa ſku þoð þnd ⁊
mode hu nauuztu giptigu rꜹða· Hu
e bꜹd nanꝛ ⁊ ſkiuꝛ þa at· þa ſk ſa ira
ſin þu raða þylg eꝛ þ þu raꝛꝛꜹ ⁊ ſ
ſk huuetna þ ſin þlei e ſaꝛkou ꞇ· Hꝙp
ting mað ſk ſkilꝛa heiꝛ þylgiu ⁊ til

gioꝛ þ ꝛudkau ſina· ꝛ ſu þu keiꝛ at
ſat þꝛ ſku ⁊ þa eindaga nꜹꝛ bꝛullaup
ſkue· Gu ſk þu at lꜹdi geſt meiꝛ til gioꝛ
mey edꝛ kou· eu til ꝺꜱ huꝛada þo að
n ſie ꝛik ⁊ lþugi menſa e þidũꝛ uꝛ þe
hꝱ· Gu eꝛ ui geꝛ y beſtu eigu ſin þa
ſku erþingi þꜱ leþſa til ſin eꝛ þn ui
ta· Hu eꝛ þa ſkilꝛ at ũ ualdaga· þa la
ti þett mað þe uiegra ũ __ ime ũ hei
ũ þylgiu hu uilt u þꝛa e þꝛa ũ· Gu eꝛ
þa ſkilꝛ at ũ til gioꝛ· þa noti giptũ ũ
uiegra uotta ũ þyra ſkꜹrdi· Gu ſkal
ſ klꜹdu menſa heiũa geþaꝛt en þaũ
g· eu þ ſin meꝛ geꝛ giptũ mað þa ſk
ua y þylgĩ þnigũ· at þ meꝛ uɖa þũ
til þꝛa· edꝛ aꝛla· e konu þꜹꝛ· Gu aug
heiũ þylgiu uia aꝛþi giptĩgaꝛ nꝛ ui
uꝛa· þa eꝛ e gioꝛ ſin uu uarſ ſkilt· e
eꝛ koa edꝛ mꜹꝛ utã ediꝛa giptiꝛꝛ· þ ut
rad þodꝛ ⁊ uad· edꝛ bꝛoð ſinſ· e þll eꝛ
gipting ĩ e þ rſadi huiaꝛ· haþi þ guꝛt
aꝛþi ept giptũg ĩ þu ſin hu ſtoðꞇ
nema ule uei uiſkũ at guͤ uﯾ gi
ptigaꝛ ĩ uili þ ꝛyꝛa lſa raꝛꝛꜹdi· þa
uia hu giptaꝛt ĩ aua ſkꝛiſaĩ ꝛnda
ſuia ꝛi· eꝛ þn liſt raꝛꝛꜹdi e bet· ⁊ ũ
egu þꝛ ũ eidi ſinu ſana· ⁊ at þo at lei
ta ſila aɖ uſad giptũg ĩ· Gu giptũg ĩ eꝛ

Iceland, in a way, was the climax of the Viking Age; in their books, the Saga-writers like Snorri Sturluson chronicled a Golden Age of challenge and achievement, a great transplant of Viking settlers and Viking culture that took root and flourished as the violence was channelled into more peaceful, more creative directions. But Iceland was not the end of the Viking road to the West; it was from the west coast of Iceland that other and even more unlikely experiments in settlement would be launched, voyages of exploration and colonisation that would take the Vikings far beyond the furthest horizons that Europeans had ever attempted – first to Greenland, and from there to North America.

Snorri's Pool: the open-air hot-spring pool built at Reykholt by Snorri Sturluson. In the background, the entrance to the passageway to the cellar of his house.

OPPOSITE A page from the sixteenth-century illuminated vellum copy of the ancient Icelandic code of laws, *Jónsbók*.

8

The Ultimate Outpost

On the west coast of Iceland the long, mountainous peninsula of Snæfellsnes points like a bony finger in the direction of Greenland, invisible beyond the western horizon. Right at the tip sits the celebrated glacier of Snæfellsjökull, a handsomely domed ice-cap covering an extinct cone-volcano, 1446 metres above sea level. More often than not it is wreathed in its own private congregation of clouds; but on a clear day a climber on the summit can sometimes see the towering glaciers of eastern Greenland in a mirage, shimmering upside-down above the horizon in an optical phenomenon known to the Norwegians as an *is-blikk* – an 'ice-glimpse'.

Snæfellsnes forms the southern reaches of Breiðafjörður (Broad Firth), rich in fish and Saga story. And it was from here, in the 980s, about a century after the discovery and colonisation of Iceland itself, that the last great Viking surges to the west were launched: first to Greenland, and from there to the ultimate outpost of North America, *Vínland*.

The story of these enterprises is closely bound up with the story of a man called Eirík the Red (*Eiríkur rauði*), as told in two separate but related Icelandic Sagas – *Grænlendinga saga* (*The Greenlanders' Saga*), which was written late in the twelfth century, and *Eiríks saga rauða* (*Eirík the Red's Saga*), which was written as a deliberate revision of the earlier *Grænlendinga saga* about a century later, probably around 1270. These two Sagas, and some occasional references in earlier historical works, are the major source of documentary information about the Viking voyages westwards, now increasingly supplemented and refined by modern archaeology.

Eirík the Red's family hailed originally from south-western Norway, but his father and he had to leave in a hurry 'because of some killings', as the Sagas succinctly put it. They made their home in Iceland, but nowhere for long; Iceland by this time (around 960) was fully settled, and it was hard for new immigrants to get good land. At first they had to make do with a remote and bleakly uninviting plot on the north-western fringe of Iceland; later, Eirík the Red married well, and was able to move to the more prosperous domains at the bottom of Breiðafjörður, where he cleared land and made himself a new home up the valley of Haukadalur, calling the farm Eiríksstaðir after himself. The site was excavated in 1938, revealing the foundations of a modest long-house and various out-buildings. It would be rash to assume that this was Eirík's actual home-stead; but it was at Eiríksstaðir that his wife, Thjóðhild, gave birth to a son, Leif Eiríksson – the man who would go down in history as Leif the Lucky, the first European explorer of North America.

But Eirík and his hasty sword were soon in trouble. His slaves acciden-tally started a landslide that destroyed a neighbour's home, indignation flared into all-out feuding, and after some bloodshed, Eirík was thrown out of Haukadalur. He made himself a new base on some of the myriad islands out in Breiðafjörður – well out of harm's way, one might think. But in no time at all he was embroiled in another bloody feud with a wealthy farmer on Snæfellsnes over the loan of some household fittings, a set of bench-boards, of all things. When Eirík came and took them back by force, there was a pitched battle in which several men were killed, including two of the farmer's sons.

Such anti-social behaviour was too much even for the relatively tolerant frontier society that Iceland still was at this time. The local court gave him a three-year sentence of full outlawry; it meant banishment from Iceland for three years, on pain of summary execution by relatives and friends of the dead men if he did not leave the country immediately.

With a vengeful band of enemies hard on his heels, Eirík the Red set sail due west along the 65th parallel, past the gleaming dome of Snæfellsjökull, heading straight for the east coast of Greenland 320 kilometres away. He had heard old seamen's tales of distant land to the west; and like every Viking before and after him he longed to conquer new worlds, make himself some elbow-room, acquire wealth and power of his own, carve out a little empire for himself somewhere. In Greenland, he was to find one.

According to *Landnámabók*, Greenland had been glimpsed, at least, around the year 900 when an Icelander on his way home from Norway had been storm-swept into unknown waters far to the west. No attempt was made to follow up this chance sighting for many years, apparently. It was not until 978, two years after Iceland had suffered a grievous famine in 976, that a party of prospective settlers from the stricken western districts tried to establish a colony on Greenland. It was a total disaster. The would-be colonists landed on Greenland's bitterly inhospitable eastern coast, spent an appalling winter snowed up there, and came to blows in a welter of manslaughter.

Mindful perhaps of the fate of the earlier expedition Eirík rounded Cape Farewell at the southern point of Greenland in 981 or 982 and spent his exile exploring the much less forbidding western coast. 'From Greenland's icy mountains', says Bishop Heber's well-known hymn; but in the folds of these icy mountains lie unexpectedly green valleys, reaching back from sheltered fjords littered with icebergs but teeming with fish.

213

The islands in Breiðafjörður where Eirík the Red made his home before his exile.

South-western Greenland in high summer is a land of extraordinary contrasts: pockets of vivid fertility surrounded by ice. It is an exotic, beautiful, rugged land; a land reasonably well suited to the kind of farming/fishing economy that Eirík was used to in Iceland, a land that could support livestock and provide desirable produce for the markets of Europe in the form of furs and hides and ivory, of narwhal and seals and walrus and polar bears. In addition, the climate then was marginally warmer than it is today.

Eirík the Red, no stranger to pioneering new homesteads, realised that he had found a land fit for settlement, a land where he would be able to exercise all the authority of First Settler. He earmarked a choice site for himself in Eiríksfjörður (modern Tunugdliarfik); and when the three years of his outlawry were up he returned to Iceland to raise a colonising expedition.

In Breiðafjörður he found no lack of volunteers to join him. Times were hard, there had been further years of famine, there were plenty of despairing men who were more than willing to uproot themselves and take a chance on a new life in a new land – especially a land which Eirík the Red, in an inspired moment, had decided to name 'Greenland' because, as the Sagas claim, he recognised that 'people would be the more eager to go there if it had a good name'.

214

And so it was, in the early summer of 985 or 986, that a motley little armada of twenty-five ships set sail from Breiðafjörður, laden with some three hundred emigrants and their livestock and domestic possessions, to brave the fogs and ice-floes of the Denmark Strait. It was a voyage of four days in good weather, an eternity in bad.

The expedition got off to a spectacularly inauspicious start; according to *Grænlendinga saga*, only fourteen of the original fleet of twenty-five reached their destination safely. Some of them foundered in what appears to have been a freak disturbance of the sea, perhaps a submarine earthquake (the Icelandic word for it was *hafgerðingar*, meaning 'sea-fences' or 'towering waves'), others were forced to turn back to Iceland. One of the battered survivors of that ill-starred voyage is a scrap of poetry from a votive lay composed on board ship by an anonymous God-fearing poet from the Hebrides. It is the oldest extant Christian verse-prayer in Icelandic:

> I beseech the immaculate Master of Monks
> To steer my journeys;
> May the Lord of the lofty heavens
> Hold His strong hand over me . . .
>
> (*Hafgerðingadrápa*, in *Grænlendinga saga*, Ch. 2)

The huge land they were on their way to colonise was apparently uninhabited, just as Iceland had actually been when the first Viking settlers arrived there. But there were tangible signs that Greenland had not always been so. Ari the Learned recorded in his *Íslendingabók* what the first Norsemen found there:

> Both to the east and the west of the country they found human habitations, and the remains of skin-boats, and stone artefacts, from which it can be concluded that the people who had been there before were of the same race as those who inhabit Vínland, whom the Greenlanders call Skrælings. (*Íslendingabók*, Ch. 6)

This twelfth-century identification of the Eskimo natives of Greenland with the natives the Norsemen were later to meet in North America, based on an observed similarity between two Stone Age material cultures, was a very reasonable deduction for its time. But there was an ominous assumption of cultural superiority implied in the Norse term for the Eskimos – *Skrælings*, literally 'wretches' or 'savages'.

The original Norse colonists split into two groups when they reached Greenland. The majority established themselves in the Julianehaab area, where they laid claim to large areas of land and founded the 'Eastern Settlement' under the patriarchal aegis of Eirík the Red. The remainder preferred to press on some 640 kilometres further up the coast to the north-west, to the Godthaab area, where they established the 'Western Settlement'. The following summers brought wave after wave of new

Brattahlíð in Greenland: formerly thought to have been the original site of 'Eirík's Hall'.

immigrants from Iceland, until every patch of farmable land in the two Settlements was occupied. The Icelandic sources mention 190 farms in the Eastern Settlement and 90 farms in the Western Settlement; but this is not meant to be definitive. Danish archaeologists have so far unearthed traces of about 330 Norse farms in the two Settlements, and it has been estimated that the Norse population of Greenland reached a peak of some 3000 at its heyday.

Those optimistic settlers found that the name, Greenland, was by no means the cynically misleading misnomer that it might seem to the arm-chair critic today. The Eastern and Western Settlements were indeed 'green land', especially during the Little Climatic Optimum the north was enjoying at the time. 'Greenland' referred exclusively to those two habit-able areas of the west coast, nowhere else; and they were quite green enough for the Norse colonists, at least for as long as the climate remained relatively kind.

The nuclear centre of the Norse colony on Greenland was the place in the Eastern Settlement that Eirík the Red had earmarked for himself. *Brattahlíð*, he called it: 'Steep Slope', or more prosaically 'Hill Farm'; today's Greenlanders call it *Qagssiarssuk* ('Little Strange Creek'). Grassy hillsides tumble down to an incredibly green plain by the foreshore of

Tunugdliarfik. Across the fjord lies the airfield at Narssarsuaq ('The Big Plain'), where a charming little hotel welcomes visitors with a refreshing lack of pretentiousness.

From his manor-farm at Brattahlíð, Eirík the Red was able to enjoy all the prestige and political power traditionally accorded to the First Settler, as Ingólf Arnarson had done in Iceland a century earlier. The grassy plain below his homestead was the site of the local assembly, or *Thing*, based on the Icelandic model, and Brattahlíð seems to have provided the hereditary chieftain of the *Thing*, just as Reykjavík had done.

But where precisely was Eirík the Red's homestead? When I first visited Greenland in 1970 the answer seemed quite clear-cut and unequivocal. I was shown a group of grass-grown ruins which had been excavated by archaeologists from the National Museum of Denmark in 1932. The farmhouse itself, 'Eirík's Hall' as it was called, was a typical Viking Age long-house with thick walls of stone and strips of turf. The interior measured 14.7 by 4.5 metres. There was a fireplace or cooking-pit opposite the main door, and a stone-flagged conduit under the floor led fresh water through the house. The outbuildings nearby consisted of four barns and two cow-byres, solidly constructed of turf and stone; the byres could house twenty-eight cows in stalls partitioned by thin slabs of stone, or the shoulder-blades of whales.

Just down the slope from the long-house are the ruins of a substantial church, a large rectangular structure of blocks of red sandstone, which has been dated to about 1300; traces of an earlier church were detected beneath it during the 1932 excavations.

That was the picture of Eirík the Red's Brattahlíð that archaeology gave us then, nice and pat. But in archaeology nothing is ever absolutely clear-cut and definitive; a new chance discovery can overnight destroy the most reasonable and logical interpretations based on previously available evidence. And so it turned out at Brattahlíð in Greenland.

The identification of the ruins at Brattahlíð as the site, at least, of Eirík's original farmstead seemed to be spectacularly confirmed by a chance find in 1961, when some workmen were digging trenches for the foundations of a school hostel some two hundred metres to the south of the farm ruins and, because of the configuration of the ground, just out of sight of Brattahlíð. Suddenly they started unearthing human skulls from an ancient cemetery – and not an Eskimo cemetery, but a Christian Viking cemetery. Archaeologists from the National Museum of Denmark were quickly called in, led by Dr Knud Krogh; and in the middle of this graveyard they found the remains of a tiny U-shaped chapel built chiefly of turf strips fortified with stones, paved with flags of red sandstone. The west gable would have been made of wood, like some of the oldest country churches still to be seen in Iceland, turf-roofed and seeming to cower into the ground against the winter gales. It really *is* tiny; the interior measures only about four metres by two, room

217

Fourteenth-century stone church beside the ruins of the long-house at Brattahlíð.

enough for scarcely a score of people standing shoulder to shoulder.

What made this new discovery so exciting was that it seemed to corroborate a telling little story in the later of the Greenland Sagas, *Eirík's Saga*. According to this, Eirík the Red's son, Leif the Lucky, was converted to Christianity in Norway by that blood-and-iron evangelist, King Ólaf Tryggvason, and returned to Greenland in the year 1000 with a missionary priest to spread the new faith:

> Leif made land at Eiríksfjörður and went home to Brattahlíð to a warm welcome. He at once began preaching Christianity and the Catholic faith throughout the country, revealing to men King Ólaf Tryggvason's message and telling what excellence and glory there was in this religion.
>
> Eirík was reluctant to abandon his old faith, but his wife, Thjóðhild, embraced it at once and had a church built, though not too close to the farmstead. This building was called Thjóðhild's Church, and there she and many others who had accepted Christianity would offer up their

prayers. Thjóðhild refused to sleep with Eirík after she was converted, which annoyed him greatly.

(*Eirík's Saga*, Ch. 5)

The tiny chapel found in 1961, 'not too close' to the ruins at Brattahlíð, was naturally assumed to be the 'Thjóðhild's Church' of *Eirík's Saga*. It was obviously very old – indeed, it is thought to be the earliest Viking Age church that has yet been found, anywhere. And its discovery in turn seemed to validate the identification of the Brattahlíð ruins, two hundred metres away, as the site of Eirík's original farmstead – particularly because in Greenland all other churches (and no fewer than twenty church sites from the Viking period have now been identified) were built right *beside* farmsteads, not at a distance from them. At Brattahlíð, archaeology and the Saga sources seemed to vindicate one another triumphantly.

But – and here comes the rub – Dr Krogh has very recently made yet another discovery at Brattahlíð which tosses the whole Saga story right out of the window.

'Thjóðhild's Church' stands a few metres away from a large hayfield. There is nothing to see there except grass stubble. But just under the surface there is a great deal to be seen: a major Viking farm complex, no less. The first traces were found by the farmer, Hans Christian Motzfeldt,

The tiny country church of Núpsstaður in the south of Iceland, with turf walls and wooden gable; 'Thjóðhild's Church' at Brattahlíð would have looked like this.

in a hollow in his field in 1975; ever since then, Dr Krogh has been carefully surveying the field, season by season, and digging trial trenches which he thoughtfully fills in again to allow the farmer to continue to use his field for hay. So far, Dr Krogh has established the outlines of several buildings, and the turf foundations of a farmhouse that could well have been Eirík the Red's original homestead only *fifty* metres north of the little church.

So what went wrong with that felicitous association of Eirík's Brattahlíð and the 'Thjóðhild's Church' of *Eirík's Saga*? Alas, it seems that the story in *Eirík's Saga* is simply inspired fiction – inspired by what was *then* visible to the Saga-writer or his informants. The earlier source, *Grænlendinga saga*, makes no reference to 'Thjóðhild's Church'; indeed, it states categorically (Ch. 5) that Eirík the Red died before the introduction of Christianity to Greenland.

According to the new scenario afforded us by archaeology, what seems to have happened is this: Eirík the Red built the first farm at Brattahlíð in what is now Farmer Motzfeldt's hayfield. After Eirík died, Christianity was introduced to Greenland (from Iceland, not from Norway) and a small chapel was built close to the homestead. Some time later, for reasons about which we can only guess, the Brattahlíð farmstead was moved two hundred metres north to the site of the present ruins of 'Eirík's Hall', and a new church was built beside it. By the time that *Eirík's Saga* was being written, late in the thirteenth century, all traces of the original farmstead had disappeared, but the tiny chapel was still in evidence. So the Saga-writer was faced with the intriguing situation that at Brattahlíð – and only at Brattahlíð – a church had apparently been built 'not too close' to the farm. Some explanation for this aberration was required; and thus the apocryphal story of Thjóðhild and her chapel came about.

The confusion over 'Thjóðhild's Church' and the introduction of Christianity to Greenland leads us straight to the heart of a major problem concerning the two Greenland Sagas and their account of the Viking discovery of Vínland, somewhere in North America. *Eirík's Saga* (the later and more polished of the two) claims that North America was first sighted, accidentally, by Leif the Lucky on his evangelising journey home from Norway to Greenland in the year 1000, when his ship was storm-swept west across the Atlantic. *Grænlendinga saga*, however, gives the credit for that first accidental sighting to someone else: a man called Bjarni Herjólfsson.

According to *Grænlendinga saga*, one of the first colonists who accompanied Eirík the Red to Greenland was an Icelander called Herjólf Bárðarson, bankrupted by the famines; his son, Bjarni Herjólfsson, was a prosperous merchant who plied the trade routes from Iceland to Norway, spending alternate winters abroad and at home with his father. Bjarni happened to be in Norway during the winter that his father made the momentous decision to sell up his farm and emigrate to Greenland with

Eirík; when he reached Iceland the following summer, it was to be met with the news that his father had upped sticks and started a new life in Greenland at a farm called Herjólfsnes, at the southernmost point of the Eastern Settlement (modern Ikigait, 'Burnt Homestead'). Bjarni was greatly taken aback; he promptly decided not to unload his cargo, but to follow his father to Greenland so that he could stay with him that winter, as was his custom. His crew, whatever their misgivings about sailing into uncharted waters, accepted his decision, and off they went:

> As soon as they were ready they put to sea, and sailed for three days until land was lost to sight below the horizon. Then the fair wind failed and northerly gales and fog set in, and for many days they had no idea what their course was. After that they saw the sun again and were able to get their bearings; they hoisted sail, and after a day's sailing they sighted land. (*Grænlendinga saga*, Ch. 2)

The land they sighted, by obvious implication, was the eastern seaboard of North America. But the Saga gives no indication of precisely where the landfall may have been; it merely says that 'the country was not mountainous, but was well wooded and with low hills', a vague description that could apply to innumerable places along that vast coastline. From what Bjarni had heard about Greenland, he reckoned it could not be that; and so, cautious by nature and perhaps mindful of his precious cargo, he decided not to go ashore to explore this unknown country. Instead he put out to sea again, 'leaving the land on the port quarter'.

Bjarni Herjólfsson, we are given to understand, realised that he had been blown much too far to the west, and was intent only on reaching Greenland. Two days later he sighted land again; this was a flat, well-forested country, and once again Bjarni refused to accept that this could be Greenland, for he had been told that there were huge glaciers on Greenland. When his crew wanted to land to collect firewood and water, Bjarni refused – a decision that caused much grumbling among his men.

On they went, arcing towards the north-east. After three days' sailing before a south-westerly breeze they sighted land for a third time. This one was high and mountainous, and capped by a glacier. But even now, Bjarni was unimpressed, 'For this land seems to me to be worthless,' he said. He hugged the coastline long enough to establish that it must be an island, and then set his prow to the open sea again. After four days of sailing before a gale-force wind he sighted a fourth land; and *this*, at long last, Bjarni was prepared to accept as being Greenland. He made land at dusk at the nearest promontory which, by happy if unlikely chance, turned out to be Herjólfsnes – his father's new home. It had been, in retrospect, an oddly inglorious voyage in comparison with the fame that history would have accorded him if he had taken the risk of going ashore and actually exploring the New World, instead of merely sighting it. Indeed, *Grænlendinga saga* reports that when Bjarni next went to Norway and talked about the

Farmer Motzfeldt's hayfield at Brattahlíð. Eirík the Red's original farm is now thought to lie under this field.

unknown lands he had seen, 'People thought he had shown a great lack of curiosity, and he was criticised for this' (Ch. 3). The Saga tells us that Bjarni now abandoned his career as a merchant, stayed with his father, and carried on farming Herjólfsnes after his father's death.

In *Eirík's Saga*, on the other hand, it is not Bjarni Herjólfsson (who is not even mentioned) but Leif Eiríksson – Leif the Lucky – who gets the credit for the first accidental sighting of North America. As we saw earlier, *Eirík's Saga* casts Leif the Lucky in a glamorised role as Greenland's evangelist. It was on his journey home to Greenland on that pious mission in the year 1000 that he is meant to have sighted unknown transatlantic lands:

> Leif set sail when he was ready; he ran into prolonged difficulties at sea, and finally came upon lands whose existence he had never suspected. There were fields of wild wheat growing there, and vines, and among the trees there were maples. They took samples of all these things.
>
> (*Eirík's Saga*, Ch. 5)

Most scholars now accept that *Eirík's Saga* is much less trustworthy, as

a historical source, than *Grænlendinga saga*, which itself has to be treated with considerable caution. It now seems quite certain that *Eirík's Saga* was written as a conscious correction, improvement indeed, of the much earlier *Grænlendinga saga* in the light of what the author considered to be more reliable information – especially about Leif the Lucky and King Ólaf Tryggvason of Norway. The traditional view used to be that *Eirík's Saga* was the 'better' of the two, from a literary standpoint, and therefore the earlier; but the problem of the relationship between the two Sagas was brilliantly resolved by the Icelandic historian, the late Professor Jón Jóhannesson.[1] It was a stunning piece of literary detective work, which proved beyond any reasonable doubt that *Grænlendinga saga*, far from being later than *Eirík's Saga*, was in fact one of the earliest of all the Icelandic Sagas, written only about 150 years after the time of the Vínland adventure.

The key to the solution lay in the role of that enigmatic character, King Ólaf Tryggvason of Norway. He was the darling of the Icelandic poets and

High summer in Greenland: the fjords of the 'Eastern Settlement' still clogged by ice-floes.

[1] '*Aldur Grænlendinga Sögu*' in *Nordæla* (Reykjavik, 1956), published in English as 'The Date of the Composition of the Saga of the Greenlanders' in *Saga-Book*, 1962.

Leif the Lucky decides to explore Vinland; Chapter 2 of *Grænlendinga saga* in *Flateyjarbók*.

Saga-historians, and was hailed as a great champion of Christianity, having played a major role in the conversion of Iceland in the year 1000 (*cf* Ch. 7). He was credited with having been instrumental in the conversion of four other lands besides – Norway, Shetland, the Orkneys and the Faroes.

This fulsome attitude towards King Ólaf Tryggvason in the Icelandic sources stands in stark contrast with the view of him expressed by medieval Continental historians like Saxo Grammaticus of Denmark and the eleventh-century German cleric, Adam of Bremen. To them, he was anathema: no evangelist, not even a Christian, more like Antichrist – a foreign usurper who seized the throne of Norway by force and wrought untold harm in that country before his unlamented death in battle in the year 1000. One can perhaps trace this ungenerous attitude to the fact that the Archbishopric of Hamburg was keen to apportion to itself the prestige and perquisites of having Christianised the northlands through its own missionaries, rather than allowing the credit to be given to an upstart king.

The Icelandic historians, however, wanted a patron saint of their own – and who better than Ólaf Tryggvason, whose ruthless power-politics had helped to bring Iceland to the true faith? And so, to give further polish to King Ólaf's lustre as the alleged evangelist of the northlands, round about the year 1200 an Icelandic monk called Odd Snorrason wrote a Latin biography of King Ólaf Tryggvason which, for the first time, added Greenland to the list of Ólaf's evangelising achievements.

Once this pious fiction was accepted, it meant that history and Saga alike had to be rewritten. Jón Jóhannesson argued that since the author of *Grænlendinga saga* made no mention of Ólaf Tryggvason's part in the conversion of Greenland, it must have been written *before* the story was invented by Odd Snorrason around 1200; whereas it was to explain *how* King Ólaf achieved the conversion of Greenland that Leif the Lucky was wheeled on stage as his evangelising agent in *Eirík's Saga*, with the happy chance discovery of Vínland as an auspicious start to his holy mission.

Through Jón Jóhannesson's masterly solution of the problem of the two Vínland Sagas, the problem of Vínland itself becomes correspondingly more manageable – although it should also caution us not to take either of the two Sagas too literally. It appears that we can now discount the version given in *Eirík's Saga* of Europe's first contacts with North America – all the more so now that the story of 'Thjóðhild's Church' has been shown up archaeologically to be an inspired rationalisation rather than reality.

In *Grænlendinga saga*, Leif Eiríksson is celebrated not as the first chance *discoverer* of Vínland, but as the first deliberate *explorer* of Vínland:

> There was now great talk [in Greenland] of discovering new countries. Leif, the son of Eirík the Red of Brattahlíð, went to see Bjarni Herjólfsson and bought his ship off him, and engaged a crew of thirty-five.
> (*Grænlendinga saga*, Ch. 3)

There is an echo there of the old adage that 'ships know the way back': Leif clearly planned to retrace Bjarni's course in reverse. The Saga indicates that Eirík the Red himself was invited to lead the expedition, but eventually declined because he felt that he was too old for it – his pioneering days were over; so it seems reasonable to assume a date sometime in the 990s for Leif's voyage of exploration westwards:

> The first landfall they made was the country that Bjarni had sighted last. They sailed right up to the shore and cast anchor, then lowered a boat and landed. There was no grass to be seen, and the hinterland was covered with great glaciers, and between glaciers and shore was like one great slab of rock. It seemed to them a worthless country.

Eskimo figurine found on Baffin Island in 1977 commemorates a Viking visit.

Dismissively, Leif Eiríksson named it *Helluland* – literally, 'Slab-Land' – and sailed on his way. There can be little doubt that this was the south coast of Baffin Island; indeed, it is now clear that Baffin Island became a regular landfall for seafarers voyaging from Greenland or Iceland to Vínland, and remained so for a very long time. There are several Saga references to this; but very recently, in 1977, tangible evidence of it came to light in Baffin Island itself, during the excavation of an ancient Eskimo winter-house at Okivilialuk on the south coast.

The site was being dug by two archaeologists from Michigan State University, George and Deborah Sabo. The house had been a substantial structure dating to the thirteenth century, with a stone-slabbed floor, walls of stone and turf, and a roof made of whale-ribs covered with turf. It was in houses like this one that the Eskimos spent the winter, cosily insulated against the cold in sleeping quarters that were dug well below ground level.

On the floor of this Eskimo house at Okivilialuk, Deborah Sabo found a tiny carved wooden figurine – a doll, perhaps, or just a casual doodle,

226

a Tom Thumb figure just over 5 cm in height. What makes it so significant is that scholars are in no doubt at all that it was meant to depict a Viking: a Viking wearing an ankle-length pleated robe, split in front from below the waist to the hem – a form of clothing quite consistent with that worn by Europeans, including the Norsemen of Greenland, in the thirteenth century. On the figurine's chest there is a lightly-incised cross, perhaps to indicate the wearing of a Christian amulet.

It represents an Eskimo view of those alien Europeans who dropped in occasionally on Baffin Island – not, I like to think, as ravening robbers, but in search of mutually profitable trade; this Viking, at least, is depicted without any weapons. The style is typically Eskimo – the flat, featureless face, for instance. It is the gravity, the fine dignity of this doll-like figure that I find so telling, as telling as any Saga. The Vikings saw the Eskimos as savages, mere 'Skrælings', but they were wrong; the material culture of the Eskimos, their life-style, their standards of civilisation, were every bit as high as those of the Norsemen who affected to despise them.

From Baffin Island, Leif the Lucky came to a second land:

> Once again they sailed right up to it and cast anchor, lowered a boat and went ashore. This country was flat and wooded, with white sandy beaches wherever they went; and the land sloped gently down to the sea.

This country, obviously the one where Bjarni Herjólfsson's crew had wanted to land to collect firewood and water, Leif named *Markland*, literally 'Forest-Land'; it is usually identified with the coast of Labrador. Later voyagers, impressed by these interminable reaches of white sand after the black volcanic sands of Iceland, would name it *Furðustrandir* – 'Wonder Strands'.

From Labrador/Markland, Leif sailed for another two days before a north-easterly wind and sighted land for a third time. He sailed towards it, and came to an island that lay to the north of it:

> They went ashore and looked about them. The weather was fine. There was dew on the grass, and the first thing they did was to get some of it on their hands and put it to their lips, and to them it seemed the sweetest thing they had ever tasted.

But Leif still did not feel that he had 'arrived' yet. He negotiated the sound between the island and the mainland promontory, sailing west round the headland. His men were now impatient to get ashore. They towed their boat up a river to a lake, where they dropped anchor. They decided to winter there, and built some large houses which would become known as *Leifsbúðir* – 'Leif's Booths' (booths were stone-and-turf enclosures which could be temporarily roofed with awnings for occupation, as at the *Althing* at Thingvellir in Iceland):

> There was no lack of salmon there in the river or the lake, larger salmon than they had ever seen before. The natural qualities of the land seemed

to them so choice that no winter fodder would be needed for livestock; there was no frost all winter, and the grass hardly withered at all. In that country, night and day were of more equal length than in either Greenland or Iceland.

Reconnaissance parties were sent out on day-long sorties to explore the interior. On one of these expeditions a German member of the crew, a man called Tyrkir, made a discovery so exciting that it reduced him to babbling incoherence: he found grapes growing wild! All wine in Greenland and Iceland had to be imported from the Continent, at considerable expense no doubt; here was a new source, free for the taking, verified by a man who ought to know all about wine if he came from Germany.

This was the jackpot. The fact of *grapes* is absolutely central to the Icelandic traditions. The adventurers gathered a boatload of grapes and vines, and felled enough timber to freight their ship; next spring they sailed back home to Greenland, grapes and all – although they must have become raisins by then! And Leif named the land after its natural qualities, and called it *Vínland* – 'Wineland', the Land of Grapes; he had clearly inherited all his father's flair for inspired name-giving.

Such is the bare outline of the discovery of Vínland, as recounted in *Grænlendinga saga*: tantalisingly vague as far as geographical details are concerned, hopelessly perfunctory in its navigational directions, intriguingly precise in certain topographical particulars. Later expeditions, led by Leif's brothers and in-laws, would add further details – and further confusion – to the story of Vínland in both *Grænlendinga saga* and *Eirík's Saga*. All these references, with their inconsistencies and mutual contradictions, have provoked an endless and acrimonious literature on the actual location of the Vínland of the Sagas; by judicious or injudicious selection of particular words and phrases from one or both of the Sagas, enthusiasts have 'located' Vínland in places as far apart as Hudson Bay in the north and Florida in the south – and practically everywhere else in between!

It is my personal opinion that the Vínland of the Sagas can never be located with any precision from the evidence of the Sagas alone. They are essentially works of literature, not geographical treatises. In them, Vínland is not so much a place as a concept, a glimpsed paradise of plenty that acquired almost Biblical or Elysian literary overtones: 'Vínland the Good', as *Eirík's Saga* would call it. It hangs over the horizon of history like some semi-tropical *is-blikk*.

At the core of the concept is the report of grapes growing wild, and fields of self-sown wheat, as *Eirík's Saga* would later claim. It was this sensational aspect of North America that flew by word of mouth round the Northlands in the eleventh century. Long before the Icelandic Saga-writers committed their version of the discovery to calfskin, the German cleric, Adam of Bremen, had heard the story from no less an informant than King Svein Úlfsson of Denmark, nephew of King Knút (Canute); and around the year 1075, Adam included it in his monumental Latin history of the Archbishopric of Hamburg (*Gesta Hammaburgensis ecclesiae pontificum*):

> [King Svein] also spoke of yet another island of the many found in that ocean. It is called Vínland because vines producing excellent wine grow wild there; moreover, self-sown wheat grows there in abundance. It is not from any fabulous imaginings that we have learned this, but from the reliable reports of the Danes. (Book IV, Ch. 38)

It sounds like proof, but it is not a 'proof' that stands up to scrutiny. Most commentators conveniently overlook the fact that Adam of Bremen wrote some extremely silly things about other islands in the Atlantic in his *Descriptio insularum Aquilonis* in the *Gesta*: about Greenland, for instance, he says, 'The salt sea there gives the inhabitants a bluish-green appearance, and from this the country gets its name.' Adam of Bremen does not 'prove' the existence of Vínland – just the existence of a *story* about Vínland.

Attempts to found a permanent Norse settlement on Vínland there certainly were, and not half-hearted attempts either. Leif the Lucky was clearly in no doubt about the potential value of Vínland as an extension of the Brattahlíð domain in Greenland: he is said to have encouraged further voyages to Vínland, but he was careful to keep his seigneurial lien on the houses he had built, 'Leif's Booths', which he was prepared to lease but not to sell.

In both the Vínland Sagas, the major attempt at colonisation was made a few years after Leif's first voyage by an Icelander called Thorfinn Karlsefni (his nickname means, literally, 'Man Material' or 'Makings of a Man'). He was a merchant of substance from Skagafjörður in the north of Iceland, who came to Greenland on a trading voyage and spent the winter enjoying the abundant hospitality of Brattahlíð. He enjoyed no less the company of Eirík the Red's widowed daughter-in-law, a strikingly beautiful and wealthy lady called Guðríð, whom he married at Christmas.

Grænlendinga saga describes in somewhat bare outline Thorfinn Karlsefni's attempt to carve out a new life for himself and his bride in Vínland, living in rented accommodation at 'Leif's Booths'. His expedition consisted of sixty men and five women in one ship, with sufficient livestock to make farming viable. They spent three years in 'Leif's Booths', where Guðríð gave birth to a son, Snorri Thorfinnsson, the first white child to be born in North America according to the written records. *Eirík's Saga* is more lavish of detail and correspondingly more confusing. Thorfinn's expedition now consisted of two ships and 160 people. But because the author of *Eirík's Saga* had deliberately discarded the story of Leif's planned voyage of exploration and substituted a chance discovery in the year 1000, there were no 'Leif's Booths' for Thorfinn to lease and

Grapes growing wild in North America – the *Vínland* (Wineland) of the Vikings.

occupy; so *Eirík's Saga* has Thorfinn and his fellow-colonists stopping off at two places, both now unidentifiable, the one called *Hóp* ('Tidal Lake'), the other called *Straumfjörður* ('Current Fjord'); but the illusion, at least, of having found Vínland is indicated by references to self-sown wheat and wild grapes.

What the two Sagas have in common, however, is their version of why the attempted colonisation of Vínland failed, after only three years; in both Sagas it was said to have been because of increasingly hostile relations with the indigenous natives, the Skrælings. *Eirík's Saga* describes them as small and evil-looking, with coarse hair, large eyes and broad cheekbones; they travelled in skin-boats (canoes or kayaks), and swung staves in the air that made a noise like flails or rattle-sticks. It is clearly impossible to decide, from these patronising Saga references alone, whether these natives were Indians or Eskimos; but Dr Robert McGhee, Arctic Archaeologist at the National Museums of Canada in Ottawa, thinks that although there may have been remnant Eskimo populations in some coastal areas at that time, the archaeological evidence from Newfoundland and Labrador suggests that these areas were occupied by Amer-Indians during this period, probably the Algonkian ancestors of the Beothuk and Montagnais tribes. Further south, of course, one would not expect to find any Eskimo occupation at all.

Whatever the ethnic identity of the Skrælings, the Sagas leave us in no doubt about their decisive effect on the Viking attempt to join Vínland to Europe. The first contacts between aborigines and would-be colonists were apparently friendly, if a little wary; the Skrælings seemed happy at first to trade their valuable furs and pelts for milk (according to *Grænlendinga saga*) or for ever-diminishing strips of red cloth (*Eirík's Saga*). But it did not take long for them to realise that they were being

230

exploited. When they returned, fighting broke out, whether accidentally or on purpose. Thorfinn Karlsefni prudently stockaded his little outpost; but still the Skrælings came at him, with increasingly hostile intent.

After three years, Thorfinn Karlsefni bowed to the inevitable. The Norse settlers were hopelessly outnumbered; their lines of communication with their northern homelands were far too stretched; their iron weapons, although superior to the Stone Age weapons of the Skrælings, were not superior enough to keep the enemy at bay indefinitely. And so, with considerable regret no doubt, Thorfinn Karlsefni turned his back on this alluring land of Vínland and returned home, first to Greenland and then to Iceland, with a rich cargo of valuable produce and an even richer cargo of exotic yarns and stories. The Vínland enterprise was over, for the time being at least; Europe, to put it simply, was not yet ready to colonise America.

Did it leave any mark, this abortive attempt to bring North America into the ambit of North Europe? Yes, indirectly – in the form of a welter of wishful thinking. Canadians would like to claim Vínland as theirs because of the Saga references to maple trees and maple wood; the maple leaf is now the national emblem of Canada, and *Grænlendinga saga* says that when Thorfinn Karlsefni visited Norway after his Vínland adventure, one of the souvenirs he traded was a carved gable-head of maple wood. Americans, on the other hand, would also like to claim Vínland as theirs because they find it hard to resist the temptation to push back the frontiers of their cultural heritage as far as possible beyond the relatively recent sixteenth century to the more distant Viking Age.

It is this kind of wishful thinking that has given birth to a major 'Spot the Viking' industry in North America. Ludicrous claims have been made for the most unlikely 'identifications': a seventeenth-century windmill at Newport on Rhode Island, alleged 'rune-stones' in Oklahoma, various 'anchor-holes' bored into rocks on the seashore, the so-called 'Beardmore Find' of genuine Viking artefacts claimed to have been found at Lake Superior in Ontario, and so on. More recently a much more serious claim has been made for a complex of stone buildings and cairns at Ungava Bay, in Hudson Strait, in the province of North Quebec. The excavator, Thomas E. Lee of the Centre d'Études Nordiques at Laval University, is the maverick of Canadian archaeology; he is passionately convinced that the Ungava Bay site is Viking, while most of his fellow archaeologists are equally convinced that it is Eskimo.

The Kensington Stone is much the most preposterous of all the so-called 'Viking relics' in North America. It now sits on a ceremonial plinth, draped with cloth of white-fringed royal blue, in the entrance hall of the Alexandria Agricultural Museum in Douglas County, Minnesota. Above it hangs a map purporting to show the Viking route to Minnesota via the St Lawrence and the Great Lakes. Outside, in the nearby 'Runestone Memorial Park', stands a monstrous reproduction of the Stone weighing some

A monstrous concrete effigy of a Viking welcomes the visitor to Alexandria, in Minnesota, now the home of the Kensington Stone.

VIKINGS!

18,000 kgs. In Main Street itself the eye is gladdened by the sight of a huge concrete sculpture of a Viking warrior with a targe bearing the words 'Alexandria – Birthplace of America'. In the museum itself, questing visitors in search of truth (about 17,000 of them a year) are welcomed by attractive young ladies carefully programmed to deal with doubters and sceptics.

The Stone originally came to light in 1898. It had allegedly been found embedded in the roots of a poplar tree in a field near the village of Kensington in western Minnesota, the most Nordic state in the USA. The man who claimed to have found it was a Swedish immigrant farmer called Olof Ohman, who had been farming the land since 1890. It was dark grey in colour, and shaped like a rough-hewn grave slab, about 76 cm high, 40 cm wide, and 13 cm thick. It weighed about 90 kgs. On the upper half of the face and along one of the edges there was an exceptionally long and elaborate inscription in what looked like medieval runic lettering. It turned out to be written in a bizarre mixture of modern Swedish, Norwegian, Danish and English, with an overlay of curiously inconsistent archaisms. Tidied up, an English translation might read something like this:

. . . 8 Goths [Swedes] and 22 Northmen on a journey of exploration westward from Vínland. Our camp was by two skerries one day's journey north from this stone. We were out fishing one day. When we came home, found 10 men red with blood and dead. AVM [Ave Maria?] save us from evil. Have ten men by the sea to look after our ships, 14 days' journey from this island. 1362.

Unfortunately the runic inscription on the Stone was promptly and brusquely dismissed by the foremost Scandinavian scholars of the day as an inept forgery. In 1907, however, it was acquired by a Wisconsin writer, impresario and self-styled 'runologist' called Hjalmar Rued Holand; and for the next fifty years, Holand devoted all his formidable skills as a special pleader to arguing the case for the authenticity of the Kensington Stone. Eventually, by sheer dogged perseverance, he managed to gain acceptance for it from many not undistinguished quarters, both lay and learned alike – including the Smithsonian Institution of Washington, which put it on display in 1948 with the implied imprimatur of its own great authority.

At this point the Swedish Academy of Sciences commissioned Professor Sven B. F. Jansson, now the doyen of runic scholars, to examine the Stone at first hand and make a report. Jansson's verdict was unequivocal: the Kensington Stone had no significance for runologists whatsoever. In 1958 a young scholar called Erik Wahlgren, of Wisconsin University, pricked the bubble with a devastating *exposé* of the Holand fable.[1] Quite simply, he took Holand and all his pretensions to scholarship apart, and proved utterly and absolutely that the Kensington Stone was a modern forgery.

[1] *The Kensington Stone – A Mystery Solved* (Madison, 1958).

232

But who did it? Wahlgren took conspicuous care not to point an accusing finger at any particular individual. But he made it pretty plain that Olof Ohman of Kensington, far from being the ignorant rustic suggested by Holand, was in reality a thoughtful, self-tutored man, with a deep interest in mysticism and numerology. Among the books in his library was a Swedish popular encyclopaedia, Carl Rosander's *The Well-Informed Schoolmaster (Den Kunskapsrike Skolmästaren)*, first issued in Stockholm in 1864 and subsequently re-issued in a number of editions in Sweden and the United States, in particular the Chicago edition of 1893; Ohman's copy was particularly well-thumbed at the section dealing with the history of the Swedish language, from runes onward.

We can now understand both the *how* and the *why* of this classic American hoax. America was in a fever of excitement over the Chicago World Fair of 1893 ('The Columbian Exposition') which had featured so dramatically Magnus Andersen's epic sailing of a near-replica of the Gokstad Ship from Norway to North America (*cf* Ch. 2). The atmosphere was right for a forgery, Scandinavian immigrants in America were in the right mood to accept one, the whole world was geared to thinking about Vikings in North America.

Another Viking forger who got away with it for a time in a blaze of publicity was the man who made the so-called 'Vinland Map', which purported to be a fifteenth-century (and therefore pre-Columbian) chart of the Atlantic depicting the Vinland of the Sagas. It was published by Yale University with much scholarly pomp and panoply in 1965 as *The Vinland Map and the Tartar Relation*. Today, the 'Vinland Map' has been shown up to be a forgery, and a laughably bad forgery at that; but at the time, a lot of people were taken in by it – myself included. I recall with some embarrassment an enthusiastic article in *The Scotsman* newspaper in which I hailed it as a major breakthrough in Old Norse studies!

The Map itself is a pen-and-ink drawing of the world on a sheet of much-scraped parchment, light greyish-brown in colour, measuring just over 27.8 cm by 41 cm and folded in two. It is an unprepossessing-looking document, spattered with exotic geographical names and Latin legends, and marred by four pairs of worm-holes. On the back of it there is a Latin inscription whose import is not immediately clear: 'Delineation of the first, second and third parts of the *Speculum*'. Much of the Map seems to be based on a copy (or even a copy of a copy) of a world map drawn by the Venetian cartographer Andrea Bianco in 1436. What made it such a sensational 'find' is the addition, in the north-western corner, of the Norse Atlantic settlements: a rather haphazardly depicted Iceland, a remarkably accurate Greenland, and a vast lumpy island labelled *Vinilanda Insula*: obviously, the Vinland of the Sagas. It is shown with two deep inlets on the eastern seaboard, very roughly corresponding to the Hudson Strait and the Gulf of St Lawrence. The *Vinilanda* label adds the information

The Kensington Stone with its fake runic inscription.

'*discovered by Bjarni and Leif in company*'. The top left-hand corner carries a lengthy legend in indifferent Latin which begins as follows:

> By God's will, after a long voyage from the island of Greenland to the south toward the most distant remaining parts of the western ocean sea, sailing southward amid the ice, the companions Bjarni and Leif Eiríksson discovered a new land, extremely fertile and even having vines, the which island they named Vínland . . .

The distinguished academic editors of the Yale volume claimed that it must have been made around 1440 by a monk working in some scriptorium in the Upper Rhineland; he had evidently modified his copy of the Bianco world map with some hitherto unknown chart made by a (presumably) Norse cartographer in the thirteenth century, based on the Saga accounts of the Viking voyages to Vínland.

It had reached Yale University in a curiously circuitous way. It is not an easy story to piece together, but an authoritative account of it was given by Dr Helen Wallis, Superintendent of the Map Room at the British Library, at a symposium on the Vinland Map held at the Royal Geographical

234

Society in February 1974, and published in *The Geographical Journal* (June 1974).

In 1957 an Italian bookseller long resident in Barcelona, the late Enzo Ferrajoli de Ry, had shown it to antiquarian booksellers in Geneva, London and Paris on behalf of an anonymous client. It was bound in a relatively modern binding with twenty-one pages of a previously unknown account of a mission to the Mongol court in 1245–7 by the Franciscan Friar John de Plano Carpini, entitled *The Tartar Relation*. This mission, undertaken at the behest of Pope Innocent IV, was one of the first links of the West with the East, and was previously known only from Friar Carpini's own account of it; *The Tartar Relation* purported to be an account of the same mission from a different source. It was hailed (but not in all quarters) as a highly significant historical document in its own right; but it was the 'Vinland Map' accompanying it that attracted the most attention.

A London bookseller now came on to the scene: the late Joseph Irving Davis, of Davis and Orioli Ltd. Davis helped Ferrajoli to have the Map volume seen at the British Museum by Dr R. A. Skelton, then Superintendent of the Map Room, and George D. Painter, Assistant Keeper in charge of incunabula in the Department of Printed Books. If genuine, the Map was obviously a spectacular catch, 'of so arresting a character as to prompt scepticism, if not incredulity', according to Dr Skelton. The British Museum experts *were* sceptical. The date of the Map, and therefore its authenticity, depended on the date of the accompanying *The Tartar Relation*, which was adjudged to be *c.* AD 1440 from the style of the handwriting and the watermarks on the paper on which it was written. Unfortunately, although both the Map and *The Tartar Relation* had worm-holes, the worm-holes did not match; in addition, the Latin of the inscriptions was adjudged to be suspect, and the reference to the *Speculum* on the back of the Map was inexplicable. So the British Museum rejected the volume.

The book was returned to Geneva, where it was bought for a reputed $3,500 by an antiquarian dealer from New Haven in Connecticut called Laurence Witten. Witten bought it because he believed that it was a genuine fifteenth-century product, and therefore an absolute snip for the 'Americana' market in the States. He showed it to Yale University, where it was examined by two experts, Thomas E. Marston, Curator of Medieval and Renaissance Literature, and Alexander O. Vietor, Curator of Maps of Yale University Library. Like the British Museum experts, they were not convinced that the Map was sufficiently well authenticated; Vietor, however, asked for a 'first refusal' option on the book. As Vietor explained on a BBC TV *Chronicle* programme for which I interviewed him in 1966, 'We were extremely interested in it. It looked right to us, it smelled right, as they say, but there were two disturbing features: one, that it was in a relatively modern binding, and two, that certain worm-holes on the surface of the Map did not coincide with what was only a single worm-hole in

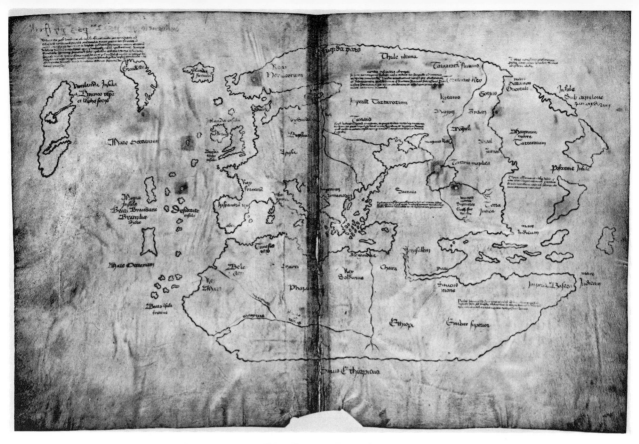

The Vinland Map.

the front page of *The Tartar Relation*. This made us feel that the two pieces did not belong together, and we did not quite know the reason.'

But now the long arm of coincidence – too long, some might think – stretched out, right on cue to allay Vietor's doubts. It just so happened that the London bookseller, Joseph Davis, had bought from Enzo Ferrajoli, the Italian bookseller, another work reputedly from that same private library which had provided the Map and *The Tartar Relation*. This was a 'rather sorry' fragment of a fifteenth-century copy of a thirteenth-century work called the *Speculum Historiale (Mirror of History)* by Vincent de Beauvais. It was advertised at a price of £75 in the 1958 Davis and Orioli catalogue, where it was spotted and purchased by Thomas Marston as a routine acquisition for the Yale University Library. He happened to show it to Laurence Witten – and now what has been sardonically called 'a miraculous reunion' occurred.

According to Alexander Vietor, 'Mr Witten eventually noticed, to his astonishment, that the worm-holes in the Vinland Map coincided with the worm-holes in the first half of the *Speculum Historiale*. He then turned to *The Tartar Relation* and discovered that its single worm-hole exactly matched the single worm-hole in the back of the *Speculum Historiale*. So, by an incredible chance, these three pieces, which had obviously once been bound together, were reunited at Yale University Library, and a strong argument was established for a fifteenth-century date for the Map and its first known delineation of the American continent.'

236

An incredible chance, indeed – but not incredible enough, apparently, for it to be disbelieved by a lot of people who probably now feel that they should have known better. Everything had literally fallen into place: the worm-holes matched up, and that mysterious reference to the '*Speculum*' in the endorsement on the back of the Vinland Map was now explained. What seemed to have happened was that the three documents – Map, *The Tartar Relation*, and *Speculum Historiale*, which all came from the same anonymous private library – had come adrift sometime previously, and had been re-bound in a different order. The *Speculum Historiale* had then come on to the market in a manner which can only be described as providential, at the right moment to help authenticate the Vinland Map.

Anyway, in the spring of 1959 the reunited manuscripts were bought by an anonymous Yale benefactor (believed to be Mr Paul Mellon of Pittsburgh) for a reputed £100,000; he donated them to the Yale University Library, and entrusted the task of editing and publishing them to Skelton, Marston and Painter.

For seven long years the three editors laboured over their *magnum opus*; at the end they produced a mountain of scholarship but only a mouse of a Map. It was immediately and roundly condemned by specialists in many disciplines, not least in Old Norse studies. In particular, scholars criticised Witten's adamant refusal to reveal the Map's provenance or pedigree. The most forthright condemnation came from one of England's leading cartographists, the late Professor Eva Taylor. Her rejection of the Map rested largely on the depiction of Greenland, which was drawn as an island – a fact which no one could possibly have known before it was established by explorations late in the nineteenth century; in addition, Greenland was drawn with such accuracy that Professor Taylor had no hesitation in saying that it had simply been traced from a modern school atlas.

In January 1967 the Map was exhibited at the British Museum in the course of a European tour, and scientists from the Research Laboratory there took the opportunity of making a brief examination of it with optical means like ultra-violet light and low-power binocular microscopy. They found the ink of the Map distinctly suspect; it did not appear to be of the same substance as the faded iron-gall ink of the other manuscripts, and they told Yale University so. Increasingly beleaguered and embarrassed by the mounting opposition to the Map, Yale eventually initiated its own scientific investigation. The task was entrusted to a Chicago firm of specialists in the field of small-particle analysis, Walter C. McCrone Associates. That was in 1968, but it was not until 1972 that everybody was satisfied that the available micro-analytical tools and techniques were adequate for the job. Micro-samples of the inks from all three manuscripts were taken and subjected to advanced electronic tests to reveal their crystalline structure.

The McCrone report was unequivocal, and devastating: the inks in *The Tartar Relation* and the *Speculum Historiale* were organic iron gallo-

L'Anse aux Meadows, in Newfoundland: site of the only indisputable Norse settlement yet found in North America.

tannate, like most other medieval inks, but the ink from the Map was not; the ink on the Map contained large proportions of an inorganic element called *titanium dioxide* (in the form of anatase) which was not developed until 1917 at the very earliest.

So the 'Vinland Map' was a twentieth-century fake after all, as many scholars had suspected. On 26 January 1974 Yale sent out a sorrowful little news release:

> Yale University Library reported today that its researches suggest that the famous Vinland Map may be a forgery. This conclusion is based on exhaustive studies initiated by the Yale Library taking advantage of techniques of chemical analysis only recently developed by scientists . . .

Ultimately it did not matter very much. Even if the 'Vinland Map' had been a genuine fifteenth-century, pre-Columbian product, it would not have had any significant impact on the basic question of the Viking discovery of the New World five centuries before Christopher Columbus. That claim was already documented in the Vínland Sagas; a 'graphic' version of it would only have proved that the map-maker, whoever he was, and in whatever century he worked, knew the Saga traditions, too.

At present the only firm and convincing archaeological evidence of a Viking presence in North America is at a site near a tiny fishing village called L'Anse aux Meadows, on the northernmost tip of Newfoundland. The locals (there are only seventy inhabitants) call it 'Lancy Meadows', thus making it an English-language name; but in fact it is a corruption of the original French name, 'L'Anse au Méduse' ('Jellyfish Creek'), dating back to the time when French fishermen started working in the area in the seventeenth century.

Today it is a remote and isolated community, perched right at the end of Newfoundland's Great Northern Peninsula; but quite shortly, I predict, it will be anything but – thanks to the Vikings, and to Parks Canada.

The site was located by the Norwegian explorer and writer Helge Ingstad in 1960. Ingstad, a specialist on life in the Arctic, was determined

Viking house-foundation at L'Anse aux Meadows, after re-excavation in the 1970s.

to find tangible proof of the Viking colonisation of Vínland. In 1959 he scoured the coastline from New England northwards, ending up in Canada at a place called Pistolet Bay on Newfoundland, which had recently been investigated by the Danish archaeologist Jørgen Meldgaard in the mid-1950s. The following summer, a L'Anse aux Meadows fisherman, Joe Dekker (his son Lloyd Dekker now works for Parks Canada at the Viking site), told Ingstad about some interesting humps and depressions to be seen near his village, which the locals called the 'Indian Camp'. Lloyd Dekker maintains that it was more or less meant as a joke; but Ingstad took it seriously, and decided that the site was worth excavating. He is not a professional archaeologist himself, but his wife, Anne Stine Ingstad, had had archaeological training; and in 1961 the Ingstad expedition started excavating at L'Anse aux Meadows. In 1968, after seven seasons of excavation, the Ingstads felt able to claim unequivocally that they had found the first indisputable remains of the Norsemen in North America: they had found the Viking settlement in Vínland, 'Leif's Booths'.

Not all scholars were convinced by the claims; there had been all too many false alarms where alleged 'Viking finds' in North America were concerned. With all due respect to the Ingstads, there were also reservations in academic circles about the validity of the results that Helge Ingstad was claiming year by year in the *National Geographic* magazine.

But now all these doubts and suspicions have been dispelled. The L'Anse aux Meadows site has recently been re-excavated (with the willing co-operation of the Ingstads) by an international team supervised by the eminent Swedish archaeologist, Dr Bengt Schönbäck of Gotland. The re-excavation was carried out for four seasons between 1973 and 1976 under the aegis of Parks Canada, after an International Advisory Committee had recognised the unique character of the site the Ingstads had unearthed. It was intended to provide a comprehensive interpretation of the site and to extract as much additional information as possible, in advance of an ambitious scheme to conserve the excavated ruins as the centrepiece of a National Historic Park. This scheme is now well under way, with Robert McNeil as its inspiring and enthusiastic Park Superintendent.

The effect of this re-excavation has been to corroborate the conclusions drawn from the Ingstad excavations, and in some cases to refine them. Dr Schönbäck's report has not yet been published at the time of writing, and obviously he would not want to pre-empt it; but he was good enough to tell me his general conclusion: 'The excavations have confirmed the Ingstad interpretation of the site as a Norse settlement.'

At L'Anse aux Meadows, the Ingstads uncovered the remains of a complex of eight turf-walled structures of a distinctly Norse type. Most of the buildings were situated on a curving marine terrace (a former beach) which lies about a hundred metres from the present shore, separated from it by a low-lying marshy area of peat bogs. A busy little stream, the Black

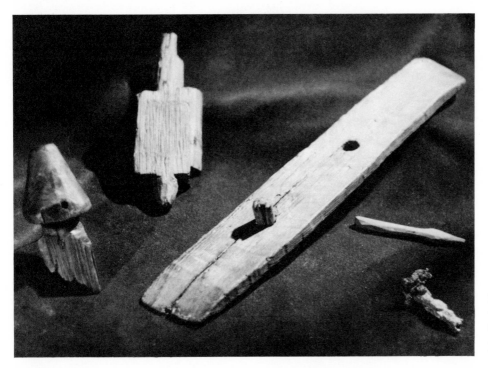

Fragments of worked wood found in the bog at L'Anse aux Meadows, dating from the Norse period.

Duck Brook, meanders through the meadowlands behind this raised terrace and cuts through it before running into the sea.

It is not, at first glance, a typically Norse site. The sea is extremely shallow for a long way out. It is not a natural harbour, although the gently shelving beach would make it easy to haul boats ashore. Indeed, on the drive north to L'Anse aux Meadows one can spot a dozen sites that would have been far more attractive as potential settlement areas. Nor has it any of the sheer lushness of the Vínland of the Sagas – no wild grapes, no self-sown wheat, and certainly no frost-free winters. Grapes have never grown north of Maine, even in the slightly improved climatic conditions of around AD 1000.

Yet there is no doubt now that Vikings nested there for a time, like migrant birds. The little settlement they built consisted of a strung-out line of traditional Norse long-houses with cooking-pits and, sometimes, curving walls – all very reminiscent of Norse buildings from contemporary Greenland and Iceland. There was even a sunken sauna bath dug into the terrace near the largest building ('House F'), identified by the large number of fire-cracked flagstones on the floor.

The Ingstads also claimed they had found the traces of five 'boat-sheds' – five depressions near the shoreline which they interpreted as having been turf-walled winter-sheds for boats. But Schönbäck's team showed that they were, in fact, natural features, formed by erosion caused by storm-driven breakers – they themselves observed this phenomenon actually happening during a storm in October 1975!

A small number of artefacts was found on the site – smaller than one

would have hoped, but consistent with a very brief occupation. The most impressive finds were a steatite spindle-whorl, a bronze ring-headed pin, a stone lamp very like the Icelandic *kola* (a lump of stone with a depression on the top surface to hold the fish-oil that fuelled the wick), and various bits and pieces like a needle-sharpener and some iron rivets. All these were of distinctively Norse manufacture. In addition, Schönbäck's team found several pieces of worked wood in the nearby peat bogs, a few of which have been dated to the Norse period – a pointed post, a decorative terminal from an article of furniture, a piece that has been interpreted as coming from the floor-board of a boat, and a very interesting cylindrical container made of sewn birch-bark that may have been intended for a net-sinker. The rest of the finds were either much earlier, or somewhat later; it is clear from the available evidence that the L'Anse aux Meadows site had previously been used by Eskimos, and was later used by Amer-Indians, of whatever tribe, although it is still not possible to clarify the occupation sequence.

To my own mind, quite apart from the indisputably Norse artefacts found at L'Anse aux Meadows, the most impressive evidence of Viking occupation, the real clincher, lies embedded in the nodules of bog-iron ore one can still grub up beside the Black Duck Brook. These small nodules are formed when particular chemical circumstances, particular bacteria, precipitate the iron that is in the water. It was from these bog-iron ores that the Vikings in Greenland and Iceland smelted and forged iron for their tools and weapons; it was an inferior iron, to be sure, but it was something that the local natives, with their Stone Age culture, by very definition never did.

Across the Black Duck Brook, facing the house-settlement, there is what can only be a Viking smithy. It was excavated in 1962 by an invited team of Scandinavian archaeologists, led by Dr Kristján Eldjárn, then Curator of the National Museum of Iceland and later the President of Iceland. It had been dug into the river bank to make a smelting furnace, which seems then to have been converted into a smithy proper. Embedded in the floor they found stones that look as if they had been used as an anvil and a forge; all around they found hundreds of lumps of iron slag. Nearby there was a kiln pit for making charcoal for the blacksmith's fires. It was just as well that the smithy had been sited across the stream from the rest of the settlement, because one day the place caught fire, burning the wooden roof-supports and leaving tell-tale scorch-marks on the turf walls.

Recent scientific analysis of all these remains suggests that there was only one, or at the most two, smeltings carried out in that little smithy. And judging by the small amount of slag found on the floor, it seems that no more than about three kilograms of iron were ever worked at L'Anse aux Meadows; obviously it was simply for occasional domestic use, certainly not on an industrial scale. It is yet another indication of just how short-lived the Viking presence at L'Anse aux Meadows must have been.

Today, the visitor there can see an impressive reconstruction of one of

OPPOSITE Black Duck Brook at L'Anse aux Meadows. On the right, cut into the bank, the site of the Viking smithy.

OPPOSITE Modern reconstruction of 'House A' at L'Anse aux Meadows.

the Norse houses, which has been specially built for the National Historic Park. Undoubtedly it brings to vivid life the sort of houses which the Vikings of Greenland and Iceland inhabited; it is about twenty-five metres long, divided into four rooms. Two had long-fires in the middle of the room, the other two each had a large cooking-pit.

Despite my admiration for the way in which Parks Canada is presenting the site, I must, however, confess to some reservations about this reconstructed building. It is too solid, too substantial, in relation to the archaeological evidence. The house on which it is based ('House A') is a relatively flimsy structure compared with similar Norse houses in Iceland. The walls are comparatively thin – only one metre thick, compared with two metres elsewhere. And the walls do not have foundation courses of stone (although there is plenty of stone lying around); they are simply layer upon layer of strips and blocks of turf, laid directly on to the ground surface. Nor was there any archaeological evidence for the elaborate wooden structuring of the interior as featured in the reconstruction; in the original house there were no traces of any post-holes to hold up a heavy roof.

It makes me think that when it was originally built, it was not a house at all, but a *booth*, deliberately left unroofed for temporary occupation – a seasonal camp for the summer exploitation of local resources, just a set of bare walls that could be roofed over with the sail of a Viking ship when required. And this leads me to the conclusion that L'Anse aux Meadows was *not* the Vínland of the Sagas, however tempting the association might be. The houses at L'Anse aux Meadows were not intended for permanent occupation, for permanent settlement. It may make them a candidate for 'Leif's Booths', but not for the Vínland of Adam of Bremen and the Saga-writers. It was simply a staging-post on the way to Vínland.

This does not in any way detract from the importance of the discovery at L'Anse aux Meadows. It is unique – the one and only authenticated Norse site yet found in North America, the only tangible and incontrovertible evidence of the Viking discovery of the New World a thousand years ago.

Another very intriguing find is the so-called 'Maine penny', which has been confidently identified by numismatists as a Viking Age coin minted during the reign of Ólaf Kyrri (Olaf the Gentle), who ruled Norway from 1067 to 1093. It was found during an excavation of an extensive Amer-Indian site by two amateurs, Edward Runge and the late Guy Mellgren, at a place called Naskeag Point, between Penobscot Bay and Blue Hill Bay, near Brooklin on the coast of Maine. They found it as long ago as August 1957 (at which time it was incorrectly identified as a twelfth-century English coin), but it is only very recently that serious scholarly attention has been devoted to it as a possibly authentic Viking Age find. It is now in the Maine State Museum in Augusta.

It is a small, fragile coin of very debased silver – indeed, a fragment is missing from it. The obverse side, now badly worn, displays a rather crude cartoon head of a maned animal, while the reverse side depicts a short voided cross in a circle. There is no visible inscription. Leading numismatists are now convinced on stylistic and technical grounds that it is a genuine Ólaf Kyrri coin.

Coins have a habit of turning up in the most unlikely places – one Ólaf Kyrri specimen turned up in England in a flower-bed outside the Usher Art Gallery in Lincoln! Coins travelled far and wide, sometimes as amulets or trade trinkets, and stray finds in unexpected contexts can easily mislead the unwary into drawing unwarranted conclusions. However, it seems likely that it could be tangible evidence of some occasional and unrecorded voyage by Norse Greenlanders late in the eleventh century who stopped off to barter their goods for pelts and furs; for all we know, they may well have been on their way further south in search of that ever-elusive Vínland.

For the time being at least, the Maine penny must be classed as an oddity, part of the flotsam of the Viking Age, washed up on a distant transatlantic shore when the Viking impetus was already spent.

It was spent in any dynamic sense – but not entirely over. After Thorfinn Karlsefni's major attempt at settlement, which is generally dated to around AD 1020, there are sporadic documentary references to further voyages to, or towards, Vínland from Greenland or Iceland. The latest is an entry in the Icelandic Annals for 1347, referring to the arrival of a storm-battered ship which had been on a voyage to Markland (Labrador). It made haven at Snæfellsnes – the very place from which the whole western adventure had begun, more than 350 years earlier:

> There came also a ship from Greenland, smaller in size than the small Icelandic boats; she was anchorless, and came into the outer Straumfjörður [on Snæfellsnes]. There were seventeen men on board. They had made a voyage to Markland, but were afterwards storm-driven here.

(Skálholtsannáll hinn forni)

There are two ways of interpreting that laconic entry: either that voyages to Markland were so rare that they deserved mention, or that *failed* voyages to Markland (and Vínland) were so rare that they deserved mention. It is impossible to tell with any certainty, now; but I incline to think that voyages westwards from Greenland continued, simply because Vínland was there and people had not forgotten it.

That is pure speculation, of course. What is not speculation is the fact that the Viking settlements on Greenland continued, and indeed flourished, for several centuries after the Vínland settlement came to grief. Like Iceland, Greenland had its own Golden Age in the eleventh and twelfth centuries, based on the new thrusting dynamic of the Church. Around 1125 the Greenlandic Church felt the need of a bishopric of its own, and the chieftain at Brattahlíð sailed to Norway to petition the king, taking a

The fragmentary Ólaf Kyrri coin, dating from the eleventh century and found on an Amer-Indian site in Maine.

Ruins of the Viking Age stone cathedral at Garðar in Greenland.

live polar bear as a gift. A Norwegian bishop duly arrived in 1126, and a magnificent stone cathedral was built for him at Garðar (modern Igaliko, 'The Deserted Cooking-Place'). It was over thirty metres long, constructed of the handsome red-and-white speckled local sandstone that some call Igaliko marble. Today, its ruins lie tumbled in the midst of a new settlement of Greenlanders who have quarried it remorselessly for building-stone; but in its time it was a formidable new spiritual and temporal power-centre for Greenland, a classic example of the sheer energy of the medieval Church.

So what happened to this brave outpost of European culture? The short answer is that we do not know. In 1261, Greenland came under the rule of the Norwegian crown, as Iceland did. It became a colony, a colony whose trade links depended entirely on the will and power of a king in far-off Norway. At the same time, the Little Climatic Optimum that had lured the first Viking settlers to a habitable Greenland had passed, and Greenland gradually became less and less inhabitable for Europeans. The weather began to worsen; ships found it harder to reach Greenland because of coastal ice, while the Eskimos found it expedient to move southward into Norse territory, towards the Viking Settlements. There are stories, in both Eskimo and Norse tradition, of violent clashes between the Eskimos and the Vikings. But the archaeological evidence suggests that the Norsemen

246

made far-reaching journeys to the north to trade with the Eskimos, not fight with them; and other legends suggest close friendships between the two races. Certainly there is no archaeological evidence to suggest that either the Eastern or the Western Settlements succumbed as a result of attacks by the Eskimos. All we know for certain is that they died out, some time late in the fifteenth century – just as Columbus was rediscovering the New World in South America and John Cabot was attempting to re-discover it in North America.

However it happened, the despised Skrælings, so much better adapted to the climate than the Vikings, had won out at last.

9

Empire of the North Sea

> Our galley is the People's Right,
>   the Dragon of the free,
> The Right that, riding in its might,
>   brings tyrants to their knee;
> The flag that flies above us
>   is the Love of Liberty;
> The waves are rolling on.
>
>   (Haldane Burgess: *Up-Helly-Aa Song*)

Every January, on the last Tuesday of the month, the people of Shetland go a little mad. When dusk falls the whole population, it seems, converges on the capital, Lerwick, to celebrate all night, with a highly individual northern blend of abandon and decorum, the annual fire-festival they call Up-Helly-Aa.

It is an exhilarating occasion, the outstanding spectacle of the Shetland year. It is the culmination of a year's hard work by a committee of volunteers who plan all the festivities and build a ten-metre model of a Viking galley to be ceremonially incinerated in the town centre. The procession through the town is led by an elected *Guizer Jarl* ('mummer earl') and his squad dressed as Vikings. Another thousand sturdy islanders are formed into smaller *guizer* squads, laboriously costumed in fancy dress based on some topically bizarre theme. At 7.30 p.m. they all muster at the Hillhead below the Town Hall; at the firing of a maroon they set light to their home-made torches of wood and sacking and set off, singing lustily and dragging the galley to the appointed place of immolation. There the ranks of *guizers* encircle the boat; a bugle sounds, and a thousand flaming torches arc through the night sky and turn the Viking galley into a funeral pyre. A splendid, heroic blaze it makes, too. Thereafter all the *guizer* squads in strict rotation make a formal round of the numerous hostelries and halls that have prepared a reception for them, where they perform a party piece, toss down a quick dram of whisky, and go on to the next venue.

Astonishingly, they are all still on their feet at dawn; despite the relentless all-night hospitality, native Shetlanders simply do not get drunk at Up-Helly-Aa.

It is the night when the islanders demonstrate spectacularly their pride in a Viking ancestry that reaches back for more than twelve centuries, a glorification of the Norse heroic spirit which they feel to be their heritage. It is not an ancient festival dating back to the days when the Northern Isles of Scotland enjoyed a golden age as a Viking earldom; in its present form it is less than a hundred years old, in fact. But that does not necessarily make it spurious, or ersatz.

Up-Helly-Aa (the name is a corruption of the Shetland term 'Uphalli-day', when the holidays or 'daft days' of Yuletide were up) is a metamorphosis of an older fire-festival marking the end of Yule and saluting the return of the sun after the winter solstice (21 December). It used to be a rather rowdy celebration of the old-style Christmas on 5 January, when young men dragged sledges of burning tar barrels through the streets and created such a nuisance that the good burghers of Lerwick banned it in 1874. Two years later they relented and allowed torchlight processions to take place, followed by *guizer* entertainments as part of the Christmas and New Year celebrations.

It was some time in the 1880s that the torchlight procession incorporated the burning of a model Viking galley, to represent the funeral of a Viking chieftain. The moving spirit behind this change was a blind Shetland poet called J. J. Haldane Burgess, who lived in Lerwick. He had had a brilliant academic career cut short by his blindness; thereafter he taught himself many languages and the violin, and made a living through journalism and private teaching. He became deeply interested in the Norse heritage of the Northern Isles and wrote a lot of verse in Shetland dialect and an adventure story called *The Viking Path*. He was a romantic Socialist, or a Socialist romantic, and was profoundly interested by the ideas of William Morris, co-translator with Eiríkur Magnússon of several Icelandic Sagas for the Saga Library series.

It was a time when the Victorians had been rediscovering the Vikings and the Icelandic Sagas. Some found in them a pleasurable *frisson* of horror at the savageries described in the late Legendary Sagas; others, like Thomas Carlyle in his major essay *On Heroes and Hero-Worship* (1840), deified a pre-Nietzschean concept of Superman by setting up Óðin as a model of the kind of strong leadership he felt necessary in the face of nineteenth-century anarchism. William Morris, however, that prototype Socialist, found in Old Norse literature a joyous independence of the spirit that inspired his own passionate ideals about the right to freedom for all. Haldane Burgess expressed this Viking inspiration in 1897 with a specially written *Up-Helly-Aa Song*, which is still sung when the procession moves off. It tells us more about the Victorians than about the Vikings, perhaps, but it is stirring stuff none the less:

Up-Helly-Aa: the climax as the galley burns furiously.

From grand old Viking centuries
   Up-Helly-Aa has come,
Then light the torch, and form the march,
   And sound the rolling drum;
And wake the mighty memories
   Of heroes that are dumb;
The waves are rolling on.

Chorus
Grand old Vikings ruled upon the ocean vast,
Their brave battle songs still thunder on the blast;
Their wild war-cry comes a-ringing from the past;
We answer it 'A-oi!'
Roll their glory down the ages,
Sons of warriors and sages,
Where the fight for freedom rages,
Be bold and strong as they!

So Up-Helly-Aa celebrates what Shetlanders felt about their Viking ancestry a century ago: a fascinating historical and social *mélange* of Methodism, Socialism, Salvation Army and piano-thumping music. Alcuin of York and his contemporaries would scarcely have approved, but it is none the worse for that. Paradoxically, the pioneers of the new-style festival were looking not to the past, but to the future. For those who looked backwards there was little enough to see apart from a rather romanticised literary view.

Very little is known with any certainty about the early days of the Vikings in the north of Scotland. Until quite recently, all the evidence has been Saga evidence, and therefore to be treated with caution. The main documentary source is *Orkneyinga saga (Saga of the Orkneymen)*, which was written in Iceland early in the thirteenth century; and it reflected faithfully the Icelandic historical tradition which cast King Harald Fine-Hair of Norway as the prime cause of the great Norwegian emigrations that led to the settlement and discovery of Iceland in the 870s (*cf* Ch. 7). Other fugitives had settled in the Orkneys and Shetland and, according to *Orkneyinga saga*, Harald Fine-Hair came over to the Northern Isles in person to annex them for the Norwegian crown:

> One summer King Harald Fine-Hair sailed west on a punitive expedition against the Vikings who were raiding the coasts of Norway from their winter-bases in Shetland or the Orkneys; for he had grown tired of their depredations. He subdued Shetland and the Orkneys and the Hebrides, and sailed all the way down to the Isle of Man and destroyed all the settlements there. He fought many battles there, and extended his dominion further west than any king of Norway has done since then.
>
> One of those killed in battle was Ívar, the son of Earl Rögnvald of Möre; so when King Harald set sail for Norway, he gave Earl Rögnvald the Orkneys and Shetland as compensation for his son. Earl Rögnvald in turn transferred both countries to his brother Sigurð, who was King Harald's prow-man. When the king sailed back to Norway he bestowed on Sigurð the title of *Jarl* [Earl], and Sigurð stayed behind on the islands.
>
> (*Orkneyinga saga*, Ch. 4)

There is no corroboration in any other source for this alleged expedition by Harald Fine-Hair, not even in the contemporary Irish annals where one would certainly not expect such an event to go unnoticed. It could well be an Icelandic elaboration to explain why a significant number of the early settlers of Iceland were second-generation Norsemen who had gone to Iceland from the Northern Isles and the Hebrides. It must always be remembered that the Icelandic Sagas are not history as such: they are *Saga* history. *Orkneyinga saga* is a historical novel, the dynastic story of the Norse earls of Orkney, a vivid narrative pageant of clashing personalities and dramatic events. That Norway exercised royal authority over the Northern Isles in the thirteenth century is not to be doubted; but whether Harald Fine-Hair was the first king to impose it is very much open to question. All we know is that for three centuries or more, it was Norse earls who ruled a miniature empire of the North Sea. From their headquarters in Orkney they controlled Shetland, the Hebrides and extensive areas of the north and west of mainland Scotland; and it is thought to have been via Viking bases in the Northern Isles that the first raids on island monasteries were launched in the 790s (*cf* Ch. 2).

In recent years, intensive archaeological excavation has done a great deal to clarify the early Viking picture. The Orkneys in particular are an archaeological paradise, with more outstanding monuments and sites than any other part of Britain of equivalent size, ranging from Neolithic chambered tombs like Maeshowe (*c.* 2700 BC), through complete villages like Skara Brae (*c.* 2500 BC) and the brooding stone circles of the same era, through the enigmatic towering stone *brochs* of the first centuries AD, and up to the start of the Viking Age. The Northern Isles, for thousands of years, had occupied a nodal position on the western seaways, and it is unsurprising that they should have attracted early attention from Norwegians on the move.

No one can be quite sure when the first Norwegians reached the Northern Isles. It has been suggested that there had been peaceful infiltration by farming settlers throughout the eighth century, before the first Viking raids, and that these Norsemen had lived in harmony with the native Pictish population at first; but not all scholars accept this view. The earliest unequivocal evidence of Viking presence is thought to be reflected in the great hoard of silver plate that was discovered in 1958 at a site on St Ninian's Isle in Shetland.

St Ninian's Isle is a small, treeless and now uninhabited island just off the south-western mainland of Shetland. It is no longer a true island, but is now connected to the mainland by a natural causeway of white sand, 550 metres long. No one has lived there since the eighteenth century, although the ruins of a small medieval church on the island continued to be used for burials until a century ago.

It was this site that was excavated by the late Professor Andrew O'Dell of the Geography Department of Aberdeen University from 1955–9. It was a tempting place to dig, because local tradition insisted that St Ninian's Church, as it was called, was the Mother Church of Shetland. In fact, the earliest Christian chapel on the site dates from the eighth century, a hundred years after Christianity was introduced to Shetland by Irish missionaries from Iona, *not* by St Ninian himself, who was working in Galloway in the fifth century. But the ecclesiastical interest of the site was suddenly overwhelmed by the sensational discovery, on 4 July 1958, of a buried hoard of Pictish silver. It consisted of twenty-eight pieces of ornamented silver (and the jawbone of a porpoise), crammed together in a larchwood box. It was found lying upside down under the nave of the medieval church ruins, covered by a small slab of grey sandstone lightly incised with a cross. The most striking of the objects were a collection of twelve penannular brooches, seven silver bowls, and a superb silver hanging-bowl.

It was the sort of find that every would-be archaeologist dreams of making, and it was made by a sixteen-year-old Shetland schoolboy, Douglas Coutts, who was working on his very first dig as a volunteer helper. But apart from its unique value as the finest collection of early native silverware yet found in Scotland, the St Ninian's Isle treasure has a story to tell as well. But what was that story?

The excavator, Professor O'Dell, thought that all the objects were precious church plate, buried upside down by the priests in panic and confusion at the approach of Viking raiders. Since then, however, the site and the hoard have been reinvestigated and reassessed by Professor Charles Thomas of Exeter University and Dr David M. Wilson, now the Director of the British Museum. Their conclusion is that the hoard represented not church treasure, but the secular wealth of a Pictish family, which had been deposited in the church for safe-keeping late in the eighth century. The silver bowls, which had been interpreted as chalices, were identified as table drinking-bowls; the hanging-bowl was probably a table hand-basin which could be hung up as an ornament when not in use. Not a single item had a specifically ecclesiastical function.

Why, if it was secular, was it buried in a church? Because the church represented sanctuary, a place of refuge for both people and valuables in time of danger; it was the local bank-vault, the most substantial building in the community and therefore the most defensible. The Vikings did not recognise these rules of the game; to them, a church was simply where the loot was. On this occasion they failed to find the silver; but the fact that it was never recovered suggests that its anonymous owner did not survive that Viking visitation. He had clearly had good reason to feel apprehensive.

It is one clue to what may have happened to the resident Picts, but only one. There is still considerable argument about whether they were driven out or even exterminated by the incoming Vikings, or whether they stayed on as a subservient people, their culture swamped, their identity obliterated. Certainly, practically every single place-name in the Northern Isles is of Norse origin. In Shetland, a Norse dialect called Norn was spoken until the nineteenth century, and the northern islanders of today still feel a distinct affinity with Norway as opposed to mainland Scotland.

The most venerable Viking site in Shetland, at Sumburgh on the southern tip of the island, has the distinction of being the first Viking homestead to be positively identified as such anywhere in the British Isles. That was in 1934, by Dr A. O. Curle. The site is familiarly known as *Jarlshof* ('Earl's Temple'), the romantic name given to the ruins of a medieval baronial building that dominates the bay by Sir Walter Scott in his 'Viking' novel, *The Pirate*. The excavations by Dr Curle and, in the 1950s, by J. C. R. Hamilton revealed an extensive Viking farmhouse complex, dating back to the first half of the ninth century, that had been established on a site previously occupied by Bronze Age people, then

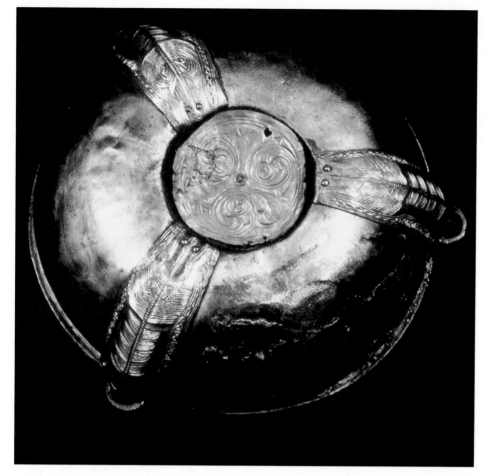

Silver hanging-bowl from the St Ninian's Isle Treasure.

Iron Age *broch*-builders, then Pictish settlers who built circular 'wheel-houses'. Each successive group of occupants had apparently been forced to abandon the site because of sand drifting in from the nearest dunes. A similar fate overtook the Norse settlement late in the thirteenth century, leaving Jarlshof under a deep shroud of sand until it was accidentally rediscovered early this century.

Today, the site is a textbook ancient monument, admirably tended by the Department of the Environment and showing very clearly the way in which the first Viking long-house with its paved floors and paths expanded into a large settlement. It was inhabited by generations of farming families who did a little fishing and seem to have been an industrious and peaceable folk. A couple of doodled portraits were found, scrawled on fragments of slate. There is nothing fierce or warlike about the faces, unlike the snarling heads from the Oseberg Ship furniture (*cf* Ch. 2). There were no signs of a violent take-over, and from the earliest levels of Norse occupation only three fragments of weapons were unearthed. Jarlshof, it seems, was certainly no nest of Viking marauders.

OPPOSITE The St Ninian's Isle Treasure: replicas from Lerwick Museum at the place the silver was found.

255

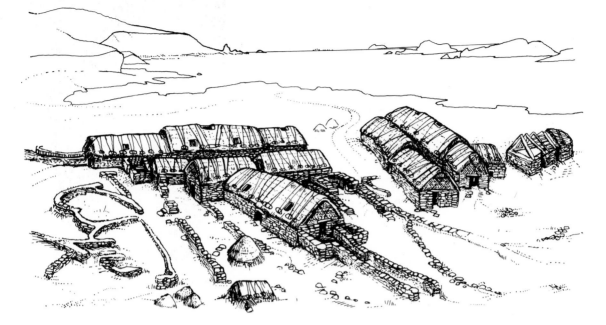

Jarlshof: artist's impression of the settlement in its heyday.

On the other hand a long and painstaking excavation of a site at Coileagan an Udail (the Udal) on the island of North Uist in the Outer Hebrides has recently revealed a very different picture. The first stage of the excavation lasted for fourteen years (155 weeks in all) from 1963–76, and was directed by Dr Iain A. Crawford of Cambridge University. It provided detailed evidence of continuous occupation from the Iron Age to the eighteenth century. Round about AD 850 there was a sudden change in material culture, which is attributable to the intrusion of the Vikings into that part of the Western Isles in circumstances that strongly suggest the use of violence. The first indication of the Viking presence came with the construction of a small fort, only seven metres across, which Dr Crawford thinks was the intruders' first positive action on taking over the site. The Udal later developed into a densely occupied settlement of some six buildings, suggesting that it was the demesne land of a major magnate; but the first fort, according to Dr Crawford, 'gives the quietus, for this region at least, to strongly held but unsubstantiated theories of a much earlier, gradual penetration'.

Meanwhile, current excavations of a clutch of threatened sites on Orkney, at the Bay of Birsay on the north-western point of the mainland, by a Durham University team led by Christopher D. Morris, may throw further light on early Viking/Pictish relations. There are at least nine sites round the bay, all under threat from severe coastal erosion, which are now being dug on a rescue basis. All the sites have already been severely damaged by erosion, and are proving hard to interpret; but there seems to have been a Norse take-over, involving the building of new houses on top of older structures – one of which was an unusual two-roomed house,

OPPOSITE Jarlshof: one of the Viking long-houses and the paved path to the byre.

257

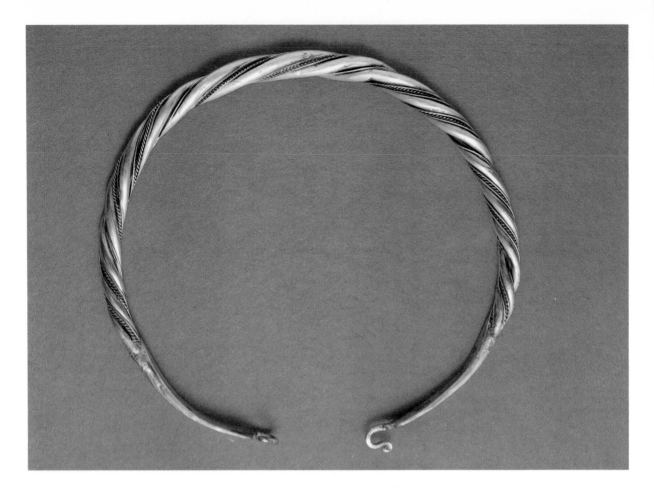

Superb silver neck-ring from the Skaill Hoard.

shaped like a figure-of-eight, which may have been Pictish. A little further along the coast there is a house site called Buckquoy which was excavated in the early 1970s by Dr Anna Ritchie of Edinburgh. It was a long, low mound which contained evidence of four major phases of human occupation from the seventh to the tenth centuries; the three earlier structures she interpreted as being Pictish, the last as being Norse. But not all archaeologists accept this view.

Orkney has proved a mine of precious finds in the past. In 1858, a boy out rabbit-hunting came across an astonishing hoard of buried silver that had been disturbed by the burrowing rabbits. This was near the beach of Skaill Bay, on the west side of the mainland of Orkney. The Skaill hoard comprised ninety silver objects weighing more than seven kilograms – great penannular brooches, neck-rings, arm-rings and ingots of silver. A large number of English and Arabic coins in the hoard proved that it had been deposited in the second half of the tenth century – a vivid indication of the prosperity of Orkney in the Viking Age.

This heyday of Viking wealth and power comes most graphically to light at the excavation site that had originally brought Christopher Morris and his Durham University colleagues to Orkney. It is a fascinating complex of

258

Norse buildings superimposed on earlier Pictish structures on the Brough of Birsay, just across from the Bay of Birsay. The Brough is now a small, encliffed tidal island, less than a kilometre across, accessible on foot only for a few hours on either side of low tide across a modern causeway a hundred metres long; during the Viking Age it may have been fully islanded. With its rearing cliffs, it had all the makings of a natural fortress.

The Brough had been the site of an early Christian monastery before it was taken over in the ninth century by Norse incomers, who built the first of a series of farmsteads on the landward slopes above the monastic site. It was to conduct further investigations of this Norse complex that the Durham team had come to Birsay in 1973, in continuation of excavations by Stewart Cruden and Dr Ralegh Radford.

The Norse newcomers had evidently respected the small Pictish chapel and graveyard that were there already: a broken head-stone has survived at the head of a triple grave, incised with Pictish symbols and depicting three richly clad figures, perhaps three army officers. In time, the original farmstead expanded into a highly complex settlement, which included workshops for metal-workers. Central to this later development was the construction of a church minster and a large palace associated with one of the most formidable of the Norse earls of Orkney, Earl Thorfinn the Mighty.

The Norse church was built in the first half of the eleventh century on top of the earlier Pictish church. It was made of split flagstone, with a rectangular nave and a square choir with a circular apse. On the slope below the church and reaching right to the cliff-edge lie the remains of what was once an extensive range of buildings. Erosion has already torn away much of the structure; but there are clear traces of a stone-built hall which had its own under-floor central heating – a system of ducts through which hot air from a fire-pit in an adjoining ante-chamber was circulated under the dais that ran down the side-walls.

According to *Orkneyinga saga*, Birsay was the 'capital' seat of Thorfinn the Mighty: 'He stayed constantly on Birsay, and there he built Christchurch, a splendid minster.' On Birsay he established the first bishopric in the Orkneys, and it is generally accepted that the ruined church there now was that 'splendid minster' of Christchurch, and the ruined palace was his royal hall.

He was a remarkable and potent man, this great Orkney earl; not for nothing did they call him 'the Mighty'. He was a huge, powerfully-built, swarthy man, ugly and sharp-featured, beetle-browed and with a prominent nose, according to the Saga. He was ambitious, ruthless and very shrewd, a born survivor. He inherited the Orkney earldom when he was five years old, in the year 1014; when he died fifty years later, in 1064, just before the Battle of Hastings, he had extended his northern domains deep into the heartlands of Scotland and over all the Western Isles as well, and was recognised as the most powerful ruler in northern Britain. He was a

The Brough of Birsay: Earl Thorfinn's palace complex at the cliff edge, and the apsidal Christchurch minster in the centre of the settlement.

man of compelling personal authority; after the turbulent years of his early reign, he spent the latter part of his life ruling his realms wisely and benevolently from his haven on the Brough of Birsay. His reign was the high point of the golden age of Viking power in the Northern Isles.

In England, the Viking Age came to an effective end in 1066 with the defeat of King Harald Harðráði of Norway at the Battle of Stamford Bridge and the subsequent Norman Conquest (*cf* Ch. 10). But in the Northern Isles it lasted for at least another century, long enough to see the creation of the most impressive and enduring Viking monument of all – St Magnus Cathedral in Kirkwall, the capital of the Orkneys. It was founded in 1137 when Kirkwall was still barely a village: a handsome, solid building of warm red sandstone that glows in the sunlight.

The story of St Magnus Cathedral is a marvellous yarn that deserves the fullest telling from *Orkneyinga saga*. It came about because early in the twelfth century the earldom of Orkney was split between two cousins, two

260

joint earls, Magnús and Hákon. After years of feuding and squabbling, they agreed to hold a peace-meeting to try to resolve their differences and come to some agreement over the earldom.

The peace-meeting was scheduled to take place on the little island of Egilsay, just off the east coast of the Mainland of Orkney, immediately after Easter; the year, as far as we can tell, was 1117. Each agreed to bring only two ships and an equal number of men, and they both swore binding oaths to keep whatever terms might be agreed between them.

Earl Magnús and his men set off in their two longships, rowing across a calm and sunlit sea. Suddenly, from nowhere, a huge breaker reared up over the ship that the earl was steering and crashed down over him. No one had ever seen anything like it before. 'I think,' said Magnús, 'that this forebodes my death.' Deeply disturbed by this ominous occurrence his men urged him not to trust Earl Hákon, and to turn back. 'No,' said Magnús. 'On with the journey; let it turn out as God wills.'

Earl Magnús was the first to reach Egilsay with his two shiploads of tried and trusted followers; but when they caught sight of Earl Hákon approaching across the sound, they saw that he was bringing not two ships as had been stipulated, but eight. Earl Magnús now realised that there was treachery afoot. He went up with his men to the church on Egilsay to pray, and there he spent the night.

There is a hauntingly beautiful ruined church on Egilsay today, situated high in the centre of the island, and conspicuous for the tall round tower at the west end of the nave. It is not the church in which Earl Magnús spent his last night on earth, although it may well stand on the same site; this one was built in the middle of the twelfth century in honour of his memory after his sanctity had been formally recognised. Architecturally, St Magnus Church on Egilsay is highly unusual, Irish in inspiration but very Orcadian in its use of split flagstones for the walls. It has a barrel-vaulted chancel at the east end, and above it there used to be an apartment known as the 'Grief House'; this is not a poignant reminder of Magnús and his vigil on Egilsay, although one feels it ought to be, but a corruption of the Old Norse word *grið*, meaning 'sanctuary'.

On that fateful night, Earl Magnús's men offered to defend him with their lives. 'No,' said Magnús, 'I do not want to put your lives at risk for my sake; and if there is not to be peace between us kinsmen, then be it as God wills.' He already seemed to have foreknowledge of the allotted hours of his life-span, and would neither flee nor shrink from a meeting with his enemies.

Early next morning Earl Hákon and his men hurried ashore and ran to the church and searched it, but found no trace of Earl Magnús; he had already gone to ground elsewhere on the island with two companions. When he saw his enemies searching for him he called out to them, telling them where he was. When Earl Hákon and his men caught sight of him they rushed towards him with a great clamour and clangour of weapons . . .

261

The ruined church on Egilsay

It is said that Earl Magnús was as blithe as if he had been invited to a feast, and uttered not a word of bitterness or anger.

Once it had been decided that Magnús was to die, Earl Hákon told his standard-bearer, Ófeig, to kill him; but Ófeig angrily refused. So Hákon ordered his cook, Lífólf, to do the execution. At that, Lífólf began to sob loudly. But Earl Magnús said to him, 'Do not weep over this; this is an honourable task that will bring you fame. Be brave and steadfast, and afterwards you shall have my clothing in accordance with the customs and laws of old. Stand now in front of me and strike me a great blow on the head, for it is not seemly that a chieftain should be beheaded like some common thief. Take heart, poor wretch, for I have prayed to God to have mercy on you.' And with that he crossed himself, and bowed his head to the stroke; and so his soul passed away to Heaven.

According to the Saga, the place where Magnús died was rocky and overgrown with moss, but overnight it turned into a green and verdant field. The traditional site of the execution, about half a kilometre from the church, is now marked by an inscribed stone pillar.

Now politics entered the scene. Magnús had a nephew, Rögnvald Kali, who harboured ambitions for the earldom himself. In a shrewd move, he vowed that if he ever became earl with the support of the people, who were already talking in terms of sanctity and miracles, he would build in his martyred uncle's memory the most magnificent minster in the Northern

262

Isles. It was one of the few election promises in history that have been honoured to the letter.

But what of St Magnús himself? His body had originally been buried in that 'splendid minster' of Christchurch that his grandfather, Thorfinn the Mighty, had built on Birsay. Later, when the partly completed cathedral in Kirkwall built by Earl Rögnvald Kali was ready for use, his holy relics were translated thither and enshrined 'above the high altar'. After that – silence. No more was heard of him.

Early in the nineteenth century a cache of bones was discovered in a crude cavity high up in the large rectangular pier of the north arcade of the choir, close to the original position of the high altar. It was popularly assumed that these must be the missing relics of St Magnús, although others argued that they were more likely to be the mortal remains of the cathedral's founder, who had himself been canonised for his good works as St Rögnvald.

It was not until a hundred years later that the mystery was finally resolved, during a massive programme of restoration of the cathedral fabric (1913–30). On 31 March 1919, the Clerk of Works was checking the stonework of the corresponding pier of the *south* arcade of the choir. He noticed that some of the ashlar facing-stones, about three metres above floor-level, appeared to be loose. So he went up a ladder with his foot-rule, which he pushed into a crack between the stones; a long way in, it struck something that sounded like wood. And that was precisely what it turned out to be; the loose stone was prised out, revealing a carefully excavated

St Magnus Cathedral in Kirkwall.

The secret recess in the south pillar of St Magnus Cathedral, with the box that held the saint's relics.

cavity behind the façade, and inside this cavity there lay a wooden casket made of oak, about seventy-five centimetres long.

The casket was removed for scientific investigation. When it was opened it was found to contain the skull and most of the bones of a man of medium height (about 170 centimetres), rather poorly developed physically, and aged between twenty-five and thirty-five. The bones were examined first by the local doctor and later by Professor R. W. Reid, Regius Professor of Anatomy at Aberdeen University. What excited most attention was the condition of the skull, because it brought irresistibly to mind the account of the death of St Magnús in *Orkneyinga saga*. It had a clean-cut gash across the parietal bones towards the back of the head, 'evidently produced by a swift blow from a heavy sharp cutting instrument such as an axe'. It showed a sharp perpendicular cut through both layers of the bone; the instrument had then turned and glanced backwards off the skull, removing a flake of the outer layer of the bone.

There was only one conclusion possible: the relics of St Magnús had been found at last, so precisely did the state of the skull conform to the Saga account ('Strike me a great blow on the head'). It followed that the bones found earlier in the other pier had to be those of his nephew, St Rögnvald. Presumably both sets of bones had been removed from their shrine above the high altar and hidden away in the pillars for safety at the time of the Reformation.

The bones of St Magnús were given a new lead-lined casket and re-placed in the cavity behind the loose stone in the south pier. The original wooden casket is now on display in Tankerness House Museum, opposite the Cathedral. Their finding had provided dramatic vindication of the

264

accuracy of the Saga tradition, which claimed to be based on the eyewitness account of one of Magnús's companions who had been present on Egilsay, a Hebridean farmer called Holdboði.

Every time I visit Kirkwall, I marvel at this brooding, wise old cathedral, preserving its own saints in such security against all vicissitudes; and it delights me to know that in this most enduring of all the monuments of the Viking Age in the British Isles, my namesake, Earl Magnús the Holy, still superintends these Northern Isles he once ruled.

Although the Northern Isles might feel remote from the centre of things today, they were not in any way remote during the Viking Age. From the west coast of Norway it was only a brief voyage of a day or two to Shetland or the Orkneys. Orkney in particular was the major staging-post of the northern seas, where many trade- and raid-routes met.

They also played a role in Viking affairs to the south. Many of the first raids had been launched from the Northern Isles, and they were a constant preoccupation of the kings of Norway. King Ólaf Tryggvason (995–1000), who would first erupt on to the English scene at the Battle of Maldon in 991, is credited in the Icelandic Sagas at least with the forcible conversion of Orkney to Christianity in 994. Orkney Vikings were embattled at

The skull of St Magnus – the wound from the 'great blow on the head'.

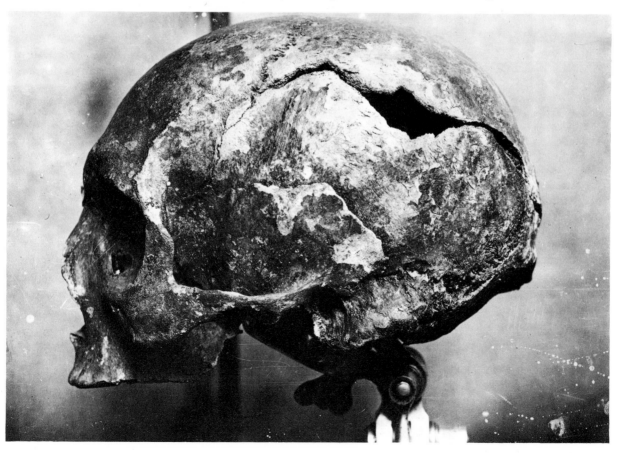

Clontarf in Ireland in 1014 (*cf* Ch. 6). The Northern Isles were always a potential source of manpower for raids or alliances, and in the fateful year of 1066 there were Viking reinforcements from the earldom of Orkney helping to swell the invasion fleet of King Harald Harðráði of Norway (*cf* Ch. 10). Indeed, had Earl Thorfinn the Mighty himself still been alive in that year, history might well have turned out rather differently.

The century that preceded 1066 was to be a troubled one for England for the most part. After twenty-five years of relative peace, the accession to the throne of England of a ten-year-old boy, Æthelred II, Æthelred the Unready, coincided with and helped to encourage a renewed phase of disruption by Viking incursions. His father, the strong King Edgar, had died in 975, and the crown was inherited by Æthelred's half-brother Edward. The succession aroused bitter dynastic disputes between rival supporters of the two brothers; and in March 978 Edward was brutally and treacherously murdered while on a visit to his young brother at Corfe Castle in Dorset. Æthelred, still only ten years old, was too young to have been implicated in the plot, although later sources would allege that his mother, Queen Ælfthryth, had been the instigator of her step-son's murder. None the less, Æthelred benefited from the crime by succeeding to the throne within a month, and his long reign of nearly forty years would always be haunted by the stigma of treachery.

Æthelred has been cast by history as one of the most disastrous and feeble of English rulers, a reputation only compounded by the popular linguistic misconception that converted his nickname *unræd* ('lacking in counsel') into 'Unready'. He was given a consistently critical and hostile 'press' from the writer of the *Anglo-Saxon Chronicle*, who clearly disliked and mistrusted him. However, Professor Peter Sawyer has argued cogently in *From Roman Britain to Norman England* that Æthelred has been unfairly blamed for England's failure to cope with the renewed Viking attacks, for the vacillations of policy and the desperate shifts with which the king tried to stave off the enemy. Sawyer points out that the new Viking armies were larger and better organised than those of the ninth century, that the kingdom was larger, less united, and less easy to defend, and, above all, that the nature of the raids was now significantly different. The Vikings were no longer would-be settlers who would become vulnerable to counter-attack once they settled anywhere, but highly mobile raiders whose one objective was to get as much as they could, anywhere they could, in the shortest possible time, and then head for home. Against such tactics, conventional defences were useless. Besides, Æthelred could not command or inspire the same sense of patriotic unity and fervour with which Alfred the Great had fired his people. Æthelred's unhappy reign was punctuated with spectacular treacheries and defections, as nobles of the former Danelaw remembered their Scandinavian ancestry and threw their lot in with the invaders in order to be on the winning side.

The troubles began almost as soon as Æthelred was on the throne. It was as if the Vikings across the North Sea could scent the taint of weakness and corruption emanating from England under its boy-king. In 980 the first attacks began, with Southampton ravaged, the Isle of Thanet sacked and Cheshire overrun. These first raids seem to have been the work of small bands of adventurers chafing under the strong royal hand of King Harald Blue-Tooth in Denmark (*cf* Ch. 3), just as the Norwegians were said to have taken to their longships to escape the despotism of King Harald Fine-Hair a century earlier (*cf* Ch. 2).

Throughout much of the 980s, with only occasional lulls when no incursions were recorded, this pattern continued: raids that were damaging to the immediate places involved, but not to the fabric of the state as a whole. London and the south coast suffered; England as a whole did not. But in 991 a major warfleet of ninety-three ships arrived in the Thames estuary. One of its leaders was a Norwegian Viking, Ólaf Tryggvason, who had been reared on piracy in the Baltic and who aspired to the throne of Norway itself (*cf* Ch. 2). Their target was the prosperous south-east. It was a larger and better organised army than any that had appeared in England before; but even so, the campaign of 991 would have been no more than yet another despairing date in a long litany of calamity were it not for a momentous battle that was fought that summer near Maldon in Essex:

991. In this year came Anlaf [Ólaf] with ninety-three ships to Folkestone, and harried outside, and sailed thence to Sandwich, and thence to Ipswich, overrunning all the countryside, and so on to Maldon.

Ealdorman Byrhtnoth came to meet them with his levies and fought them, but they slew the ealdorman there [10 August] and had possession of the place of slaughter.

(*Anglo-Saxon Chronicle*, Parker MS)

Harald Fine-Hair; the Saga text says that Norway was in danger of depopulation because of his despotism. Manuscript illumination from *Flateyjarbók*.

VIKINGS!

And that is all we would have known about it, just a brief reference in an annal; but an anonymous Anglo-Saxon poet wrote a poem about the battle, a poem that expresses better than anything else the old Germanic warrior ethic of heroic valour. In that poem, *The Battle of Maldon*, the defeat and death of Byrhtnoth are celebrated not as a failure but as the ultimate triumph of courage and loyalty.

The Viking army had come up the Blackwater estuary and made camp on Northey Island, just to the east of the town of Maldon, poised to attack. Then as now it was joined to the mainland by a tidal ford or causeway about eighty metres long. A defence force led by Byrhtnoth, the senior ealdorman of Essex, and consisting of the local militia and his own personal hearth-troops, marched out from Maldon and drew up in battle array at the landward end of the causeway.

Byrhtnoth was an old man by then. He had been appointed to office as an ealdorman as long ago as 956, and was one of the leading men responsible for the defence of eastern England. He had been brought up in the old school, in which loyalty to one's leader was the paramount virtue, even at the cost of life itself. He was not a man to back away, whatever the odds.

It was high tide at Northey, the causeway submerged. From the island, a Viking herald shouted an offer of truce in exchange for Danegeld: they were quite prepared to be bought off without a fight – it would be better for both sides. Contemptuously, Byrhtnoth rejected the offer. When the tide began to ebb, the Viking host came charging across the causeway. But like Horatius and his companions on the bridge, three of Byrhtnoth's retainers held the narrow causeway against them with ease. So now the Viking leader made a crafty request perfectly calculated to appeal to Byrhtnoth's stiff-legged pride: withdraw from the shore, he said, and let my men come across so that we can fight this out fair and square. And Byrhtnoth, trapped by his quixotic sense of chivalry, or 'overswayed by his pride of heart', as the poem puts it, agreed to let the Vikings cross over to the mainland.

It was a suicidal act of gallantry. Byrhtnoth withdrew, and regrouped his men to await the Viking charge. A fierce battle ensued. The Anglo-Saxons were outnumbered, yet fought with desperate bravery. All too soon, however, Byrhtnoth, that prototype English sportsman, was mortally wounded by javelin and spear. As he fell dying, he exhorted his followers to continue the battle; but some of the English broke and fled. Byrhtnoth's own retainers, however, his *comitatus*, stood their ground, determined to avenge their fallen lord by selling their own lives dearly. One elderly retainer, Byrhtwold, who had grown old in his master's service, expressed it all with perfect, epic simplicity:

> Mind must be mightier, heart the fiercer,
> Courage the greater, as our strength lessens.

Here lies our lord, cut down in battle.
Hero in the dust. Long will he mourn
Who thinks to dodge this battle-play.
I am an old man now; I shall not go from here.
By the side of my lord I mean to lie,
Lie in the dust with the man I loved.

That proud last stand, that epic bravura of hopeless resistance, gloriously exemplified the virtue of absolute unwavering loyalty to the leader, the ring-giver. As Marshal Bosquet is reported to have said of the Charge of the Light Brigade, it was magnificent but it was not war. Certainly, no Viking would have done it; the Vikings always preferred survival to defeat, however glorious, if they had the choice. *The Battle of Maldon* celebrates a warrior ethic that was by this time considered anachronistic; it is a superb epitaph for the Anglo-Saxon England that once had been, and was now no more.

As it turned out, the flamboyant gesture by Byrhtnoth and his *comitatus* was unavailing anyway. Byrhtnoth had scornfully refused to pay the Vikings to go away; but that is precisely what King Æthelred now did. On the advice of Sigeric, the Archbishop of Canterbury, he concluded a peace treaty with Ólaf Tryggvason designed to protect English shipping abroad and grant similar immunity from attack for Viking merchants; no compensation was to be paid for all the slaughter and ravaging that had taken place before the truce was established – and, in a final clause, 'Twenty-two thousand pounds in gold and silver were paid to the army for this truce.' With that formal legal agreement, Æthelred had set foot on the slippery path of paying Danegeld in ever-increasing quantities to buy off trouble for a time – money that only helped to pay the wages of warriors enlisted for the *next* assault.

The Viking army sailed away with a down payment of £10,000 safely tucked away in their sea-chests; but they did not leave England. The following year, Æthelred raised a fleet to try to trap the enemy ships at sea, but the plan was betrayed to the Vikings by no less a person than the ealdorman of East Anglia, Ælfric, 'one of those in whom the king had most trust' according to the *Anglo-Saxon Chronicle*, and the Viking fleet escaped. Treachery and betrayal would become endemic in England, and so would the viciousness of revenge – in 993, Æthelred had Ealdorman Ælfric's son blinded.

The year 994 saw another ominous development – the arrival of a crowned king of Denmark at the head of a large raiding fleet. This was King Svein Fork-Beard (*tjúguskegg*), son of King Harald Blue-Tooth Gormsson (*cf* Ch. 3). Svein Fork-Beard had fallen out with his father, and by 988 had ousted him from the throne and seized the crown for himself. Now he was in the Thames estuary with ninety-four ships and Ólaf Tryggvason by his side. They launched an all-out attack on London, but

The causeway from the island of Northey to the mainland at Maldon, scene of the Battle of Maldon.

the Londoners threw them back. Foiled there, the Vikings hurled themselves at the south-east coast, burning and ravaging, riding freely into the interior whenever and wherever they wanted. At last Æthelred felt compelled to offer terms again; the Vikings were given winter quarters in Southampton, provisions for them were gathered from all over Wessex, and in addition they were paid £16,000 in cash.

That winter another event occurred that would have considerable impact on Norway and other northern countries: Ólaf Tryggvason, that relentless Viking, was converted to Christianity. An unlikely legend claims that he was converted by a hermit in the Scilly Isles; but the *Anglo-Saxon Chronicle* affirms that he received instruction from the Bishop of Winchester, and that King Æthelred himself stood sponsor at his baptism at Andover. With that, Ólaf Tryggvason left England for good; he had achieved his purpose of amassing sufficient money to finance a challenge for the throne of Norway, which he won and held for five violently evangelistic years (995–1000).

The invasion by Svein Fork-Beard reflected a new pattern in Viking attitudes to England. The attacks were no longer casual and sporadic. The armies that came over now were professional and highly organised. It used to be thought that the four Danish 'Trelleborgs' (*cf* Ch. 3) had been built by Svein Fork-Beard specifically as military barracks for the purpose of invading England. This view is no longer tenable – recent dendro-chronological dates prove beyond any doubt that they were built during Harald Blue-Tooth's reign; but they indicate a degree of discipline and a potential for organised manpower that must have made Danish armies at the end of the tenth century alarmingly formidable opponents. All Svein Fork-Beard had to do was to find the money to pay for them – and that he was able to do, with ease, with English silver extorted as Danegeld.

The price of peace kept on escalating; the scale of the invasions kept on increasing. In 1002 King Æthelred 'No-Counsel', goaded perhaps beyond endurance, decided on a course of despair. He paid Danegeld of £24,000 – but still the raiders would not let up. He married Emma, the daughter of the Duke of Normandy, in an attempt to shore up his position by an alliance with a powerful foreign state – which would lead to complicated dynastic problems later (*cf* Ch. 10). And then, that same summer, he risked everything in a desperate gamble to extirpate the cancer of 'fifth column' treachery within his own borders: he ordered that every single Dane resident in England should be exterminated on St Brice's Day, in November 1002. The *Anglo-Saxon Chronicle* makes only the barest reference to the event; but in the thirteenth century the chronicler John of Wallingford had much more to say about it:

This day was the Saturday, on which the Danes are in the habit of bathing; and accordingly, at the set time they were destroyed most ruthlessly, from the least even to the greatest. They spared neither age nor sex, destroying together with them those women of their own nation who had consented to intermix with the Danes, and the children who

Hack-silver hoard in Denmark. Danegeld from England?

had sprung from that foul adultery. Some women had their breasts cut off; others were buried alive in the ground; while the children were dashed to pieces against posts and stones.

It did not work, of course. Inevitably some Danes escaped, to take the news to Denmark, where King Svein Fork-Beard used it as an excuse for yet more violent assaults on England in the following years – driven to ever greater excesses, some said, because his own sister was thought to have been one of the victims of the massacre.

The English nightmare went on. Every year the *Anglo-Saxon Chronicle* had more disasters to report, more horrors to mourn. In 1007 the price of Danegeld rose to £36,000. It seemed as if everyone in Scandinavia who could carry weapons was jumping on the band-wagon. In 1010, for instance, one of the leaders was another would-be king of Norway, Óláf Haraldsson (Óláf the Stout, later to be canonised as St Óláf, *cf* Ch. 10). During an abortive attack on the sturdy defenders of London, it was Óláf Haraldsson who had the bright idea of tearing down London Bridge by fixing grappling irons to its piers and wrenching them free by the muscle-power of his oarsmen. The tactic worked, and the bridge fell, but London did not; the stock of nursery rhymes in Britain was enriched by a new song still sung to this day: *London Bridge is falling down*.

England was disintegrating, and the writer of the *Anglo-Saxon Chronicle* could only shake his head in dismayed bewilderment:

1010. Then they [the Vikings] turned back to their ships with their booty. And while they were on their way to the ships, the English levies should have been out in case they tried to go inland; but our men were on their way home instead. And when the enemy was in the east, our levies were in the west; and when the enemy was in the south, our levies were in the north . . . Whatever course of action was decided upon, it was not followed even for a single month . . .

1011. All these calamities befell us by reason of bad policy, in that the enemy were never offered payment in time, nor fought against; but when they had done their worst, only then was peace and a truce made with them. Yet for all the payments, the truces and the peace treaties, they went about everywhere in bands, harrying and robbing and slaying our wretched people.

1011 was probably the nadir of England's humiliation. In that year the Vikings took Canterbury and captured for ransom Archbishop Ælfheah, the eminent cleric who, as Bishop of Winchester, had baptised Óláf Tryggvason. Despite a payment of £48,000, the Vikings killed him during a drunken orgy. That was enough to turn even the most hardened stomach, and forty-five Danish ships under the command of Thorkel the Tall switched their allegiance and stayed on in England for a time to act as protectors of the kingdom against their former friends.

Vast quantities of Anglo-Saxon silver coins from this period have been found in buried hoards in Scandinavia, particularly in Sweden. Swedish mercenaries seem to have played a large part in the invasions, and a number of Swedish memorial rune-stones record their exploits. One stone at Orkestad in Uppland tells the whole story in one terse epitaph:

> Karsi and Gerbjörn had this stone raised in memory of Úlf their father. God and God's Mother help his soul. And Úlf received Danegeld three times in England. The first was that which Tosti paid. Then Thorkel paid. Then Knút paid.

The names of the paymasters summarise neatly the years of Danish attrition that led to the conquest of England. 'Tosti' was probably an eminent Swedish leader known to us from *Heimskringla (St Ólaf's Saga)* as Sköglar-Tosti, who 'was a very great warrior and spent long periods on raids abroad'; 'Thorkel' was Thorkel the Tall, Svein Fork-Beard's lieutenant, later famed throughout the northlands as the leader of the Jómsvikings of Jómsborg, a dedicated band of professional Danish Vikings, but now serving under King Æthelred; and 'Knút' was the great Knút himself (Canute), the first and only king of a North Sea empire that embraced both Scandinavia and England.

By 1013, Svein Fork-Beard must have realised that England was ready to fall into his lap. In July of that year, accompanied by his eighteen-year-old son, Knút, he set sail from Denmark with a huge invasion fleet. The author of the *Encomium Emmae*, a near-contemporary account, could scarcely contain his enthusiasm:

> When at last the soldiers were all assembled they went on board the towered ships, each man having picked out by observation his own leader on the brazen prows. On one side lions moulded in gold were seen on the ships, on the other side birds on the mast-tops veered with the direction of the wind, or dragons of various kinds breathed fire through their nostrils. Here were glittering men of solid gold or silver, almost as real as living people; over there were bulls with arching necks and legs outstretched, carved as if they were alive . . .

Svein set course for the north of England, where the Anglo-Scandinavians of Northumbria and what used to be the Danelaw were quick to make submission to him. He made a lunge at London, but once again the city held firm, so Svein moved elsewhere; within weeks he was in command of Wessex as well as Mercia and Northumbria. London was now hopelessly beleaguered. By the end of the year, Æthelred knew his cause was lost. He sent Emma and their sons to safety in Normandy, and later that year fled there himself. Svein Fork-Beard was king of England in all but name; but five weeks later he died, on 3 February 1014. Once again, the fate of England was in the melting pot. Æthelred was recalled from Normandy in return for a promise of just government and reform, and young Knút, still inexperienced, thought it prudent to withdraw his

father's army back to Denmark, where his older brother Harald had succeeded to the throne. In the late summer of 1015, Knút sailed for England again with a fleet of two hundred ships and a refurbished army stiffened by veterans of many campaigns, including Thorkel the Tall, who had inexplicably changed sides once again. Æthelred's son, Edmund Ironside, offered resistance, but once again England lurched into a chaos of treachery and shameful double-dealing.

In April 1016 Knút marched on London for a final showdown with Æthelred; but before he reached there, Æthelred died, and the Londoners, no doubt resigned to the inevitable, acknowledged Knút as their king. For the rest of the summer he fought a series of engagements with Edmund Ironside; in the autumn they called it quits, and agreed to partition the kingdom, Edmund to have Wessex and Knút to have Mercia and the Danelaw. But within a month Edmund Ironside, too, died, on 30 November 1016, and Knút Sveinsson became king of all England.

Knút, better known in English as Canute, brought to England twenty years of sorely-needed peace; he also reissued English laws that emphasised justice and the proper rights of individuals. Yet he is one of the most underrated of kings, despite his achievements – the English have never really forgiven him for being a Dane! Today he is best known in popular folklore as the foolish king who tried to command the tide not to come in – and even that is a travesty of what is actually meant to have happened on that celebrated occasion.

The story was first recorded a century after his death by the English chronicler Henry of Huntingdon, in his *Historia Anglorum* compiled around 1130. He wrote that when Knút was at the height of his political power he gave orders for his throne to be placed on the seashore as the tide came in. The traditional site for this curious episode is Bosham Beach, near Chichester on the south coast of England; perhaps it is because Bosham village stands on a little peninsula between two tidal creeks, where the tide comes in very fast, and also has a fine Saxon church which claims to house the mortal remains of one of Knút's young daughters.

So there you have Knút sitting on his throne at the water's edge, surrounded by a gaggle of puzzled courtiers. And he said to the rising tide, according to Henry of Huntingdon, 'You are within my jurisdiction, and the land on which I sit is mine; no one has ever resisted my command with impunity. I therefore command you not to rise over my land, and not to presume to wet the clothes or limbs of your lord.' But the sea rose as usual, and wetted the king's feet and legs without respect.

That is about as much of the story as most people know, getting the impression that Canute the Great had grown too big for his boots, which got a good soaking as a consequence. But in Henry of Huntingdon's version it does not end there. That is only the first half. And the second half of the story makes it quite clear that the king *intended* the tide to give him a wetting, as an object lesson in humility for the benefit of the assembled

OPPOSITE The Orkestad Stone in Sweden: three Danegelds paid to one man.

courtiers. It goes on:

> And so the king jumped back on to dry land, and said, 'Be it known to all inhabitants of the world that the power of kings is empty and superficial, and that no one is worthy of the name of king except for Him whose will is obeyed by Heaven, earth and sea in accordance with eternal laws.'

And with that he took off his golden crown and never put it on his head again.

It is the sort of parable beloved of medieval historians, who liked nothing better than a good moral tale. There is no way of telling, now, whether the episode ever took place. But the contemporary *Liber Vitae* of Hyde Abbey in Winchester depicts King Knút and his English consort Ælfgifu (*cf* Ch. 10) giving to the New Minster at Winchester a magnificent gold cross, covered with jewels, which they placed on the altar, and which was still there in Henry of Huntingdon's day – it disappeared soon afterwards during the troubled reign of King Stephen in the middle of the twelfth century. The copy of the *Liber Vitae* in the British Museum has a drawing of the scene, which shows Christ witnessing the event, flanked by the Virgin Mary and St Peter, the patron saints of the monastery, watched by the monks of the abbey in their stalls. The picture shows an angel lifting the crown from King Knút's head and indicating that it belonged to the Heavenly king, Christ himself, and not to Knút. Professor Sir Robert Birley has made the inspired suggestion that the story of Knút and the waves may originally have grown out of this drawing.

Throughout his reign, Knút courted the Church zealously as the only institution that could reconcile the tensions that had racked England for the last forty years. The ecclesiastical sources speak glowingly of his generosity, his humility, his devotion to Christianity. To a nation exhausted with horrors he brought balm; to a land saturated with blood he brought security from external attack by dealing briskly with any potential threats from abroad; to a realm that had lost all confidence in kingship he restored respect for the crown by a subtle combination of giving and taking. Concessions on one side were matched by punitive taxes on the other. Those whom he trusted, prospered; those whom he did not, died. The smack of firm government was heard in the land, and the land liked it.

To be sure, there were virulent racial prejudices and suspicions between Saxon and Dane to allay. There were the cruel decades of bitterness to soothe. The long-settled Danes in the Danelaw had never changed their spots, and had recently sided with the invaders against the English. It is a measure of Knút's greatness that he made himself acceptable to all, and harmonised these deep-seated antagonisms.

One aspect of this racial strife has lingered on in the national consciousness, however, in the popular belief that any Danes who were captured during the invasion years were skinned alive in revenge, and their hides fastened to church doors as a grisly warning to others. Several of these so-

Drawing of Knút and his English consort Ælfgifu at Winchester, from the contemporary *Liber Vitae* of Hyde Abbey, now in the British Museum.

called 'Daneskins' have been reported. The earliest record of this belief is given by Samuel Pepys, who noted in his *Diary* on 10 April 1661: 'To Rochester and there saw the Cathedral . . . observing the great doors of the church, as they say, covered with the skins of the Danes.'

Only a few of these alleged Daneskins are extant today. One, from a door in Westminster Abbey, has been examined microscopically, and was adjudged to be almost certainly ordinary cow-hide. Another, from Copford Church near Colchester in Essex, showed many of the structural features of human skin, however, and could possibly be human in origin. Perhaps the most interesting example comes from Hadstock Church near Saffron Walden in Essex, which dates back in parts to Anglo-Saxon times. A small portion of leather was found under the hinges of the North door, and is now in the Saffron Walden Museum. The fragment is about five centimetres long; it is pale brown in colour, and perforated by large holes where it had been pierced by the nails attaching the hinge to the door. Hadstock

277

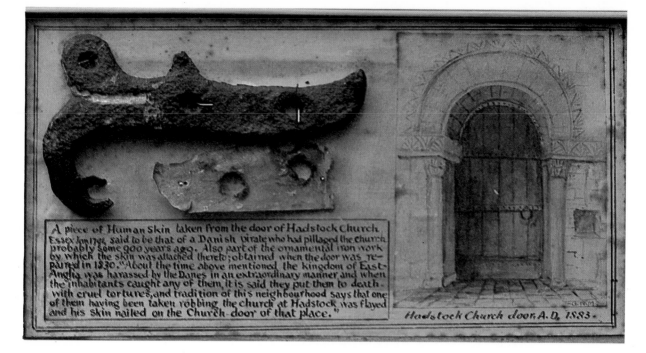

A piece of Human Skin taken from the door of Hadstock Church, Essex [in 1791] said to be that of a Danish pirate who had pillaged the church probably some 900 years ago. Also part of the ornamental iron work by which the skin was attached thereto; obtained when the door was re-painted in 1830. "About the time above mentioned, the kingdom of East-Anglia was harassed by the Danes in an extraordinary manner and when the inhabitants caught any of them, it is said they put them to death with cruel tortures, and tradition of this neighbourhood says that one of them having been taken robbing the church at Hadstock was flayed and his skin nailed on the Church-door of that place."

Hadstock Church door, A.D. 1883.

The 'Daneskin' fragment from Hadstock Church near Saffron Walden.

Church is an unlikely setting for such a macabre idea; the surroundings are rurally idyllic, housewives drive up to deposit their young at play-school in the church hall. Yet there is thought to be a distinct possibility that the skin from the Hadstock Church door is, in fact, human – a piece of Daneskin. Structurally it resembles human skin, and it also has blond (grey-yellow) hair still attached to it which, from its surface scale markings, looks human in origin. This has been used as an argument to reinforce the belief that it came off the back of some villainous flaxen-haired Viking who had been caught pillaging the church, and was flayed in punishment for such sacrilege.

It makes a splendidly gruesome story. Unfortunately the tradition relating to it was not recorded until early in the eighteenth century, by the antiquarian William Stukely, who noted that 'at Hadstock they talk of the skin of a Danish king nailed upon the door'. In 1974 the Hadstock fragment was carefully examined by Dr Ronald Reed of the Procter Department of Food and Leather Science at Leeds University. In his report to the Saffron Walden Museum he concluded that it was '*probably* human skin'; he was being suitably cautious, as befits a scientist, but in a letter to me he wrote that 'I can honestly say that of the various samples of suspected Daneskins I have looked at, the Hadstock one was the only one I would stake my money on as being human in origin.'

This is not an opinion to be lightly dismissed; but I remain sceptical. It was relatively common for doors in medieval times to be covered with painted leather as a protection against the elements, and leather of that age is difficult to identify at the best of times. Also, because the Hadstock fragment was found under the hinge (the only reason it survived), it means that the door was covered before it was installed — it was not a question of applying it after the door was in position. Nor would any one miscreant have been able to provide enough skin to cover a whole door — the largest piece of hide available from a human victim is only about a metre square.

Most significantly, perhaps, Hadstock also has claims to having been *founded* by a Dane, not pillaged by one — and that Dane was King Knút himself, after his victory over Edmund Ironside at Ashingdon in Essex in 1016 that led to the short-lived treaty of partition just before Edmund's death. Would King Knút have approved the use of 'Daneskins' to adorn the doors of his church? The traditions seem incompatible; one cannot have it both ways. My own opinion, for what it is worth, is that the Hadstock leather is not so much a piece of genuine Viking Daneskin as a piece of genuine Viking nonsense!

We know only the barest outlines of Knút's reign. The writer of the *Anglo-Saxon Chronicle*, who catalogued King Æthelred's failings with such relish after his death, did not say much about Knút: perhaps he did not dare. Knút acted decisively to get rid of potential claimants to the throne from the royal dynasty of Wessex, either by banishment or execution. He ordered Emma, Æthelred's widow, to be fetched from Normandy to be his wife. He hurried to Denmark in 1019 when his brother Harald died, to ensure his own succession to the throne there. In 1028 he drove King Ólaf Haraldsson (Ólaf the Stout) from the throne of Norway, and assumed the crown himself (*cf* Ch. 10). When he died at Shaftesbury in 1035, still a relatively young man, he was, according to Henry of Huntingdon, 'lord of the whole of Denmark, England and Norway, as also of Scotland'. For a few short years he had been the ruler of a North Sea empire that many had aspired to but none had achieved before him.

His mortal remains are said to be interred in one of the six mortuary chests which rest on the glazed stone screen in the South Presbytery Aisle of Winchester Cathedral. It is known that when he died in 1035 he was buried at Winchester in the minster that was demolished to make room for the superb Norman cathedral that stands there today, and that his relics were transferred to the new building because he was regarded as something of a saint.

With his death, the Anglo-Scandinavian empire he had built up began to fall apart. It had been very much his own personal achievement; dynastic politics and rivalries now caused immense confusion, and not one of his sons had either the calibre or the longevity to hold it together (*cf* Ch. 10). By 1042 England was ruled by an Englishman again — Edward the Confessor, the son of Æthelred the Unready, recalled from exile in Normandy. Norway and Denmark recoiled into their own preoccupations, Knút's empire disintegrated as if it had never been. The tide of Viking power had finally turned.

Mortuary chest in
Winchester Cathedral,
said to contain the bones
of King Knút and
others.

But England continued to be the key country in the North Sea power
struggle, symbolised perhaps by the fact that Knút the Great had chosen
to be buried in England and not in his native Denmark. That struggle
would reach its climax in the most famous year in English history – 1066.

10

'Here King Harold is Killed'

To all intents and purposes the year 1066 marks, or symbolises at least, the end of the Viking Age. History is never as neat and tidy as that, of course, but the date is not entirely arbitrary; 1066 has an air of culmination about it, with two climactic battles on English soil within three weeks of one another – Stamford Bridge in the north and Hastings in the south.

There were to be other Viking threats in the years that followed 1066, other Viking lunges to be dealt with, including a menacing invasion from Denmark in 1085 that was threatened but never launched. But 1066 saw the annihilation of the last major attempt at foreign expansion to be mounted by a Viking ruler; and by an irony of history, England was successfully invaded that year by a descendant of the Vikings who had settled in Normandy 150 years earlier.

Apart from the Normans, by 1066 most of the Viking peoples who had started bursting out of their homelands so exuberantly at the start of the Viking Age were back inside their original boundaries. From then on, for a variety of reasons – political, economic, military, technological, mercantile – the Viking dynamic was in decline. They had neither the man-power nor the staying-power, neither the wealth nor the political experience, neither the cohesion at home nor the confidence abroad, to master effectively the older and richer states overseas which they attacked. Those warriors who had settled in other lands had quickly become absorbed and lost their individual identity as Vikings. Only the Atlantic colonies that had been founded on virgin territory survived as recognisably Viking states abroad.

The decisive events of 1066 can be portrayed, in true Saga style, in terms of the personalities of three compelling but very different men: King Harald Sigurðsson of Norway, King Harold Godwinsson of England, and Duke William of Normandy. All three were after the same rich prize – the throne of England with all its prestige and perquisites; all three had claims to it, of a sort; only one of them could emerge the victor. And all of them had their roots deep in the Viking Age.

The story of Normandy as a Viking duchy starts with a man called Hrólf, who was 'a great Viking' according to Snorri Sturluson in *Heimskringla*. He was such a huge man that no horse could bear his weight, and so he had to go everywhere on foot; for that reason he was known as Göngu-Hrólf – Hrólf the Ganger, Ganger-Hrólf. History would get to know him better as Rollo, the founder of the Duchy of Normandy.

According to Icelandic historical tradition he was the son of Earl Rögnvald of Möre and brother of Earl Turf-Einar, one of the first Norse earls of Orkney. He took early to a career of piracy in the Baltic; but on one expedition he tactlessly helped himself to some cattle from Oslo Fjord, in Norway. It so happened that King Harald Fine-Hair was staying in the area at the time and was so incensed by this impertinent violation of his territory that he had Göngu-Hrólf declared an outlaw, even though Hrólf was the son of the man who had given the king his epic haircut (*cf* Ch. 2).

Göngu-Hrólf, or Rollo, sailed off to exile in the Hebrides. From there he took the well-worn Viking trail to join the war-bands that were harrying on both sides of the English Channel, late in the ninth century. We know nothing for certain of his movements; but it is not improbable that he was a member of the 'Great Heathen Host' that descended on England from the Continent between 892 and 896, during the latter years of King Alfred's reign, only to return to France with empty hands (*cf* Ch. 5). This army, or the remnants of it, went up the Seine, according to the *Anglo-Saxon Chronicle*, where Viking raiders had been on the rampage for many years. Rouen and several other towns had been taken over by Viking freebooters, and much of the Normandy countryside had been overrun.

We know nothing of Rollo's activities in France until 911, when he is reliably reported as the leader of a force that laid siege to Chartres. But on this occasion the Vikings suffered a severe reverse, and withdrew. King Charles III of France saw the chance of a diplomatic initiative to reach an accord with these particular Viking marauders after their setback, and summoned Rollo to a parley.

They met in the chapel at St Clair-sur-Epte, which is now a little village on a tributary of the Seine beside the old highway, the N14, between Paris and Rouen. Today, the somewhat decayed-looking church there has a stained-glass window commemorating that historic meeting. At that time, St Clair-sur-Epte marked the eastern limits of the Viking occupation of Normandy; later, William the Conqueror's son, William Rufus, would build a fortress at Château-sur-Epte, whose ruined keep still commands the hilltop and keeps watch over the village.

At their meeting in 911, King Charles III agreed to grant to the Viking invaders the lands they already occupied. He was therefore not giving much away; indeed, he was shrewdly using the Vikings as settlers who would be sure to defend that part of his realm against any future Viking invaders. In return, the Vikings swore to him oaths of allegiance as their king.

The stained-glass window in the church depicts a pious scene, with Rollo on one knee before King Charles. But legend has it that the giant Rollo treated the act of making homage with something less than the

Falaise Castle:
birthplace of Duke
William of Normandy.

respect due to majesty. When the time came for him to kiss the royal foot
he bent down and grasped it and then, straightening to his full height,
hauled the foot up to his lips. The king, naturally, fell flat on his back,
much to the merriment of the assembled Vikings, who always liked
their fun to be on the boisterous side. And thus was born the Duchy of
Normandy – *Northmandy*, the province of the Northmen (Old Norse
Normenn).

It was a classic case of turning poachers into gamekeepers, and not for
the first time. The cession of towns or lands that were already virtually lost
had been going on since the earliest Viking assaults in the previous
century, to stiffen the Frankish Empire's defences. Throughout the
second half of the ninth century, the Franks and the English had been
learning how to deal with the Vikings after absorbing the fury of the first
assaults. In France, fortified bridges were built to block the river-routes.
In England, King Alfred built fortified *burhs* (towns) to hold garrisons that
could contain the invaders. It is noticeable that the *Anglo-Saxon Chronicle*, which normally paid scant attention to events outside Wessex, anx-
iously recorded the deeds of Viking armies across the Channel that might
turn their attention to England. This shared concern seems to have led to a
sharing of ideas as well.

283

VIKINGS!

By the treaty of St Clair-sur-Epte, King Charles ensured that garrisons of erstwhile Vikings would hold Rouen, Lisieux, Evereux and all the lands between the Bresle and the Epte. He also ensured that the pagan invaders would be baptised and become Christian. This stipulation does not seem to have worried Rollo at all – indeed, he seems to have taken his 'conversion' seriously. He renounced his paganism as robustly as he had previously practised it.

No doubt the French kings thought they could wrest Normandy back for themselves at any time they wished; but in this they underestimated these new Normans. Rollo seems to have realised that the strength of the older Frankish system lay in a different concept of kingship and authority. Whereas the Vikings had favoured a loosely democratic or oligarchic system in which the authority of the king rested upon the freely-given support of his subjects, the Franks imposed authority from above. All land, all law, all loyalty belonged to the ruler. This was the meaning of feudalism, which Rollo grasped and put into effect. For the next century and a half he and his descendants would have a very rough ride, from rivals within the Duchy and attempted encroachments from without. But Normandy stood firm, and Rollo's Norman dynasty survived. A century and a half later it was strong enough to mount a major foreign invasion – the Norman Conquest of England, under Duke William.

The second major figure in the 1066 scenario, King Harald Sigurðsson of Norway, was the last of the great Viking sea-kings: the 'thunderbolt of the north', as Adam of Bremen called him. Later historians would dub him *harðráði* (Norwegian *Hardraade*), meaning 'hard-ruler': Harald the Ruthless. He has a Saga to himself in Snorri Sturluson's *Heimskringla – Haralds saga Sigurðarsonar* (*King Harald's Saga*):

> King Harald surpassed all other men in shrewdness and resourcefulness. He was an outstandingly brave warrior, and he also had great victory luck. He was brutal to his enemies, and dealt ruthlessly with any opposition. He was exceptionally greedy for power and wealth; but he was very generous to those of his friends who were dear to him.
>
> Harald was a handsome man of great presence. He was fair-haired, with a fair beard and long moustaches. One of his eyebrows was set slightly higher than the other. He had large well-shaped hands and feet. He was five ells tall [well over six feet].
>
> (*King Harald's Saga*, Ch. 99)

Harald was half-brother to King Ólaf Haraldsson, later to be canonised as St Ólaf, patron saint of Norway, who ruled Norway from 1014 until his death in battle in 1030. They had the same mother, Queen Ásta, and Harald was born in the year that Ólaf was fighting his way to the Norwegian throne.

Ólaf Haraldsson – Ólaf the Stout, as he was called during his lifetime – had been a professional Viking since the age of twelve. He had harried in the Baltic and much of northern Europe. He had fought in England, changing sides like any shrewd mercenary as pay and conditions dictated, and it was he who tore down London Bridge with his grappling irons and thus gave birth to the nursery rhyme that 'London Bridge is falling down' (*cf* Ch. 9). He saw service in Normandy, too, and it was in Rouen around the year 1013 that he was converted to Christianity.

When he seized the throne in 1014, Norway had lapsed into paganism after the brief 'conversion' by King Ólaf Tryggvason fifteen years earlier. Ólaf the Stout, doubtless well aware of the political advantages of an institutionalised State church to support him, set about the task of reconverting Norway with considerable missionary zeal. He was no milk-and-holy-water Christian, for he evangelised Norway with all the blood-and-iron ferocity he had shown on the battlefield. He scoured the length and breadth of the country, especially the recalcitrant northern regions, to root out paganism, building churches and despoiling heathen shrines and sanctuaries. Those Norwegians who bowed to his uncompromising will were rewarded with baptism and the royal favour. Those who tried to withstand him were less fortunate; some he simply killed on the spot, some he had maimed and mutilated, others had their eyes put out. The rest were driven from their homes, their lands confiscated, their families made hostage. Not surprisingly most people saw the error of their ways and meekly succumbed to the blandishments of the new religion. Norway, however reluctantly, became a Christian country, and was thus drawn more closely into the mainstream of European progress.

The magnificent old stave-churches of Norway (so called because their walls consist of vertical tree-trunks split in two), dating in some cases to within the first century of Norwegian Christianity, express a fascinating blend of the Christian and the lingering pagan. The towering Borgund church at Fagusnes counterpoints its serried pinnacles with Christian crosses and fearsome dragon-heads as well, to make doubly sure that the old gods were kept at bay no less than the Biblical devil. The splendid little Urnes church, islanded in the district of Sogn, has given its name to a whole art-style, intricate interlacing patterns of ribbon-like animals biting one another. By great good fortune some decorated timbers from the original eleventh-century church at Urnes were re-used when it was reconstructed in the middle of the twelfth century; and one of the panels of the north portal represents a distinct motif from pagan Norse mythology – a stag browsing on the foliage and bark of Yggdrasil, the World Tree that held the fabric of the Universe together.

King Ólaf also introduced – and enforced – new legislation and a new respect for justice and the rule of law. It was popular with the farmers who had often suffered at the hands of rapacious earls, and correspondingly unpopular with the powerful men who had formerly lorded it with impunity over their domains. One by one, the strong men of the realm began to turn against him; and at the same time Ólaf became hopelessly em-

Detail of Christian crosses and pagan dragons on Borgund stave-church.

broiled in the inter-domestic politics of the Scandinavian nations that so often bedevilled Viking affairs. To shore up his weakening position in Norway, he made alliance with Sweden by marrying a daughter of the Swedish king, Ólaf Sköttkonung.

In England, King Knút (Canute) must have viewed this development with concern. He had put a regent, his brother-in-law, Earl Úlf, on the throne of Denmark to rule the country on his behalf while his attentions were engaged in England; and he had secretly been using English wealth to bribe and suborn the disaffected lords in Norway. A Norwegian–Swedish alliance represented a clear threat to the trade and stability of the Anglo-Scandinavian empire he had built across the North Sea.

When Ólaf with a combined Norwegian and Swedish fleet began to harry the coasts of Denmark, King Knút, decisive as ever, made his move. He sailed across the North Sea and thrashed the invaders in a sea-battle at the mouth of the Holy River on the Baltic coast of Skåne (now in Sweden, but then part of the Danish kingdom). Two years later, in 1028, he arrived off the Norwegian coast with a huge fleet. Suddenly, King Ólaf found he had no friends left amongst the alienated aristocracy; while Norwegians flocked to Knút's standard, hailing him as a deliverer from tyranny, Ólaf fled the country into exile in Russia at the court of his brother-in-law Yaroslav the Wise, the ruler of Kiev. King Knút, well content to add Norway to his Scandinavian empire, placed a Norwegian earl, Earl Hákon, on the throne as regent, and returned to England.

The following year, however, Earl Hákon died, and Knút decided to put

OPPOSITE Borgund stave-church at Fagusnes in Norway.

Eleventh-century carved panels from the north portal of Urnes stave-church in Sogn.

his own son, Svein, on the Norwegian throne. Deep in the heart of Russia, exiled King Ólaf the Stout saw this political upheaval as a chance to regain his kingdom. Early in 1030 he set off along the frozen Russian rivers with a small detachment of 240 troops. In Sweden, his father-in-law lent him another 480, and with this ragtag little army he crossed the mountains and forests of the hinterland into northern Norway, hoping to rally support on the way. But little support materialised. The farmers on whom he had relied to answer his call, those farmers whom he had helped with his legal enactments and strict dispensation of justice for high and low alike, had in the meantime turned against him.

288

One person did not let him down, however – Harald Sigurðsson, his half-brother, now fifteen years old and itching to play his part in the showdown battle that everyone knew lay ahead. King Ólaf demurred: 'I think it better that my brother should not take part in the battle, for he is still only a child.'

'I shall certainly take part in the battle,' said Harald. 'And if I am too weak to grasp the sword, I know what to do – I shall bind my hand to the hilt. There is no one more eager than I to have a go at these farmers. I intend to be with my comrades.'

The fateful battle took place on a day of high summer at Stiklestad (*Stiklarstaðir* in the Saga sources) in the Tröndelag in northern Norway, seventy kilometres north-east of Trondheim. The traditional date is 29 July 1030; but the Saga accounts make much of an eclipse of the sun that took place during the battle, and there was an eclipse on 31 August. Oral tradition and piety may have telescoped the two events into one – indeed, the later canonisation of King Ólaf has cast a glow of martyrdom over all accounts of the battle.

The result was a foregone conclusion. Olaf's motley muster numbered fewer than 4000 men; facing him was reputedly the largest army ever gathered in Norway, which outnumbered his own forces by four to one. The battle was over almost before it had begun; we are told that it was joined before half-past one, and was over before three o'clock. Ólaf's men, desperately shouting their war-cry of *Fram, fram, Kristmenn, krossmenn, konungsmenn!* ('Forward, forward, Christ's men, cross-men, king's men'), broke almost at once and were routed. The king fought on with ferocious courage, but as the sky darkened he was brought to bay with his back against a rock and cut down by three fearsome blows to leg, belly and neck. Around him the men of his shield-wall, scorning flight, fought to the last.

His half-brother, Harald Sigurðsson, was severely wounded in the fighting, but managed to escape from the battlefield into the forests, where he was hidden in a remote farmhouse while his wounds were healed.

At once the miracles began. A wounded courtier who wiped the blood from the king's face and covered the body had his own injuries instantly healed. A blind man who that night accidentally rubbed his eyes with the water in which the king's body had been washed had his sight restored. The king's surviving followers were determined to prevent his body falling into the hands of the victors, who were equally determined to destroy it lest it become the focus for a cult and a political rallying-point. His friends managed to smuggle it back to Trondheim itself, by letting a decoy coffin weighted with stones be seized by their enemies, who promptly and unsuspectingly consigned it to the bottom of the sea.

In Trondheim the body was hidden in a derelict outbuilding 'above the town', and later that night it was secretly buried in an unmarked grave in a sandbank by the River Nid. And now what his opponents had feared

The death of St Ólaf at Stiklestad: illumination from *Flateyjarbók*.

would happen did happen: a cult sprang up, centred on the dead king's body, that was to prove the undoing of his successor, King Svein, son of Knút.

Svein Knútsson's reign proved to be uneasy, unsuccessful and brief. Beside his throne, as the *éminence grise*, sat his English mother, Ælfgifu (*Álfífa* in the Saga sources), Knút's consort, now being suitably rewarded for her years of faithful concubinage. According to the Sagas, Svein turned out to be a harsh and oppressive ruler; nor was his popularity enhanced by the fact that he was a foreigner, an Anglo-Dane, puppet of a Danish emperor in far-off England. In a belated access of patriotism, Norwegians started looking back wistfully to the days of King Ólaf the Stout. As more and more stories of miracles attributable to the fallen king circulated, a campaign was started to have him canonised, led by his old friend and spiritual mentor, Bishop Grimkel. Soon it was gaining increasing support amongst the disgruntled northern lords, who now resented having an avaricious foreigner on the throne of Norway: had they killed a perfectly good Norwegian king only to have a bad Danish one foisted on them?

And so, just a year after Ólaf's death, Grimkel sought King Svein's permission to exhume the body from its secret grave. Most surprisingly in the circumstances, permission was granted. The coffin was dug up with great ceremony; when it was opened, the body was found to have all the hallmarks of sanctity – it was totally uncorrupted, fresh and fragrant and glowing with colour. What is more, the hair and beard and nails had grown as much as if he had been alive all that time.

Queen Ælfgifu, at least, saw the danger signs. When she was shown the new-grown hair shorn from the dead king's head she refused to accept it as a token of sanctity unless it did not burn when put into a fire. Bishop

290

Grimkel duly consecrated a blaze, and lo! the hair was not consumed. Ælfgifu protested angrily that the fire should not have been consecrated, and demanded another demonstration with unconsecrated flames; but the northern earls, sensing the way the wind was blowing, growled her down.

Ólaf's holiness was now deemed to be beyond further question: within the space of one short year, the Viking warrior king had been translated into a Christian saint. His body was transferred to St Clement's Church, which Ólaf himself had founded in Trondheim; and by 1032 the centuries of pilgrimage had begun.

Snorri Sturluson's account of these momentous happenings in *St Ólaf's Saga* is detailed, colourful and circumstantial – suspiciously detailed, perhaps, for events that had taken place two centuries earlier. The evidence of archaeology is, as usual, less emphatic, and it cautions us to treat the Saga material with due care.

According to these Saga traditions, the town of Trondheim (*Niðaróss* – 'mouth of the Nid') had been founded on virgin soil in 997 by Ólaf Tryggvason, who established a trading-centre (*kaupstaðr, kaupangr*) on the delta-shaped peninsula where the River Nid enters the fjord. He laid out properties for his men and built himself a royal palace there. Recent archaeological indications from rescue digs in the heart of Trondheim, however, conducted by the Norwegian Central Office of Historical Monu-

Floor planking of a Viking Age house during excavations in Trondheim. Eleventh century.

Foundations of the twelfth-century church in Trondheim during the early stages of excavation – possibly St Gregory's.

ments (*Riksantikvaren*) and led by an English director, Clifford Long, suggest that there may well have been limited occupation on the peninsula *before* Ólaf Tryggvason's foundation; indeed, it would be surprising if a small settlement of merchants had not been in existence there already, which King Ólaf merely formalised and boosted into a northern base for himself.

Clifford Long's excavations are also throwing some new light on the problem of the extraordinary and complex sequence of church-building associated with St Ólaf and his remains, as reported in the Sagas. After the fall of Ólaf Tryggvason in the year 1000 the Trondheim settlement, we are told, was abandoned. It was King Ólaf the Stout who revived it and made it the effective capital of all Norway for the next two centuries. He built St Clement's Church, and a new royal palace. His son, Magnús the Good, built a new church, St Ólav's, to house his father's remains on the site

292

of the derelict outbuilding 'above the town' where they had first been hidden, and also started work on a new palace with a stone-built hall.

After Harald Harðráði came to the Norwegian throne in 1047, he is said to have converted this unfinished stone hall into a church dedicated to St Gregory, and to have built himself yet another palace and yet another church, St Mary's, on the spot where St Ólaf's body had lain for a year in its secret grave in the sandbank by the River Nid. Finally, it was Harald's son, Ólaf Kyrri (the Gentle), who built the minster of Christ Church, where the saint's remains finally came to rest and which, in the twelfth century, was incorporated into the present-day Trondheim Cathedral.

Clifford Long has now found and excavated a medieval stone-built church. It consists of the foundations and sunken crypt of an early church under the western side of Sondre Gate; it is now preserved and excellently displayed as an integral part of the basement of the new Trondhjems Savings Bank which was built on the vacant site. It is a fascinating little building: rectangular (apart from one wall which is askew), with an apsidal chancel, and steps leading down into the crypt from the nave. The apsidal chancel was later replaced by a square one, but the little vaulted crypt was retained.

But which church was it? And who built it? Its existence had long been suspected from frequent stray finds of human bones in the vicinity. Local sentiment insisted that it must be St Gregory's Church, the stone-built hall started by King Magnús the Good and completed as a church by Harald Harðráði. Unfortunately, the archaeological evidence does not square with the Saga accounts. In the first place there was no indication of the original secular building, as reported by Snorri Sturluson. In the

From the eleventh-century waterfront at Trondheim – a length of osier rôpe perfectly preserved, and the handle of an oar sticking out of the clay.

293

Bronze ship's weather vane from Heggen in Norway.

second place the church had been built on top of a thick layer of occupation material including at least five building phases or even more, and can therefore hardly be dated earlier than the twelfth century – a century later than Magnús the Good and Harald Harðráði. It may well be St Gregory's; but in that case, Snorri Sturluson was mistaken in ascribing it to Magnús and Harald.

And what of the other church that Harald is said to have built on the site of his kinsman's secret grave – St Mary's Church? According to Snorri, a fine spring whose water had miraculous healing properties had welled forth from the spot. It so happens that there *is* a spring down on the river bank, but there are no discernible signs of a church ever having stood there. It seems much more likely that Snorri's sources were garbled, and that Harald's church in honour of his sainted half-brother was built on the highest point of the peninsula, where the magnificent Trondheim Cathedral now stands, and that it was covered over by the building of the cathedral.

Whatever the precise location of his various shrines, there is no doubt that Ólaf's popularity as a national saint was immediate and overwhelming. Ælfgifu's misgivings were proved all too correct, and Svein's days as king of Norway were soon numbered. By 1035 he had been ousted by the patriotic Norwegian party. His successor was St Ólaf's twelve-year-old son, Magnús Ólafsson (Magnús the Good), who had been left behind for safety and tutelage with Yaroslav in Kiev when his father set off on his winter journey to defeat and martyrdom at Stiklestad. The boy, who was illegitimate and had been named after the Emperor Charlemagne (Carolus Magnus), was fetched back from Russia; and with him, the royal Yngling line was restored to the throne of Norway.

I must confess I find it hard not to feel a little sorry for Ólaf the Stout. As *King* Ólaf of Norway he never had much luck during his earthly reign; but as *Saint* Ólaf of Norway he really worked wonders, both for the church he had established and for the throne he had lost at the Battle of Stiklestad.

But let us return to Harald Sigurðsson where we left him after the battle, hidden in a farmhouse recovering from his wounds. As soon as he was fit to travel he was smuggled over the Norwegian border to friendly Sweden, and from there he also made his way to Kiev, at that time and for centuries thereafter the heart and capital of the Russian empire. In Kiev he was given political asylum by the ever-hospitable Yaroslav.

Yaroslav the Wise, Lord of Kiev and Novgorod, was one of the greatest princes of the Viking Age, revered as a patron and founder of learning and literature in Russia during his thirty-year reign. A shrewd and energetic statesman, he was always careful to foster his ancestral connections with Scandinavia and with the 'Varangians' (*cf* Ch. 4). He had married a daughter of the King of Sweden; his contacts with the Viking kingdoms to the west were obviously close and calculated.

Trondheim Cathedral.

At Kiev he took the young Harald as his fosterling. At Yaroslav's court, Harald met up again with Magnús Ólafsson, now heir-apparent to the Norwegian throne – two future kings of Norway learning the crafts of kingship at the Russian court. At Kiev, too, Harald would have seen the foundations being laid by Yaroslav of Russia's first cathedral, the superb minster of St Sophia which has so miraculously survived the troubled centuries.

Harald stayed with Yaroslav for three years, being taught the art of warfare as an officer in the Russian army, taking part in various military campaigns. Yaroslav must have recognised in him the steeliness and ambition that would earn him his nickname of Harðráði, and decided to give him one of his daughters, Elizabeth, in marriage. But first, to complete his education, he sent him down the Dnieper to Constantinople, capital of the Byzantine Empire, with a personal command of five hundred hand-picked warriors, to join the élite bodyguard of the Emperor, the feared and famous Varangian Guard:

> Bleak showers lashed dark prows
> Hard along the coast-line;
> Iron-shielded longships
> Flaunted coloured rigging.
> The great prince saw ahead
> The copper roofs of Constantinople;
> His swan-breasted ships swept
> Towards the tall-towered city.
>
> (*King Harald's Saga*, Ch. 2)

The Varangian Guard was the most glamorous unit in the Byzantine army: Brigade of Guards, Royal Marines and Commandos in one. It was, in effect, the Viking Foreign Legion. It has perhaps been over-glamorised in Icelandic tradition, for the Saga-writers were inordinately proud of any young Icelanders who served in it and returned home dressed in exotic raiment and laden with royal gifts and honours. Nevertheless it was undoubtedly regarded as a crack regiment, for which only the best were chosen.

Swedish Vikings had been fighting in the service of the Byzantine Emperor in Constantinople through the tenth century. The word for them, 'Varangians' (*Væringjar*), seems to derive from the Old Norse word *vár*, meaning 'pledge': they were men pledged to stand together and support one another loyally. They were the Companions, the Fellowship, the *comitatus*. Late in the tenth century the Emperor formed them into a separate unit of his Household Guard. They continued as a mainly Scandinavian company until after the Norman Conquest of 1066, when Anglo-Saxon and Danish champions, chafing under Norman rule, started to emigrate from England to join the Varangians. But by then the Varangian Guard, like the Viking Age itself, had passed its zenith, and it virtually ceased to exist after the sack of Constantinople by the Crusaders in 1204.

It was as a Varangian in Constantinople that Harald Sigurðsson mastered his trade as a Viking leader of men, and laid the foundations for his future bid for the crown of Norway. He spent about ten years in the imperial army, incognito for most of the time according to some sources, serving under three successive emperors. He campaigned vigorously and successfully all over the eastern Mediterranean: against the Arabs on the banks of the Euphrates, against Normans and Muslims in Sicily, against the Bulgars in Thessalonica. He may also have visited Jerusalem as captain of a special military escort for pilgrims or craftsmen bound for the Church of the Holy Sepulchre. His career prospered, and he was promoted to the rank of commander with the title of *spatharokanditates*, the third level in the hierarchy of the Imperial court.

Snorri Sturluson includes a number of entertaining tales of his ingenuity as a commander and his love of bizarre and crafty stratagems. He is said to have captured one town he was besieging in Sicily by fastening incendiary devices of fir chips, melted wax and brimstone to small birds, so that when they flew back to their nests under the thatched eaves of the houses, they set the town alight. But such tricks were part of the stock-in-trade of classical and medieval story-telling, and Harald was the sort of charismatic leader to attract to his name stories of this kind.

Embroidered as much of Snorri's account of Harald's career with the Varangians undoubtedly is, there is independent and contemporary corroboration of its main outlines in an anonymous Greek work called *Book of Advice to an Emperor*, written by a man who claimed to have campaigned with Harald in Bulgaria in 1040–1. It is a dry and brief biography, but clearly well-informed and an extremely valuable historical source; but it has none of the vividness of story-telling with which Snorri Sturluson brings out the key aspects of Harald's personality – his lust for fame, his resourcefulness, his single-mindedness, his cunning, his greed, his capacity for double-dealing.

He certainly played a characteristically ruthless part in some of the Byzantine intrigues that surrounded the imperial throne. When the cruel and unpopular Emperor Michael V was deposed and dragged from sanctuary in a church by a howling mob, Harald was the leader of a Varangian detachment that was given the grisly task of blinding him; according to the Sagas, it was Harald himself who gouged the victim's eyes out. But on the whole he seems to have kept himself aloof; he was certainly careful to keep his own hand-picked body of troops as a separate unit under his personal command. And with his eyes firmly fixed on his ultimate goal of gaining Norway, he secretly salted away in Kiev, in Yaroslav's safe-keeping, all the immense plunder he took on his various campaigns: 'In this way,' says Snorri blandly, 'Harald amassed a vast hoard of wealth.'

When the time came for him to leave Constantinople to fulfil his am-

Constantinople (modern Istanbul): bridging Europe and Asia.

bitions in Scandinavia, he seems to have left under a cloud, although there are conflicting versions of this. According to Snorri, the Empress Zoe had begun to suspect (no doubt rightly) that Harald had been misappropriating the Emperor's proper share of the spoils of war. She had him flung into prison, from which he escaped with the aid of a divinely-inspired fair lady, and then stole out of the city. The Greek source says that when Harald asked the new emperor, Constantine Monomachus (1042–5), Zoe's fourth husband, for permission to return to Norway, it was refused, 'and obstacles were put in his way', but that even so he got away by stealth. These obstacles included a massive iron anti-shipping chain across the Bosphorus. Harald overcame this problem by literally rocking his longship over the chain; he packed the stern with all his men and equipment to lift the bows, then rowed hard at the chain, and as the vessel came to a stop on top of it all the men ran forward and tilted the bows into a slide over the other side. A second ship that was with him broke its back on the chain, with considerable loss of life.

Safely into the freedom of the Black Sea with a hard-knit troop of battle-seasoned Varangians, Harald Harðráði now headed for home: first to Kiev to claim from Yaroslav the hand of his daughter Elizabeth and his accumulated loot, and then to Norway to claim a share at least of the throne from his nephew, Magnús the Good – if necessary by force.

Once again, political upheavals in Scandinavia were providing the opportunity for a seizure of power. The great King Knút, emperor of England, Denmark and, briefly, Norway, had died late in 1035. So had his discredited

OPPOSITE The magnificent cathedral of St Sophia in Kiev, founded in the eleventh century.

son, the deposed King Svein Knútsson of Norway. Another of his sons, Hörða-Knút, legitimate heir to the Danish crown, was now heir to England as well, but dared not leave Denmark to claim his English throne because of the threat of attack from Norway. In the meantime Knút's other illegitimate son by Ælfgifu, Harald Harefoot, was declared regent of England, and later, in 1037, usurped the throne. Goaded by his half-brother's perfidy, Hörða-Knút at last concluded a peace treaty with Magnús of Norway which left him free to sail for England with a punitive fleet.

By the time he reached England, Harald Harefoot had providentially died, in 1040, and Hörða-Knút assumed the throne. Two years later he was dead, apparently of an excessive consumption of drink; so now, in 1042, the thrones of both England and Denmark were empty. The English promptly chose an English ruler, Edward, son of Æthelred the Unready, whose widow, Emma, Knút had married for sound political reasons if nothing else; Edward, in fact, was Hörða-Knút's step-brother. He would become better known as Edward the Confessor.

The succession in Denmark had already been decided by the peace treaty that Hörða-Knút had concluded with Magnús of Norway: each was pledged to be the other's heir if one died without male issue. There was only one other legitimate claimant: Svein Úlfsson, son of the former regent Earl Úlf and Knút's sister, Estrid (*Ástrið*). As Knút's nephew he was the proper heir by blood to Denmark; but Magnús the Good gave him no time to advance his claim. He came sweeping down from Norway with a formidable fleet and simply took possession; he then magnanimously appointed Svein Úlfsson his regent in Denmark. But not for long; when Svein began to betray ambitions to wear the crown himself, Magnús once more descended with a fleet and drove him into exile.

This was the confused and intricate dynastic situation that prevailed in Scandinavia when Harald Harðráði returned to the northern arena from Constantinople in 1045. He reckoned that since his nephew Magnús now had two kingdoms, he, Harald, deserved at least a share in one. As an opening gambit he joined forces with the exiled Svein Úlfsson and raided Zealand, just to concentrate Magnús's mind. Magnús agreed to give Harald half of Norway in return for half of the Varangian gold, while he continued to keep Denmark for himself. They ruled jointly in Norway for two uneasy years, until Magnús resolved the situation by conveniently dying in 1047. In a flash, Svein Úlfsson was into Denmark, where he was acclaimed and enthroned as king.

Sole king of Norway now, Harald Harðráði immediately turned his baleful attention on Denmark. For the next two decades he was to conduct a wasteful, vicious and ultimately futile war of attrition against the man who was now his arch enemy, King Svein Úlfsson. Over and over again some part of Denmark was devastated as Harald relentlessly raided its undefended coasts. Again and again, King Svein was defeated but, despite all the punishment the Danes took, they stubbornly refused to countenance a forcible union of the two countries under the Norwegian crown, and their loyalty to King Svein never faltered.

The only beneficiary of these destructive years has been posterity, in the form of two outstanding archaeological legacies.

From the Kattegat, the sea that separates Denmark from Sweden, a long fjord cuts deep into the island of Zealand, a few kilometres west of Copenhagen. At its head sits the town that used to be the royal capital of medieval Denmark: the city of Roskilde. The water is very shallow in places – only half a fathom or so. It has always been a difficult fjord for shipping to negotiate, which is why Copenhagen itself was founded as a new port to accommodate larger ships. There is now a channel up the fjord for modern shipping, kept open by dredging; there is also a natural passage, just deep enough for fishing-boats, but it is a difficult and winding route, known only to locals. In Viking times there was another, more direct fairway through the fjord that led straight to Roskilde. At its shallowest point, in the area known as Skuldelev, that channel was blocked some time in antiquity, and it has been out of use for centuries.

In 1956 two amateur frogmen exploring the blockage found a rather unusual oaken frame, which archaeologists identified as part of the mast structure of a Viking ship. In 1962 the area of the blockage was enclosed within a coffer-dam in mid-fjord to pump the water away, and there lay revealed a whole cemetery of Viking Age ships, five in all, which had been deliberately scuttled to make the main navigational channel impassable. They were a longship, a light warship, a ferry boat, a small Baltic merchant-man, and 'Skuldelev 1', the deep-sea *knörr* (*cf* Ch. 7).

The five ships were carefully lifted from the sea-bed, piece by piece. Their timbers were by then as soft as putty, and had been flattened out of shape by the stones that had filled them when they were scuttled. They have now been conserved and moulded back into their original lines, and all the ships (except for the unusually lengthy longship, which was in the most fragmentary state) have been put together again in their original form in the handsome new Viking Ship Museum that was specially built to receive them on the waterfront of Roskilde.

Dr Ole Crumlin-Pedersen, a leading authority on medieval ships, was one of the joint leaders of the delicate operation of raising and restoring the ships; he is now Director of the new museum in Roskilde. From the type and age of the ships involved, he deduced that they had been scuttled around the period 1040–50; and it is a reasonable assumption that they were sacrificed in order to block the channel against the depredations of Harald Harðráði of Norway.

The tactic worked, better than even its planners could have dreamed. Roskilde escaped Harald's fury, and was never destroyed; and nine centuries later, modern science and technology were given the opportunity of salvaging this unique collection of five priceless ships of different types, all from the late Viking Age.

Roskilde Fjord: the coffer-dam in mid-fjord built in the 1960s for the excavation of five scuttled Viking ships.

Dr Ole Crumlin-Pedersen has more recently been involved in the salvage of yet another archaeological memento of Harald's assaults on Denmark. In 1049, Harald Harðráði made a sudden attack on Denmark's major trading-town, Hedeby (*cf* Ch. 3), and burned it to the ground:

> All Hedeby was blazing,
> Fired by Harald's fury;
> There's no limit to the boldness
> Of Norway's warrior sea-king.
> King Svein now feels the havoc
> Of Harald's deadly vengeance.
> At dawn on Hedeby's outskirts
> I saw the tall fires raging.
>
> (*King Harald's Saga*, Ch. 34)

The razing of Hedeby was a pointless exercise in vengefulness – and surely self-defeating, too, for a would-be king to destroy his hoped-for kingdom's major mart. As it turned out, Hedeby recovered, albeit briefly – wooden towns were not hard to rebuild – and King Svein remained on his precarious throne. But Hedeby was in decline by that time anyway, because the pattern of European trade was changing. The classic luxury trade of the Viking Age, high-priced exotic goods like furs, ivories, precious jewellery, weapons, amber, slaves, and so on, was being superseded by a growing trade in bulk goods like stone, timber, foodstuffs (especially dried fish for the Christian Friday market) and textiles. They called for larger ships, which needed larger and deeper ports.

Today, a spectacular new excavation in the harbour area of Hedeby has produced vivid evidence of the town's death-throes at Harald's hands. Some twenty-seven years ago, in 1953, divers found rich traces of all kinds of debris on the seabed where the old harbour had been, including the remains of what seemed to be a fortified stockade round the harbour area. In particular, they found the remains of a Viking boat lying in three metres of water, about forty metres off-shore, near the entrance to the fortified stockade. From bits and pieces brought to the surface, it became clear that it had been a Viking warship; what is more, there were strong indications that the ship had been ablaze when it sank, and had burned down to the water-line.

In 1979 a full-scale excavation was mounted, using the same coffer-dam technique that had been employed so successfully in Roskilde Fjord, and the ship was lifted. Only about a third of it has survived, unfortunately. The stern section was missing, and only about seventeen metres of the estimated original length of twenty-three metres remained. It was very slender, only about two and a half metres wide. And now speculation hardened. It was a beautifully-built ship of the right period, and it had been blazing furiously when it sank in the entrance to the harbour. It seems very likely to have been a fireship propelled by Harald Harðráði's men against the wooden fortifications of the harbour during that raid in 1049.

For another fifteen years Harald's depredations went on, in fits and starts, until even that 'thunderbolt of the north' grew tired of the game. At a peace-meeting in 1064, Harald and Svein agreed that the old frontiers would stay as they were. No war reparations would be paid on either side; Harald would keep Norway, and Svein would keep Denmark. The man who had lost all the battles had effectively won the war, and Svein would outlive Harald Harðráði by eight years.

So Harald withdrew into Norway, where he laid about him robustly for a time, cuffing upstarts and confiscating lands at will. He was almost fifty

The small trading ship (Wreck 3) at the Roskilde Ship Museum, after restoration.

Excavation of the Hedeby 'fireship' in 1979.

years old when, early in January 1066, Edward the Confessor, King of England, died. Once again, dynastic imperatives were about to throw the royalties of Europe into the melting-pot; and once again, all the old Viking compulsions stirred in Harald's veins. Here was another crown for the taking, rightly his by inheritance by virtue of the old treaty between his nephew Magnús the Good and King Hörða-Knút of Denmark and England – each had nominated the other as heir to his crown. Magnús had been too preoccupied with home affairs to claim the throne of England at the time of Edward the Confessor's accession, and Harald too busy with Denmark since then. But now, clear for once of other embroilments, Harald prepared for his Enterprise of England.

Harald Harðráði would have been well aware that there was another and perhaps equally formidable claimant to the throne in the offing – Duke William of Normandy, direct descendant of the Viking founding father of the Norman dynasty, Rollo. Like Harald, William had lived with the hurly-burly of battle for most of his life. He was the illegitimate son of Duke Robert I (Robert the Devil) and a tanner's daughter, Herleve (sometimes called Arletta); to his unfastidious contemporaries, he was known bluntly as William the Bastard.

He was born and brought up in the pleasant little town of Falaise. He was only seven years old when his father died and he inherited the Duchy, in 1035. His minority was a nightmare of danger and treachery from rival family claimants. This was not all that unusual; for several generations the Dukes of Normandy had had a hard time controlling their rebellious barons and fending off attacks from outside. Gradually the old Viking capacity for survival, by whatever devious means, had mobilised and elaborated the feudal forms which strengthened the hand of the overlord. The descendants of the Northmen had learned the realities of power-politics, how to organise, how to centralise, how to systematise feudal fiefdoms for the ultimate benefit of the Duke and his dukedom.

Somehow William survived. Even when he reached manhood there were seven more years of incessant warfare and rebellion, between 1047 and 1054, before he was able to establish his authority over Normandy beyond serious dispute. By the age of thirty he had matured into a ruthless and resourceful warrior and ruler. He had also developed a shrewd politician's eye for the main chance, and in his case the main chance, he decided, was England. He had been careful to foster friendly relations with Edward the Confessor, who had spent twenty-five years of his early life as an exile in Normandy during Knút's reign before his recall to England and the throne in 1042. Edward never lost his fondness for all things Norman, and William was later to claim that Edward had actually promised him the throne of England, nominated him as his heir, in fact, during a visit to England in 1051.

In England, the most powerful and ambitious family dynasty outside the royal line was that of the kingmaker Earl Godwin of Wessex and his five sons. It was an upstart, *nouveau-riche* family: Godwin's father had been a footloose Danish Viking who had come to England as a raider during the reign of Æthelred the Unready and settled in Sussex. Within the space of a generation, Godwin effectively controlled the whole of the south of England; his earldom extended from Cornwall to Kent, and the king was his son-in-law to boot. He had helped Edward the Confessor to the throne in 1042, but there was always an element of friction between them. Perhaps King Edward resented Earl Godwin's power; no doubt Godwin resented Edward's blatant favouritism towards his Norman friends. At any rate the friction exploded into open enmity in 1051, when Edward ordered Godwin to punish the inhabitants of Dover for a bloody brawl in which they had attacked a flock of Norman courtiers on their way home to Normandy. Godwin refused – Dover, after all, was within his earldom. The king, supported by other earls who were jealous of the Godwin family power, felt strong enough to exile Godwin and his sons for insubordination.

Within a year, Godwin and his sons were back in England in strength – sufficient strength to cow King Edward into restoring them to power and purging his court of Norman elements. Not long afterwards, Godwin died, and his eldest son, Harold Godwinsson, succeeded to the earldom as the strong man of England. He proved his military ability in crushing campaigns against insurrections in Wales. He had his brother Tostig installed in the vacant earldom of Northumbria. For the last ten years of the childless Edward the Confessor's reign, Harold ruled England in all but name.

In 1064 or thereabouts there occurred yet another cross-Channel visit, this time in reverse. For some reason that no historian can now unravel, Harold Godwinsson seems to have gone to Normandy, either at the king's bidding or storm-blown there by accident or on some private mission of his own. According to Norman sources he was sent by King Edward, who was feeling his advancing years (he was now in his sixties), to confirm William's nomination as his heir. William behaved towards Harold like a feudal patron, took him campaigning in Brittany, knighted him, and accepted an oath of allegiance from him.

Contemporary English chroniclers make no reference at all to this alleged visit; but there is one priceless contemporary document that does – the Bayeux Tapestry.

The Bayeux Tapestry is one of the most remarkable historical documents of all time. It is not in fact a tapestry at all; it is an embroidery – an incredibly long strip of embroidered linen measuring forty metres by fifty centimetres. It was commissioned by Duke William's half-brother, Bishop Odo of Bayeux, soon after 1066 to celebrate the Conqueror's victory, and embroidered in the famous needlework school at Canterbury. It is not known for what purpose it was intended, whether for William's coronation, or the consecration of Bishop Odo's new cathedral at Bayeux in 1077, or for some unknown castle. All we know is that it is a magnificent political strip-cartoon, a masterpiece of Norman propaganda, and a superb work of art: an epic *chanson de geste* in graphic form. It is now preserved in the Old Archbishop's Palace at Bayeux, in Normandy; there is also a splendid facsimile of it in the Reading Art Gallery, embroidered by thirty-five industrious needlewomen from Leek in Staffordshire in 1885–6, and now mounted and framed in twenty-five dust-proof panels.

The Tapestry tells in pictures, from the Norman point of view, the series of events that led up to William's invasion of England and his victory at the Battle of Hastings. So pronounced is the Norman bias that English historians do not consider it 'sound', historically; but it is a spectacular

source of information about the technology, dress, ships and military methods of the time.

It starts by showing '*Edwardus Rex*' giving instructions to two attentive people, followed by a scene of Harold riding to his ship at Bosham. The ship comes to land in the demesnes of William's vassal, the evil Count Guy of Ponthieu, who seizes and imprisons Harold. William sends messengers to Guy, sternly demanding Harold's release into his own custody in Rouen. We see the campaigning in Brittany, and William 'giving arms' to Harold (thus making him 'William's man' for ever), and then the enigmatic oath which Harold swore to William, hallowed by holy relics. Next we see King Edward on his deathbed, and Harold assuming the kingship with sceptre and orb. William sends word to Harold to remind him of his oath, but Harold replies, 'It is true that I took an oath to William, but I took it under duress.' So William promptly starts building an invasion fleet: another Enterprise of England.

Looking at the Tapestry is like studying history through a telescope. The field of vision is foreshortened and limited by the lens. The Tapestry totally ignores the third side of the triangle in the fateful events of 1066: Harald Harðráði of Norway. Yet it was the direct Viking challenge from Norway that so weakened the military strength of the grandson of a

Bayeux Tapestry: the Norman version of the oath sworn by Harold Godwinsson to Duke William. Harold (with moustache) in the middle, with his hands on sacred relics on either side. William seated on the left.

Bayeux Tapestry: on the left, the death of Edward the Confessor. In the centre, Harold Godwinsson is crowned king.

VIKINGS!

Viking, Harold of England, that the door to England was left open for a Norman descendant of the Vikings, William the Conqueror.

Edward the Confessor had died on 5 January 1066, and was buried in the precursor of Westminster Abbey. The very next day, Harold Godwinsson had himself proclaimed king of England. He was destined to reign for precisely nine months and eight days.

When the news of Harold's accession reached Norway, Harald Harðráði must have decided very quickly that he had the beating of both Harold and William, if need be, and started preparing an invasion fleet of two hundred ships. He knew he could rely on support from Scotland and the Orkney earldom; but he must have been heartened to receive overtures from an unexpected ally – Harold's brother, Tostig, Earl of Northumbria. After ten years of suffering Tostig's oppressive rule in the north, the Northumbrians had risen against him and turned him out. His brother Harold had done nothing to help him; and now Tostig was thirsting for revenge, and would lend his sword to any bidder who would help him gain it.

And so, while William's shipwrights felled and adzed and hammered to make a fleet of landing craft, and William sent out a rallying call to all the soldiers of fortune of Europe to join him in his pounce on the rich pickings of England, Harald of Norway was assembling his own fleet and army – secretly, it seems, because no word of his preparations reached England. Instead, the English were preoccupied with the threat from the south, from Normandy. High in the heavens, Halley's Comet seared across the sky on 24 April: 'At that time, throughout all England, there was seen in the heavens such a portent as men had never seen before' (*Anglo-Saxon Chronicle*). In May, Tostig appeared with a fleet off the Isle of Wight; a diversionary attack, perhaps, but on whose behalf? William's or Harald's? Harold of England raced south to Sandwich with an army, and Tostig backed off. For the rest of the summer, English eyes were trained uneasily across the Channel. But no Norman hulls hove into view and by the second week of September, with provisions and morale running low, Harold called off the alert; the militia was disbanded, the assembled fleet was ordered from the Isle of Wight to London, only to come to severe grief in a storm on the way.

And then suddenly, shockingly, the enemy was there; but not in the south – in the north-east. Harald Harðráði had arrived, with Tostig at his side and weighty reinforcements from Scotland that boosted his fleet to 300 ships and his army to 9000 men. Sailing down the Yorkshire coast he slashed idly at the coastal towns on his route – at Cleveland, Scarborough, Holderness. Then he swung his armada into the Humber and up the Ouse to Riccall, where he landed. The die was now cast:

> The ogress flaunts her crimson
> Shield as battle nears;
> The troll-woman sees clearly

Stamford Bridge: the original bridge probably stood near the weir in the background. The English army approached from the left (north), and the battle probably took place on the higher ground of the south bank, on the right.

> The doom awaiting Harald.
> With greedy mouth she rends
> The flesh of fallen warriors;
> With frenzied hands she stains
> The wolf's jaws crimson –
> Wolf's jaws red with blood.
>
> (*King Harald's Saga*, Ch. 81)

It was York, the key to the north, that he was after. His way was barred by an army of Northumbrians and Mercians at Gate Fulford on the Ouse. There, on Wednesday 20 September, Harald fought his first pitched battle on English soil, carrying his celebrated banner, *Landeyðan* ('Land-Waster') before him. The fighting was unexpectedly hard. It was eventide before the English broke and fled, badly mauled; but the Norwegian toll had been ominously high, too.

York prudently capitulated without further fight, and Harald went about the usual business of arranging for hostages for good behaviour and recruiting volunteers for his march south. It was all very leisurely, very confident. He did not even bother to leave a garrison in York; York, he reckoned, was now secure. Instead, he marched the main body of his army to Stamford Bridge on the Derwent, twelve kilometres north-east of York, a useful focal point of road communications but, fatally, nineteen kilometres from his fleet anchored at Riccall. As it turned out, it was a dreadful tactical mistake.

The moment that news of the Battle of Gate Fulford reached Harold of

Bayeux Tapestry: part of William's huge invasion fleet of specially constructed landing-craft on the Viking longship model.

England, he had swung into action. Summoning his army, he was now striding north in a breathtaking series of forced marches. By the evening of 24 September he was at Tadcaster, only twenty-eight kilometres away; early next morning he was marching fast through York, and by noon he was at Stamford Bridge.

For once Harald Harðráði had been caught napping. It was a warm, sunny autumn day; his troops, most of their armour discarded, were relaxing on the far bank of the Derwent. The bridge itself was unguarded. Harald looked up, surprised, as the dust-cloud of an army on the move appeared in the distance: 'And the closer the army came, the greater it grew, and their glittering weapons sparkled like a field of broken ice' (*King Harald's Saga*, Ch. 87). And so the scene was set for the battle that would decide England's destiny, for the winner would be in little shape to deal with the challenge that would inevitably follow from Normandy.

It was a heroic engagement, resplendent with Saga bravura. A giant Norwegian defended the bridge like a latter-day Horatius to give his comrades time to muster; he killed countless assailants with his battle-axe before someone crept underneath the bridge and killed him with an upward jab through a gap in the timbers . . . King Harald's black horse stumbled and threw him, and Harold of England commented, 'What a big and formidable-looking man he is – let us hope his luck has run out' . . . Harald of Norway said of Harold of England, 'What a little man he is – but he stood proudly in his stirrups' . . . Harold of England, answering Harald of Norway's demand for land, replied that he was prepared to grant him 'seven feet of ground, or as much more as he is taller than other men'.

Throughout that sunny afternoon the battle raged, swaying first one way and then the other. At a critical point, Harald Harðráði 'fell into such a fury of battle that he rushed forward ahead of his troops, hewing with both hands. Neither helmet nor armour could withstand him, and everyone in his path gave way before him. It looked then as if the English were on the point of being routed . . . But now King Harald Sigurðsson was struck in the throat by an arrow, and that was his death-wound' (*King Harald's Saga*, Ch. 92).

Reinforcements hastily summoned from the ships at Riccall nineteen kilometres away now came panting on to the scene, but it was too late; the

Last of the Vikings lay dead. All fought hard and bravely none the less, the banner 'Land-Waster' waved· defiance for a little longer, but in the end it was Harold's axe-wielding Housecarls who won the day. When the slaughter was over, and Harold gave quarter to the defeated, there were only twenty-four shiploads of survivors left alive to limp back home across the North Sea.

Two days later, William of Normandy at last set sail across the Channel from St Valéry. It was not a matter of inspired timing and tactics to exploit the situation created by Stamford Bridge – he had no way of knowing about that at the time. Indeed, if his plans had gone the way he intended, he would have been trying to force a landing on the south coast of England in the middle of August, when Harold was waiting for him.

The huge Norman invasion fleet – 700 craft of every shape and size, and an army estimated at some 10,000 men – had gathered at the mouth of the River Dives on schedule, but contrary winds kept it from moving; only in the most favourable conditions could this motley armada travel safely across the Channel. Not until early in September did the wind veer, just as Harold Godwinsson was standing down his defence forces. William set sail. But on 8 September, the sudden storm that shattered Harold's fleet on its homeward way to London drove William's fleet back into port at St Valéry. By the time the wind changed again on 27 September, everything else had changed too; the Channel was empty, the English army was bandaging its wounds 400 kilometres away to the north after the bruising battle at Stamford Bridge, and the south coast of England lay open and undefended.

On the morning of 28 September, less than twenty-four hours after leaving St Valéry, William landed on Pevensey beach, sixteen kilometres west of Hastings. The shoreline has changed very considerably since then; Pevensey was then a wide and sheltered lagoon, ideal for harbouring an invasion fleet. There was no opposition to the landing. Not a defender in sight anywhere. By nightfall the invaders were all safely ashore, men and horses and equipment, and fanning out over the Pevensey peninsula to consolidate the beachhead.

The news must have reached Harold of England within hours, perhaps by a chain of signal beacons. Once again he set off on a series of forced marches with his exhausted army. And now events were galloping towards

Bayeux Tapestry: '*Hic Haroldus rex interfectus est*': Here King Harold is killed. The panel under '*interfectus est*' shows Harold being cut down by a Norman knight; to the left, an English warrior plucks at an arrow in his eye – thus giving rise to the popular misconception that this was how Harold died.

the very climax of the Viking Age; the Norseman–Norman pincer on England was closing, and closing very fast.

Harold reached London by 5 October – an astonishing feat under the circumstances. He spent five days there, no more, raising more levies, all bustle and organisation, and then he was off again to confront the new invaders. He has been blamed for impetuousness: critics have said he should have waited longer to amass a larger army, to give his embattled troops respite after their exertions. But his strategy was theoretically impeccable. He knew that Pevensey was a geological peninsula, hemmed in by a ridge through which there was only one exit; he wanted to stop a Norman break-out and keep William bottled up for the winter.

In the event William simply outmanoeuvred him by the speed of his reactions. Before Harold's troops had had time to dig in properly along the Senlac ridge, the full Norman host was facing them in battle array, coming at them up the slope. It was the morning of Saturday 14 October.

The Norman army was divided into three component parts: infantry, cavalry, and archers. The infantry were used to hammer away at the Anglo-Saxon shield-wall, wave after wave of them, to weaken it by sheer attrition. The heavy cavalry would then try to punch a way through the weakened front ranks to wreak havoc in the rear. The archers were the equivalent of modern artillery, laying down a barrage of arrows (twelve a minute from each bow) to soften up the target beforehand. And horribly effective they were, too. They used various kinds of bows; on the meadow-land round Battle Abbey, I tried out a modern replica specially made by archery enthusiast and historian Dick Galloway. At fifty paces a war-arrow plumed with snow-goose feathers and tipped with a wicked metal barb could smash its way through double chain-mail. For long-range bombardment, in the hands of a skilled archer, its effective range would be well over two hundred metres.

As the light began to fade late in the afternoon of that October day, yet another 'arrow-storm' showering down on the depleted English ranks had a devastating effect . . .

'Hic Haroldus rex interfectus est': 'Here King Harold is killed', says the Bayeux Tapestry. There is a popular misconception that Harold of England was fatally wounded in the right eye by one of these volleys of arrows. But this is not what happened, seemingly; it is based on a mis-interpretation of the Tapestry, which shows an English warrior plucking at an arrow in his eye under the start of the embroidered caption. In fact the caption straddles two scenes, and it is the second panel, under the words interfectus est, which shows Harold being killed – hacked down by the sword of a Norman knight.

How he actually died is an academic question now. The fact of his fall signalled the end of the Battle of Hastings, the rout of the English.

And what an irony there is in that. Where the Vikings from the home-lands had failed, the émigré descendants of the Vikings had succeeded.

The Viking threat to England had been finally destroyed at Stamford Bridge by the grandson of a Viking – Harold Godwinsson. But it had been a Pyrrhic victory, which left England at the mercy of those other Viking descendants, the Northmen of Normandy, their traditional combative energy honed and disciplined by 150 years of feudal living in France. It was they who notched up the last – and the most lasting – achievement of the Viking Age: the military conquest and permanent occupation of a major European nation.

At 6 p.m. on Saturday 14 October 1066 the world changed. The Viking Age was effectively over.

Bibliography

Books in English for further reading

Almgren, B. (ed.), *The Viking*, C. A. Watts, 1966
Brønsted, J., *The Vikings*, Penguin Books, 1965
Brown, D., *Anglo-Saxon England*, Bodley Head, 1978
Dronke, U. (ed.), *The Poetic Edda, Vol. 1*, OUP, 1969
Ellis Davidson, H. R., *The Viking Road to Byzantium*, Allen & Unwin, 1976; *Scandinavian Mythology*, Paul Hamlyn, 1969
Foote, P. G., & Wilson, D. M., *The Viking Achievement*, Sidgwick & Jackson, 1970
Graham-Campbell, J., & Kydd, D., *The Vikings*, British Museum Publications, 1980
Greenhill, B., *Archaeology of the Boat*, A. & C. Black, 1976
Harbison, P., *The Archaeology of Ireland*, Bodley Head, 1976
Helm, P. J., *Alfred the Great*, Robert Hale, 1963
Hollander, L. M., *Heimskringla*, University of Texas Press, 1944
Hunter Blair, P., *An Introduction to Anglo-Saxon England*, CUP, 1956
Ingstad, H., *Westward to Vinland*, Jonathan Cape, 1969
Jansson, S. V. F., *The Runes of Sweden*, Phoenix House, 1962
Jones, G., *History of the Vikings*, OUP, 1968; *The Norse Atlantic Saga*, OUP, 1964
Kristjánsson, J., *Icelandic Sagas and Manuscripts*, Saga Publishing Co., Reykjavik, 1970
Krogh, K. J., *Viking Greenland*, Copenhagen National Museum, 1967
Loyn, H. R., *The Vikings in Britain*, Batsford, 1977
Magnusson, M., *Viking Expansion Westwards*, Bodley Head, 1973; *Hammer of the North*, Orbis, 1976

Magnusson, M., & Pálsson, H., *Njal's Saga*, Penguin Classics, 1960; *The Vínland Sagas*, Penguin Classics, 1965; *King Harald's Saga*, Penguin Classics, 1966; *Laxdæla saga*, Penguin Classics, 1969
Mongait, A., *Archaeology in the USSR*, Foreign Languages Publishing House, Moscow, 1959
Ó Corráin, D., *Ireland before the Normans*, Gill & Macmillan, Dublin, 1972
Pálsson, H., & Edwards, P., *Egíl's Saga*, Penguin Classics, 1976; *Orkneyinga saga*, Hogarth Press, 1978; *The Book of Settlements – Landnámabók*, University of Manitoba Press, 1972
Paor, M., & L. de, *Early Christian Ireland*, Thames & Hudson, 1958
Sawyer, P. H., *The Age of the Vikings*, Edward Arnold, 2nd edn, 1971; *From Roman Britain to Norman England*, Methuen, 1978
Smyth, A. P., *Scandinavian Kings in the British Isles 850–880*, OUP, 1977
Stenton, F. M., *Anglo-Saxon England*, OUP, 3rd edn, 1971
Thomson, M. W., *Novgorod the Great*, Evelyn, Adams & Mackay, 1967
Turville-Peter, G., *Myth and Religion of the North*, Weidenfeld & Nicolson, 1964; *Origins of Icelandic Literature*, OUP, 1953
Wilson, D. M., *The Vikings and their Origins*, Thames & Hudson, 1970; (ed.) *The Northern World*, Thames & Hudson, 1980
Wilson, D. M., & Klindt-Jensen, O., *Viking Art*, Allen & Unwin, 1966

Acknowledgements

In the preparation of this book I have been greatly helped by a host of scholars right across the northern hemisphere, from Russia to North America. Many of them are named in the text, but most of them are not individually credited; my debt to them all, however, is evident on every page.

One scholar I must single out, and I do so with profound gratitude: Peter Sawyer, Professor of Medieval History at the University of Leeds. He was mentor and guide to the whole project, both this book and its associated television series of the same name, and gave unsparingly of his erudition and sage counsel.

It is also with pleasure and affection that I record my thanks to my friends and colleagues on the BBC production unit: to Jane Mayes and Susan Stanyon (producer's assistants) and Liz Wright (researcher); to producer Ray Sutcliffe, who helped to make our voyage of discovery to the Viking world so enjoyable and illuminating; and above all to series producer David Collison and his assistant Alexandra Branson. We worked together on *BC: The Archaeology of the Bible Lands* four years ago; *Vikings!* was a happy resumption of a rewarding and much-valued partnership.

I am grateful to the late Dr J. M. Stern and Ralf Pinder-Wilson for the translation of Ibn Fadlan that appears in Chapter 4.

The publishers wish to thank the following for their kind permission to use copyright photographic material: Ray Sutcliffe, pages 10, 14, 15, 26, 42, 46, 63, 66 (bottom), 70 (bottom), 94 (margin), 95, 98, 99, 106, 107, 155, 158, 159, 162, 163, 166, 183, 186, 187, 190, 195, 202, 203, 207 (bottom), 211, 214, 219, 222, 223, 246, 271, 291, 295, frontispiece and jacket photographs; David Collison, pages 18, 27, 34, 55, 70 (top), 79, 83, 86, 102, 110, 114 (bottom), 115, 118, 119, 142, 146, 151, 168, 198, 230, 231, 234, 238, 239, 241, 242, 254, 264, 270, 278, 280, 286, 287, 288, 298, 299; Bob Julian, pages 91, 94, 114 (top); Liz Wright, pages 66 (top), 75; Mats Wibe Lund Jr, pages 12, 193; Per Simonnaes, page 22; The National Museum, Copenhagen, pages 21, 82, 87, 89, 216, 218; Associated Newspapers, page 24; Universitets Oldsaksamling, Oslo, pages 23, 35, 36, 39, 48, 49, 50, 51; The British Library, page 31; The Trustees of the British Museum, pages 72, 127, 167, 175, 179, 277; Crown Copyright: Controller of HMSO, page 32; Crown Copyright: The Scottish Development Department, pages 256, 260, 263; Manuscript Institute of Iceland, pages 54, 224, 267, 290; Research in Norway – '77, page 58; Aalborg Museum, page 67; The Utrecht Library (MS 32, fol. 51v), page 74; Roger Viollet, Paris, pages 77, 283; Cambridge University Collection, page 124; York Archaeological Trust, pages 128, 129, 134, 135, 136, 137, 139, 309; Ashmolean Museum, Oxford, pages 131, 150; Corpus Christi College, Cambridge, page 147; The Board of Trinity College, Dublin, page 154; National Museum of Ireland, page 161; The Manx Museum, Douglas, pages 170, 171, 173; Viking Ship Museum, Roskilde, pages 189, 191, 302, 303; National Museum of Iceland, page 206; The Royal Library, Copenhagen (Gl. kgl. Saml. 3269 A, 4°), page 207 (top); Arnamagnean Institute, Copenhagen, page 210; Michigan State University Museum, page 226; Yale University Press, from *The Vinland Map and the Tartar Relation* by R. A. Skelton, Thomas E. Marston and George D. Painter. Copyright © 1965 by Yale University, page 236; Museum of Maine, page 245; Das Photo, page 250; Peter Hall, page 262; The University of Aberdeen Anthropological Museum, page 255; The National Museum of Antiquities of Scotland, page 258; The Library, Kirkwall, page 265; Statens Historiska Museum, Stockholm, page 274; Riksantikvaren, Oslo, pages 291, 292, 293; Schleswig-Holstein Landesmuseum, page 304; The Fotomas Index, pages 307, 310, 311.

The drawings on pages 19 and 37 are by Pippa Brand, and those on pages 60, 92, 93, 199 and 257 are by Rosemonde Nairac. The maps are by John Payne.

Index